XML
and PHP

Contents At a Glance

XML and PHP

Vikram Vaswani

New Riders

www.newriders.com

201 West 103rd Street, Indianapolis, Indiana 46290
An Imprint of Pearson Education
Boston • Indianapolis • London • Munich • New York • San Francisco

XML and PHP

Trademarks

Warning and Disclaimer

Publisher
David Dwyer

Associate Publisher
Stephanie Wall

Production Manager
Gina Kanouse

Managing Editor
Kristy Knoop

Acquisitions Editor
Deborah Hittel-Shoaf

Development Editor
Laura Loveall

Product Marketing Manager
Tammy Detrich

Publicity Manager
Susan Nixon

Project Editors
Todd Zellers
Lori Lyons

Copy Editor
Nancy Sixsmith

Indexer
Fred Brown

Manufacturing Coordinator
Jim Conway

Book Designer
Louisa Klucznik

Cover Designer
Brainstorm Design, Inc.

Cover Production
Aren Howell

Composition
Scan Communications Group, Inc.

To my family and friends, for putting up with me.

"Finally, I came to regard as sacred the disorder of my mind."
—*Rimbaud*

TABLE OF CONTENTS

About the Author

Vikram Vaswani is the founder and CEO of Melonfire
(http://www.melonfire.com), a company specializing in software
consultancy, and content creation and syndication services.
Vikram is also the author of numerous well-received articles on
open-source technologies (including Perl, Python, XML, and the
very popular PHP 101 series), all written with the goal of making
complex technologies accessible and understandable to novice users.
He has been developing software since 1995, was first introduced to
PHP in 1998, and hasn't looked back since. His favorite activities
include reading, sleeping, watching movies, playing squash, and
fiddling with his PalmPilot.

About the Technical Reviewers

These reviewers contributed their considerable hands-on expertise to the entire
development process for *XML and PHP*. As the book was being written, these dedi-
cated professionals reviewed all the material for technical content, organization, and
flow. Their feedback was critical to ensure that *XML and PHP* fits our readers' need
for the highest-quality technical information.

Zak Greant is lead developer for 51 Degrees North, and is the
founder of the Foo & Associates programmer's cooperative. He
leads the PHP Quality Assurance Team, and is an active contributor
to the PHP documentation, mailing lists, and source code. (See
http://www.zend.com/comm_person.php?id=56 for his PHP
community profile.)

Mark Nenadov is a bright, young software developer living in
Canada (he does not reside in an igloo or speak French, however).
Mark specializes in Open Source technology, and has lots of expe-
rience with technologies such as PHP, XML, MySQL, and Python.
He is currently employed at a growing e-commerce company in
Windsor, Ontario. When he isn't hunched over his keyboard, he
is usually trying to learn new things, playing ice hockey, writing,
reading books, and wishing it were a bit warmer in Canada.

Acknowledgments

This book would not have been possible without the support and assistance of a whole bunch of people. Their reward? Embarrassment (and possible immortality) in this section.

First and foremost, I'd like to thank my family for providing me with a quiet place to work, and for putting up with my odd work hours (and even odder behavior) while this book was being written.

A big thank-you to my "co-CEO" and friend, Harish Kamath, for the professionalism he exhibited in doing my job (as well as his own) while I was working on this book.

Many thanks to Sterling Hughes, Phillip Gühring, Dan Libby, Manuel Lemos, Stephan Schmidt, Nigel Swinson, Edd Dumbill, Dietrich Ayala, and Bård Farstad for sharing their code and their time with me; and for their professionalism in answering my (numerous!) questions.

For keeping things interesting, thanks to: Popeye and Olive, Dennis Lehane, Lawrence Block, Bryan Adams, the Stones, Scott Adams, Gary Larson, MTV, Buffy, Stephen King, Barry White, Robert Crais, Robert B. Parker, Baz Luhrmann, HBO, Mark Twain, Mahtab Marker, Tim Burton, everyone at "the other company," the entire cast of *Friends*, Dido, Google.com, Alfred Hitchcock, Michael Schumacher, Humphrey Bogart, Amazon.com, U2, The Three Stooges, Ling's Pavilion, Britney Spears, Kylie Minogue, Oscar Wilde, Bill Watterson, Punch, Harry Potter, Scott Turow, Blizzard Entertainment, Xerxes Antia, Dire Straits, David Mitchell, and all my friends at home and elsewhere.

A special mention must be made here of the great team at New Riders Publishing—especially my Acquisitions Editor, Deborah Hittel-Shoaf; my Development Editor, Laura Loveall; and my Technical Editors, Zak Greant and Mark Nenadov, who guided this book through the development process. This is a very professional team, and if you, dear reader, ever have the opportunity to work with them, I encourage you to do so. Thanks much, guys!

Tell Us What You Think

As the reader of this book, you are the most important critic and commentator. We value your opinion and want to know what we're doing right, what we could do better, what areas you'd like to see us publish in, and any other words of wisdom you're willing to pass our way.

As the Associate Publisher for New Riders Publishing, I welcome your comments. You can fax, email, or write me directly to let me know what you did or didn't like about this book—as well as what we can do to make our books stronger.

Please note that I cannot help you with technical problems related to the topic of this book, and that due to the high volume of mail I receive, I might not be able to reply to every message.

When you write, please be sure to include this book's title and author as well as your name and phone or fax number. I will carefully review your comments and share them with the author and editors who worked on the book.

Fax: 317-581-4663
Email: stephanie.wall@newriders.com
Mail: Stephanie Wall
          Associate Publisher
          New Riders Publishing
          201 West 103rd Street
          Indianapolis, IN 46290 USA

Introduction

"There are more things in heaven and earth, Horatio,
Than are dreamt of in your philosophy."

~WILLIAM SHAKESPEARE, *Hamlet*

Unless you've been doing a Rip Van Winkle for the past few years, you've heard about PHP and XML.

Probably not in the same context, I'll grant you—one is, after all, a programming language for the web, whereas the other is a standard toolkit for describing data. Individually, they're both long-time sweethearts of the notoriously fickle web community—PHP for its rapid application development capabilities and XML for its capability to make data more useful by attaching descriptive tags to it.

Although there is no shortage of information on either of these two technologies individually, there are very few resources that explain how to use them in combination with each other. Which was exactly the problem I had about a year ago, when I decided to use XML as one of the components of a web-based project I was working on. PHP was my development language of choice. (I'd long since given up on Perl and JSP.) Although I knew very little about how PHP and XML could be integrated with each other, I blithely assumed that the web, with its gargantuan knowledge bases, would have more than enough information to help me complete the project.

Imagine my horror, then, when I was able to find only the sketchiest information on the topic, despite hours spent tapping different permutations of "php xml development" into Google's search box. With time running out, I decided to go to plan B: I printed a copy of the XML and XSL specs, stocked up on microwave dinners, and started experimenting with PHP's built-in XML functions.

I soon realized that combining PHP with XML wasn't hard at all—in fact, it was pretty easy. Before long, I had worked out the basics of the SAX and DOM functions, installed my own copy of the XSLT extension, and figured out just what I needed to do to deliver the project on time. All it took was patience, a little research . . . and a lot of time.

In the highly competitive world of web development, in which contracts often turn on how quickly a project can be executed, time is a valuable commodity. Working with picky customers against aggressive deadlines is stressful enough for most developers; having to spend most of the day on research, rather than implementation, isn't likely to make their day any sunnier. And so, one of my most important reasons for writing this book was that it might serve as a starting point and reference for other developers looking to build XML- and PHP-enabled web applications.

This book is the book I wish I'd had a year ago. It includes detailed explanations of PHP's XML extensions, together with illustrations of using PHP to parse, validate, and transform XML markup. I've also discussed, among other things, how to traverse XML data trees, exchange data between web applications, overlay remote procedure calls over HTTP, and use free open-source tools to add new capabilities to your XML/PHP applications. You can read it all the way through, or use it in traditional cookbook style, flipping it open to the chapter that addresses your specific problem. Either way, I hope you find it useful, informative, and (dare I say it?) fun.

Over the past year, I've written a few articles on how XML and PHP can be used together, and I've even given a couple of presentations on the topic. From the feedback I've received, it seems that there are still many, many people—developers, consultants, educators, webmasters, systems engineers, or just good ol' PHP enthusiasts—who would love to know how XML and PHP can be combined together, but don't know where to start.

If you're one of those people, this book is for you.

Who Should Read This Book

You should read this book if you're a developer looking to create XML-based web applications with PHP. This book examines PHP's support for different XML technologies, explaining how to develop XML-based web applications using standard PHP libraries and tools.

Regardless of whether you want to format marked-up XML data with XSLT stylesheets, create XML documents from SQL-compliant databases, exchange information with WDDX, or implement remote procedure calls with SOAP, this book has the theory and practical, hands-on code to get you started.

Who This Book Is Not For

If you're new to PHP or XML, you shouldn't be reading this book. Throughout the material that follows, I'll be assuming that you have a working knowledge of PHP (its variables, syntax, structures, and methods), and are comfortable with using it for standard web programming tasks. I'll also be assuming that you have some prior knowledge of XML and XSLT, at least to the extent of being able to construct XML files and apply XSLT transformations to them, and that you are comfortable with using SQL to retrieve and manipulate records from a database.

That said, the very first chapter of this book includes a brief discussion of basic XML and PHP concepts, and many of the subsequent chapters also include introductory primers for readers new to the technology. However, this material is intended more as a refresher course than an exhaustive reference, and you should make it a point to look up other more-specialized works if you find it insufficient.

Some of the titles you might want to consider adding to your shopping list are the following:

- *Inside XML,* by Steven Holzner (New Riders, 2000) ISBN: 0735710201.
- *Inside XSLT,* by Steven Holzner (New Riders, 2001) ISBN: 0735711364.

- *MySQL*, by Paul DuBois (New Riders, 2000) ISBN: 0735709211.

- *Web Application Development with PHP 4.0*, by Tobias Ratschiller and Till Gerken (New Riders, 2000) ISBN: 0735709971.

- *PHP Functions Essential Reference*, by Zak Greant, Graeme Merrall, Torben Wilson, and Brett Michlitsch (New Riders, 2001) ISBN: 0-7357-0970-X.

Development Environment

This book assumes that you have a working PHP 4.1 development environment, and that your PHP build supports the various XML extensions discussed in this book (instructions on how to compile PHP to include this support are available in Appendix A, "Recompiling PHP to Add XML Support.")

Some of the chapters in this book require additional development tools—for example, the MySQL database server. Wherever such additional tools are required, I've included links to online resources that should assist you in obtaining and installing them.

Finally, the examples and code listings in this book have been tested on both UNIX (specifically Linux) and Windows. So, the platform you're using shouldn't matter too much. In places where it does, I've made it a point to flag the section and explain the issues involved.

How to Use This Book

You can approach the material in this book in two ways:

- Do the traditional thing and read it through from beginning to end. If you're just getting started with the XML/PHP combo, this is the approach I'd recommend because it will teach you the basics in a structured manner, and prepare you for the more advanced topics in the latter half of the book.

- Use it as a desktop reference, reading only those chapters that address specific topics or problems you may be facing. If you've already played with PHP's XML functions in the past, you might find this approach quicker and more convenient.

However you decide to approach the subject, you should ensure that the experience is a participatory one. Make it a point to try out the examples within each chapter, and futz around with the code listings to see what happens. You're not likely to break anything, and you'll learn a lot more by actually putting the theory into practice.

Overview

Here's a quick preview of what each chapter contains:

- Chapter 1: "XML and PHP Basics"—Context is everything. And this introductory chapter attempts to put XML and PHP in context with a discussion of the history, features, capabilities, and applications of these two technologies. It then goes on to explain the rationale for using PHP to process XML, and provides an introduction to how the two can be combined together.

- Chapter 2: "PHP and the Simple API for XML (SAX)"—With the basics out of the way, this chapter discusses the Simple API for XML, lists SAX functions available in PHP, and explains how to use them to traverse and parse an XML document.

- Chapter 3: "PHP and the Document Object Model (DOM)"—There's more than one way to skin a cat—a fact amply demonstrated by this chapter, which discusses an alternative to the SAX method of parsing XML data. It explains basic DOM concepts, lists DOM functions available in PHP, and explains how to use them to traverse and parse an XML document using both recursive and non-recursive techniques.

- Chapter 4: "PHP and Extensible Stylesheet Language Transformations (XSLT)"—Now that you know how to parse an XML document with PHP, take things to the next level with a discussion of the PHP XSLT API, which is used to transform XML documents on the server using XSLT stylesheets.

- Chapter 5: "PHP and Web Distributed Data eXchange (WDDX)"—WDDX is an open framework for distributing XML-encoded data across systems. This chapter explores the possibilities for using PHP to transmit WDDX-encoded XML data, and illustrates the process of building a PHP-based WDDX server and client to handle this type of information exchange.

- Chapter 6: "PHP and XML-Based Remote Procedure Calls (RPC)"—XML-RPC makes it possible to transmit XML-encoded Remote Procedure Calls from one system to another, and retrieve the response. SOAP is an evolution of XML-RPC, which offers more features and flexibility. This chapter explores the PHP implementation of XML-RPC and SOAP.

- Chapter 7: "PHP, XML, and Databases"—Thus far, you've been dealing with static XML documents. Now, add a database to the equation by generating XML data dynamically from a MySQL database and applying XSL Transformations to it.

- Chapter 8: "Open Source PHP/XML Alternatives"—What do you do if your PHP build doesn't include support for certain XML processing functions? Turn to the open-source community for help, of course! This chapter examines four open-source projects that allow you to simulate PHP's native XML processing functions, with detailed usage examples and explanations.

- Chapter 9: "Case Studies"—There's nothing better than a good example— except maybe two good examples. And so, this concluding chapter demonstrates the fundamental premise of this book—the synergy between XML and PHP— with case studies of two real-world development projects.

Finally, instructions on how to compile PHP with XML support, the open source licenses, and a glossary are available in the appendixes.

Conventions

This book follows a few typographical conventions:

- A new term is set in *italic* the first time it is introduced.
- Program text, functions, variables, and other "computer language" are set in a fixed-width font—for example, `<?xml version="1.0" encoding="UTF-8"?>`.
- Some of the listing headings include a filename (for example, *Listing 4.1 Simple XML Book List (list.xml)*—where *(list.xml)* is the filename). This filename is a reference to filenames used in subsequent code listings.

"Toto, I've a feeling we're not in Kansas anymore."

~DOROTHY, *THE WIZARD OF OZ*

1

XML and PHP Basics

XML AND PHP ARE BOTH POWERFUL TECHNOLOGIES and open up tremendous possibilities for the creative developer. Each has its own advantages and unique capabilities; but together they form an integrated whole which is far greater than just the sum of its parts.

Before getting into the nitty-gritty of program code or tackling the intricacies of PHP's XML functions, it's important to step back a little and look at things in context. This chapter is designed to accomplish just that—it contains a quick overview of both XML and PHP; discusses the design goals, capabilities, and features of each; and puts the material that follows within a larger context.

If you're new to PHP or XML (or both), you should make it a point to browse the material in this chapter; it will explain some fundamental concepts and principles and prepare you for the journey ahead. If you're an experienced PHP or XML user, you might want to skip the introductory comments (found in the "XML" and "PHP" sections) and jump straight to the concluding material (in the section, "PHP and XML"), which explains just how PHP and XML fit together and offers a preview of the possibilities that arise from their union.

XML

This section is designed to give you a broad overview of the Extensible Markup Language (XML). It discusses XML's history, need, and rationale, together with a quick look at some basic XML constructs and applications.

XML actually is a subset of the Standardized General Markup Language (SGML). SGML is an internationally accepted standard for describing just about any type of information; however, it's way too complex for the relatively simple world of the web. And so, the World Wide Web Consortium (W3C) created a modified version of SGML specifically for the web, named it *XML*, and released it on an unsuspecting public sometime in 1998.

Over the past few years, XML has received more than its allotted fifteen minutes of fame, with technology pundits and business leaders alike singing its praises. It's been crowned the Next Big Thing, both on account of its ease of use and its potential for revolutionizing the way information is exchanged and used. Some of this is hype and some of it isn't; either way, it's quite clear that XML is going to be around for a while, and that, wisely used, it can indeed be a powerful tool for the management and effective exploitation of information.

XML works by "marking up" data with descriptive tags, in much the same way HTML does. The difference is that HTML was designed specifically to format data for web browsers and, as such, is limited to a predefined set of tags and functions. XML, by contrast, was designed as a web-friendly meta-data language and, therefore, merely lays down the rules for document markup (leaving it to the document author to define his or her own tags). As an example, consider the following block of text:

A Man and His Mouse

J. Gilbert Gumpfinch III, 23 Nov 2001

In a development many consider to be the first of its kind, the Hungarian scientist, Professor Haarbert Floopshot, today announced that he had succeeded in inventing "a better mouse." The new mouse, created using advanced genetic splicing techniques and "some good old-fashioned SuperGlue," can emit ultrasonic squeals to frighten off predators twice its size, leap tall mousetraps in a single bound, and comes equipped with a built-in CatDetector to detect approaching felines.

Sure, *you* can tell that it's a newspaper report, primarily because you read newspapers, can see the similarities, and can make a conclusion based on those similarities. You can even break it up conceptually into the headline, the byline, and the body of the article. But a computer can't do those things—to a computer, the block of text above is simply a bunch of alphanumeric characters, with very little to distinguish the headline from the body.

That's where XML comes in. It can be used to transform the anonymous block of text above into something that even a computer can make sense of (see Listing 1.1).

Listing 1.1   **A Simple XML Document**

```xml
<?xml version="1.0"?>

<story id="34" category="weird">
    <slug>A Man And His Mouse</slug>
    <author>J. Gilbert Gumpfinch III</author>
    <date>11-23-2001-</date>
    <body>
        <para>In a development many consider to be the first of its kind, the
Hungarian scientist <person type="scientist">Professor Haarbert Floopshot</person>
today announced that he had succeeded in inventing "a better mouse." The new
mouse, created using advanced genetic splicing techniques and "some good old-
fashioned SuperGlue," can emit ultrasonic squeals to frighten off predators twice
its size, leap tall mousetraps in a single bound, and comes equipped with a built-
in CatDetector to detect approaching felines.</para>
    </body>
</story>
```

By marking up the data with descriptive tags, XML makes it easy to distinguish between different types of information—even for a computer. In today's wired world, this capability is more valuable than you might surmise; with many of today's business decisions handled by computer, XML can significantly improve the accuracy of information processing, thereby increasing overall business efficiency, streamlining business processes, and (ultimately) fattening the bottom line—which probably also explains why the industry's so enthusiastic about it.

Features

XML was designed to incorporate the following features:

- **Ease of use.** By virtue of the descriptive tags they contain, XML documents are easy to read and understand, even for users with little or no computer knowledge. They're also exceedingly simple to create: a non-technical user is typically able to create an XML document in far less time than it takes to create a corresponding HTML document.

  This simplicity is perhaps XML's greatest selling point. Think about it—adopting a markup language that can be understood and used by all employees without any special training makes it easier and more cost-effective for businesses to exchange information between individuals, departments, and business units.

- **Formal structure.** Although XML offers document authors tremendous flexibility in naming and using their own tags, it nonetheless does impose some formal structure on a document. Tags must be named and nested correctly; opening tags must have corresponding closing tags; and namespaces must be defined wherever they are required. These rules ensure that every XML document meets some minimum expectations of structure and syntax, and make it easier for applications and processors to deal with XML data.

This emphasis on structured markup is in stark contrast to the "anything-goes" approach of HTML, which frequently sacrifices conformance in the name of greater flexibility. An HTML document containing incorrectly nested tags, for example, would immediately generate conformance errors when passed through an XML parser; the same document would likely be displayed correctly, with no errors recorded, when viewed in any of today's web browsers (many of which incorporate their own error-correction routines for precisely this sort of situation).

- **Internet-friendly.** XML was designed to be used on the Internet, where it plays two very important roles.

  First, XML provides a toolkit that enables users to describe the huge amount of data floating around on the Internet—this immediately opens the door to better organization and classification of information on the web, more intelligent search engines, and new types of links between data.

  Second, XML provides a standard mechanism for information exchange, encoding data in a format that is easily transmittable from one computer to another using existing Internet protocols and transport mechanisms. Because XML is essentially text, it can be used to transmit information over email, FTP, HTTP, or any other text-capable protocol. This feature makes it an ideal candidate for information sharing between businesses or individuals located in different geographical areas.

  Examples of technologies that use XML to exchange data include Resource Description Framework (RDF), Channel Definition Format (CDF), Web Distributed Data Exchange (WDDX), and Simple Object Access Protocol (SOAP).

- **Wide application support.** Because XML is easy to use and easy to move around, it's not hard to write an application that uses XML-encoded data. A number of XML parsers are available online; XML editors, validators, and similar tools are gaining market share; and most popular web browsers now support XML.

- **SGML-compatible.** As mentioned earlier in this chapter, XML is an offshoot of SGML, and XML documents comply with all the rules and constraints of SGML markup. That being said, XML is far easier to use than SGML because its focus is much narrower. By straddling both worlds, XML combines the power of SGML with the flexibility and ease of use we've come to expect from the Internet.

Basic Concepts

XML documents come in two flavors: well-formed and valid.

A *well-formed document* is one that adheres to the basic rules laid down in the XML specification; for example, all elements must be properly nested; attribute values must be enclosed within quotation marks; and the document must contain at least one non-empty element.

A *valid document* is one that, in addition to being well-formed, meets the requirements and constraints laid down in a Document Type Definition (DTD) or XML schema. This DTD or schema is an additional ruleset an author can use to specify the element names and data types that are allowed in the document. This helps to reduce the risk of corrupted or invalid data. Listing 1.2 shows well-formed XML document, which describes an invoice for materials purchased. It's a slightly contrived example, but it will serve to illustrate XML's most commonly used constructs.

Listing 1.2 **An XML Document Demonstrating Most of the Language's Basic Constructs**

```
<?xml version="1.0" encoding="UTF-8"?>

<!DOCTYPE invoice
[
<!ENTITY  terms "Payment on delivery. Cash only, no checks or money orders
➥accepted. Returns within 15 days.">
<!ENTITY logo SYSTEM "images/logo.gif" NDATA gif>
<!NOTATION gif SYSTEM "gifviewer.exe">
]>

<invoice id="AS2354R">

    <logo src="logo" />

    <date>03-12-2000</date>

    <!-- consignor address -->
    <vendor>
        <name>Bobby's Biotech Bazaar</name>
        <address>
            <street>25, Main Street</street>
            <city>Purple River Town</city>
            <zip>457929</zip>
            <country>South America</country>
        </address>
    </vendor>

    <!-- consignee address -->
    <customer>
        <name>Floopshot, Haarbert.</name>
        <address>
            <street>15, Booger Avenue</street>
            <city>Nowheresville</city>
            <zip>64732</zip>
            <state>TY</state>
            <country>US</country>
        </address>
    </customer>
```

continues

Listing 1.2 **Continued**

```
<!-- consignment details -->
<material>

    <item id="23">
        <name>Gray mouse</name>
        <quantity>12</quantity>
        <price currency="USD">11.99</price>
    </item>

    <item id="23">
        <name>Vampire bat (DNA sequence)</name>
        <quantity>1</quantity>
        <price currency="USD">34.99</price>
        <dna_sequence>
            <![CDATA[
            1627 3494 #190 2230 8549 0732 #232 8238 2833 01&6 9929
            ]]>
        </dna_sequence>
    </item>

    <item id="856">
        <name>Australian kangaroo (DNA sequence)</name>
        <quantity>1</quantity>
        <price currency="USD">34.99</price>
        <dna_sequence>
            <![CDATA[
            0101 9394 %42$ 9393 0209 2020 8348 #577 7493 2543 &646
            ]]>
        </dna_sequence>
    </item>

</material>

<terms>&terms;</terms>

<note>Include current product catalog with purchase</note>

<?sales_agent include_promotional_message="1"?>

</invoice>
```

As you can see, an XML document is merely ASCII text, broken into separate sections by markup. This markup has several components, each with its own distinct role:

- document prolog
- elements

- attributes
- entities
- notations
- CDATA blocks
- processing instructions
- comments

These components are explained in the sections that follow.

Document Prolog

Every XML document begins with a special identifier called the document *prolog*, such as

```
<?xml version="1.0" encoding="UTF-8"?>
```

This prolog appears at the top of an XML document and specifies things like the XML version and type of encoding used, the location of any DTD that may be used to validate the document, and one or more entity definitions.

In Listing 1.2, the prolog contained two entity definitions and one notation:

```
<!DOCTYPE invoice
[
<!ENTITY  terms "Payment on delivery. Cash only, no checks or money orders
➥accepted. Returns within 15 days.">
<!ENTITY logo SYSTEM "images/logo.gif" NDATA gif>
<!NOTATION gif SYSTEM "gifviewer.exe">
]>
```

Elements

The document prolog is followed by one or more elements. *Elements* are the most basic units of XML data—they consist of attributes and content (or *character data*) surrounded by descriptive tags (or *markup*). Here are three examples:

```
<street>15, Booger Avenue</street>
```

```
<rate>9.99</rate>
```

```
<name>Vampire bat (DNA sequence)</name>
```

To be well-formed, an XML document must contain at least one nonempty element. This outermost element, sometimes referred to as the *root element*, serves as the container for the remainder of the document.

Elements can be empty, contain other elements nested within them, or enclose a combination of both character data and elements.

Attributes

Elements can be enhanced further by the addition of *attributes*, which are name–value pairs that can be used to attach any type of additional descriptive information to an element. Here are two examples:

```
<invoice id="AS2354R">

<price currency="USD">9.99</price>
```

In order to be well-formed, attribute values must be enclosed within quotation marks, and attribute names cannot be repeated within the same element.

Entities

Entities serve as placeholders for frequently used pieces of text within an XML document. They provide a convenient shortcut for document authors to store and easily update commonly used text snippets.

Entities consist of two components:

- The *entity definition*, which links an entity name to the text block it represents:

  ```
  <!ENTITY terms "Payment on delivery. Cash only, no checks or money orders
  ↩accepted. Returns within 15 days.">
  ```

- The *entity reference*, which serves as a placeholder for the longer text block:

  ```
  &terms;
  ```

When an XML parser processes an XML document, entity references automatically are replaced with their actual values.

XML comes with five predefined entities. You might already be familiar with them if you have worked with HTML (see Table 1.1).

Table 1.1 **XML's Five Predefined Entities**

Entity	Represents
&lt;	The less-than (<) symbol
&gt;	The greater-than (>) symbol
&apos;	The single-quote (') symbol
&quot;	The double-quote(") symbol
&amp;	The ampersand (&) symbol

A variant of the regular entity just described is the *unparsed entity*, typically used to reference data that should *not* be processed by the XML parser. This is usually binary data—images, audio files, video streams, and the like. The preceding example demonstrates one such unparsed entity, which holds the path to the company logo:

```
<!ENTITY logo SYSTEM "images/logo.gif" NDATA gif>
```

Note the NDATA keyword, which tells the parser that it should look up the appropriate *notation* to find out how to handle this data (notations are discussed next).

In order for a document to be well-formed, entities cannot contain references to themselves—think infinite loop and you'll understand why.

Notations

A *notation* is an XML construct designed to help the parser identify non-XML data— for example, images or sound files—and typically goes hand in hand with unparsed entities. A notation is always enclosed within a *notation declaration*, which appears either within a DTD or the document prolog, and looks like this:

```
<!NOTATION notation-name notation-identifier>
```

The notation name is a unique identifier used within unparsed entities, while the notation identifier is a string that tells the XML processor how to handle that particular entity. This string could be anything from a URL that identifies the data type to the location of a program that can decode the data. Here's an example:

```
<!NOTATION gif SYSTEM "gifviewer.exe">
```

CDATA Blocks

CDATA blocks are "boxes" within an XML document, identified by special opening and closing delimiters. The text within these boxes is treated by the parser as character data, not markup, and can therefore contain special characters which would normally cause the parser to generate an error.

CDATA blocks begin with the special sequence <![CDATA[and end with the sequence]]>. For example,

```
<dna_sequence>
    <![CDATA[
    0101 9394 %42$ 9393 0209 2020 8348 #577 7493 2543 &646
    ]]>
</dna_sequence>
```

The option to CDATA blocks is, of course, using the predefined entities discussed earlier to represent special characters like the less-than (<), greater-than (>), and ampersand (&) symbols. Because entities allow for reusability within the document, using entities is sometimes preferable to using CDATA blocks.

Processing Instructions

Processing instructions (PIs) are special instructions embedded within an XML document. These PIs are not usually intended for human readers; rather, they provide special information or commands to the XML application responsible for parsing the document. Parsers that do not recognize these instructions will simply ignore them.

PIs are typically enclosed within <? ... ?> tags, as demonstrated here:

```
<?sales_agent include_promotional_message="1"?>
```

Notice that the very first line in an XML document is actually a PI indicating the version number and encoding to the parser:

```
<?xml version="1.0" encoding="UTF-8"?>
```

The parser can use this information to make decisions on how to process the XML— for example, reject the document if the XML version is unsupported, or switch its internal character handling routines to use the encoding specified in the prolog.

Comments

Finally, *comments* provide a simple and convenient way for document authors to include human-readable notes within their XML markup. Comments must be placed within <!-- ... --> markers, and they are usually ignored by the parser.

Ancillary Technologies

As XML's popularity has grown, so has an understanding of its capabilities and potential; and this, in turn, has spawned a new generation of related technologies. Together, they are an oft-confusing morass of acronyms and buzzwords; individually, they each make an important contribution to the overall picture.

Here's a brief list of the better-known XML development efforts underway at the W3C:

- **XSL and XSLT.** The Extensible Stylesheet Language (XSL) is a language designed to handle the presentation of XML-encoded data. The language has three components: XSL Transformations (XSLT), which is responsible for restructuring XML data into something new and different; XML Path Language (XPath), which provides constructs to address specific parts of an XML document; and XSL Formatting Objects (XSL-FO), which is responsible for the formatting and presentation of the new-and-different result.

  You can find out more about XSL at http://www.w3.org/Style/XSL/. Also, see *Inside XML* by Steven Holzner (ISBN: 0735710201, New Riders Publishing, 2001) and *Inside XSLT* by Steven Holzner (ISBN:0735711364, New Riders Publishing, 2001)

- **XPointer.** XPointer is a mechanism for locating specific nodes within an XML document. XPointer "addresses" use both relative and absolute paths to find and identify particular nodes in an XML document and are sometimes used with XLink for more precise links between data fragments.

  You can find out more about XPointer at http://www.w3.org/XML/Linking.

- **XLink.** XLink makes it possible to link resources in much the same way as standard HTML hyperlinks. However, XLink takes things a step further, allowing for single links that have multiple destinations and offering link authors the ability to control the direction of link traversal.

  You can find out more about XLink at `http://www.w3.org/XML/Linking`.

- **XHTML.** XHTML is a re-write of HTML 4.0 that makes it compliant with the XML 1.0 specification, combining standard XML rules with HTML markup for more efficient and structured web pages. By incorporating the best features of both versions, XHTML hopes to lay the groundwork for the next generation of web applications.

  You can find out more about XHTML at `http://www.w3.org/MarkUp/`. Also, see *XHTML* by Chelsea Valentine and Chris Minnick (New Riders Publishing, 2001).

- **XML Query.** XML Query hopes to do for XML what SQL did for databases: provide a standard interface to query XML documents and extract specific subsets of the data contained within them. Possible applications of this technology include more efficient full-text searches, multilanguage search engines, and easier access to XML-encoded information and the relationships they embody.

  You can find out more about XML Query at `http://www.w3.org/XML/Query`.

- **XML Schema.** Like DTDs, XML Schemas are rulesets specifying constraints on XML data. Unlike DTDs, they include support for namespaces, derived types and inheritance, and merged rulesets, and are expected to quickly supplant DTDs as the tool of choice for imposing conformance on XML documents.

  You can find out more about XML Schema at `http://www.w3.org/XML/Schema`.

- **XML Signature.** XML Signature offers a mechanism to digitally sign electronic—usually XML—content and verify this signature in an error-free manner at the other end.

  You can find out more about XML Signature at `http://www.w3.org/Signature/`.

Applications

As the preceding list demonstrates, XML has the potential to change the way we deal with web-based content. Here are four of XML's most important applications:

- **Better search engines.** Because XML describes data, it can significantly improve the indexing techniques used by most popular search engines, thereby resulting in faster, more efficient searches and more relevant results. Today, given the search term "rock," search engines can't distinguish between rock, a mass of stone, and rock, the musical genre. Tomorrow, document authors will be able to use XML to ensure that the distinction between the two is clear.

- **Better analysis of data.** XSLT makes it possible to create different views of the same XML data, simplifying the task of understanding and acting on complex business information. Using XSLT, the same XML document can be sliced, diced, and served up in an innumerable amount of ways, making it easier to see hidden relationships between the data and to gain a better understanding of the big picture.

- **More efficient content management.** By providing document authors with standard ways to describe data, XML opens the door to more efficient content management and publishing solutions. Content publishers can use XML to create, classify, and publish data in a standard format; because this data now meets certain basic rules of structure and syntax, it can easily be shared with other XML-compliant organizations.

- **More efficient information exchange.** To businesses, the ease and flexibility of the web and the inherent power of XML make a powerful combination, one which enables a new generation of web applications. These new applications are capable of receiving XML data from different sources, integrating these data fragments to create a composite picture, and using this information to make crucial business decisions on purchases, inventory, and billing. This is good for the organization, for the employees, and (let's not forget!) the bottom line.

Of course, this is just the tip of the iceberg. XML and its related technologies are still coming to full fruition, and new applications for this family of powerful technologies appear all the time.

If you'd like to learn more about XML, there are a number of very good books available to get you up to speed. The book's companion web site (http://www.xmlphp.com or http://www.newriders.com) has details, together with a list of useful web sites and mailing lists.

PHP

Let's move on to PHP, easily my favorite web development language. This section provides a brief overview of PHP's history, capabilities, and applications.

PHP (the name actually is a recursive acronym for PHP: Hypertext Pre-Processor—you know how geeks are!) began life as a glint in the eye of Rasmus Lerdorf in late 1994. (For the full story, visit http://www.php.net/manual/phpfi2.php#history.) Rasmus needed a tool to log visitors to his personal web page; his solution, using a C wrapper and special tags embedded into the HTML code, became the first version of PHP.

PHP hit the big time between 1997 and 2000 as more and more sites adopted it. The release of PHP 4.0 in late 2000 only served to widen its fan base. As a complete rewrite of the PHP engine, PHP 4.0 is faster, more scalable, and more full-featured than any of its predecessors. It is in use on more than six million web sites today, and that number is climbing rapidly.

Still wondering what exactly PHP is? Well, to quote its authors, PHP is "...a server-side HTML-embedded scripting language...".[1] In English, this means that PHP code is typically embedded within HTML documents; this code—variables, functions, commands—is interpreted and executed by the server, with the resulting output returned to the browser. Special PHP tags are used to distinguish between PHP commands and regular HTML markup.

That's not all, though—PHP also happens to be the most fun language I've had the opportunity to work with over the past few years.

Unlike other scripting languages, which seem to delight in convoluted syntax and tortuous structures, PHP code is clean, easy to read and understand, and incredibly user-friendly. The language comes with great documentation, a friendly and knowledgeable user community, and a feature set that would turn most other web scripting languages green. And its development team (more than 300 people across the globe) is constantly innovating and adding support for new technologies, thereby ensuring that it's on the cutting edge of new technology. What's more, PHP's huge library of built-in functions ensures that even the most complex tasks can be accomplished in less time than you thought possible.

All this, of course, would come to naught without the active support of real-world developers. Fortunately, PHP has that too. The latest Netcraft survey (`http://www.netcraft.com/survey/`) reveals that PHP usage is growing at the rate of more than 20 percent per month, with over 40 percent of the web's Apache servers running PHP. This widespread acceptance can only be music to the ears of PHP's many devotees, who have elevated PHP's developers to the status of gods and the language itself to the forefront of the popularity sweepstakes.

Language Features

PHP is a remarkably full-featured programming language, making it the ideal tool for developers looking to build complex, high-traffic web sites. Here's why:

- **Portability.** PHP distributions are available for a wide variety of platforms, including Windows, Macintosh, OS/2, and most flavors of UNIX, including Linux. Because PHP code written on one platform *usually* works "as is" on any other supported platform, using PHP can significantly reduce development time in a multiplatform environment. (Some PHP functions are platform-specific.)

- **Performance.** Independent evaluations have demonstrated that PHP is faster and more reliable that most other scripting languages. Both Fortune 500 companies and Mom-and-Pop businesses use it to run their web sites. And the completely reworked engine in PHP 4.0 raises the performance bar even further. Zend Technologies, Ltd. (`http://zend.com/zend/aboutphp.php`), which played a

---

1. Stig Sæther Bakken, Egon Schmid, et al. *PHP Manual.* Available from Internet: `http://www.php.net/manual/en`

pivotal role in the development of PHP 4.0, claims a 50-fold performance increase over previous versions; the reality is a little less staggering, but still impressive. (For numbers and benchmarks, visit the research done at http://www.linuxplanet.com/linuxplanet/reviews/1891/2/.)

- **Ease of use.** PHP is easy to learn—even a novice developer can pick up the basics in a few hours, and there are many online tutorials and books available to speed up the process. (I've even written a few myself. See the resources listed at http://www.xmlphp.com or http://www.newriders.com for more information.) PHP code is elegant and easy on the eyes, and the language comes with extensive documentation and usage examples. Because PHP is so easy to use, but packs so much power under its unassuming surface, it's become extremely popular as a tool for rapid application development, with more and more developers using it to construct high-traffic web sites and complex web-based applications.

- **Open source.** PHP is a child of the open source community—its source code is freely available, and developers are encouraged to make their own contributions to it. This open source approach has been the single most important factor responsible for the widespread acceptance of PHP all over the world. By sharing the code with other developers, the PHP development team has been able to stay abreast of current technologies and incorporate them into the language faster than their more traditional counterparts. And this open source approach has also given rise to a network of skilled PHP developers, who throng mailing lists and chat rooms with questions, comments, and knowledgeable advice.

- **Modular extensions.** Support for new technologies can easily be added to PHP through its modular extensions, which make it possible for developers to quickly incorporate new features and capabilities into their PHP build. Extensions available today allow developers to use PHP to perform FTP, IMAP, and POP3 operations; dynamically generate GIF, JPEG, and PNG images, Shockwave Flash files and Adobe PDF documents; validate credit card transactions; perform encryption of sensitive data; connect to Java; and process XML-encoded data.

- **Database support.** With most of today's web pages built dynamically from a database, PHP, with its out-of-the-box support for a variety of different databases, comes as a breath of fresh air. PHP comes with built-in support for MySQL, the extremely popular open-source database system, and can easily be configured to support a variety of other databases, including IBM DB2, mSQL, Oracle, PostgreSQL, Sybase, dBase, and ODBC. And, to simplify things even further, PHP 4.0 includes a database abstraction layer (conceptually similar to Perl's DBI module) that makes it possible to easily migrate from one DBMS to another.

- **OOP support.** Classes and objects have been available to PHP developers since version 3.0 of the languages; however, PHP's OO support has always been a little incomplete. Version 4.0 takes PHP closer to being a true object-oriented language. Among the new features, you'll find operator overloading, object nesting, and reference counting.

- **Built-in session management.** Unlike many other languages, PHP comes with native session management support, making it possible to track individual client sessions on a web site and create web applications that respond to the needs of individual users. With personalization features now almost *de facto* on popular web sites, PHP's built-in session management can significantly reduce both the time spent on developing and testing such sites.

Listing 1.3 demonstrates some of these features.

Listing 1.3   **A simple PHP script**

```php
<?php
///////////////////////////////////////////////////////////
//
// this is a simple login script that accepts a username
// and password and validates them against a database
//
// if the validation is successful, a new session is
// created and a customized template generated
//
// if the validation fails, the user is redirected
// to an error page
//
///////////////////////////////////////////////////////////

// includes
// DB variables are sourced from db_config.php
include("db_config.php");
include("TemplateClass.php");

// check login and password
// connect and execute query
$connection = mysql_connect($hostname, $user, $pass) or die ("Unable to
➥connect!");
$query = "SELECT id, username, nickname FROM user WHERE username = '$frmuser' AND
➥password = PASSWORD('$frmpass')";
mysql_select_db($database) or die ("Unable to select database!");
$result = mysql_query($query) or die ("Error in query: $query. " . mysql_error());

// if row exists - login/pass is correct
if (mysql_num_rows($result) == 1)
{

    // initiate a session
    session_start();

    // register the user's ID as a session variable
    session_register("SESSION_UID");
```

continues

Listing 1.3 **Continued**

```php
    list($id, $username, $nickname) = mysql_fetch_row($result);
    $SESSION_UID = $id;
    $welcome_msg = "Welcome back, " . $nickname;

    // close connection
    mysql_close($connection);

    // create an instance of the Template object
    $obj = new Template("welcome.tmpl", "#000000", "#FFFF00");

    // and execute some class methods
    $obj->set_welcome_msg($welcome_msg);
    $obj->print_template();
}
else
// login/pass check failed
{
    mysql_close($connection);
    // redirect to error page
    header("Location: error.php?ec=0");
    exit;
}
?>
```

Listing 1.3 demonstrates many of the most common PHP features. PHP's native MySQL support simplifies the task of connecting to a database to validate the user's account, although the built-in session functions make it easy to retain important user information as the user browses from page to page within the site. Object support is demonstrated by the use of a custom Template object, which creates the final web page seen by the user and provides developers with a robust and portable mechanism for page generation throughout the site.

Applications

In the old days, web sites consisted of static HTML pages with a few images thrown in for variety. That is no longer the case: today's web sites are complex and demanding, with movie-quality animation, high-res audio and video, and web pages built on-the-fly from immense databases churning away in the background. And, as you might imagine, PHP's ease of use, performance, and proven track record ensure that the language's primary application lies in the field of these dynamic, high-traffic web sites and applications.

PHP is well-suited to such complex web applications for a number of reasons. The language's built-in database capabilities ensure that it can connect easily to a variety of different databases for dynamic page generation; its payment processing and validation capabilities make it a good choice for online commerce; and its portability across platforms and support for important web technologies like Java and Flash make it suitable for a diverse range of other applications.

Today, PHP is used by businesses (such as Mitsubishi and Ericsson), government organizations (such as the United States Naval Research Laboratory), and popular open-source portals (for example, freshmeat.net and phpbuilder.com) for applications ranging from content management to wireless data transfer. This fact again demonstrates the versatility of the language.

If you're interested in PHP's numerous applications for business, you'll find some very interesting case studies at `http://www.zend.com/zend/cs/`.

I'm not going to get into the details of PHP's syntax and structure here, but will assume you know the basics. If you don't, you should take a look at *PHP Functions Essential Reference* by Zak Greant, Greame Merral, Torben Wilson, and Brett Michlitsch (New Riders Publishing, 2001) ISBN: 073570970X.

PHP and XML

Now that you've seen what PHP and XML are each about individually, you're probably wondering how the two of them fit together.

The overall vision of XML and its ancillary technologies is very clear—mark up data in XML, format it with XSL, link it together with XLink, and use it in a myriad of different ways. In reality, though, this overarching vision hits an obstacle at the first stage itself—most browsers don't come with either an XML parser or an XSL processor. The latest versions of Internet Explorer and Netscape Communicator do support XML, but older versions don't. And this begs an obvious question: given that these browsers do not support XML (or support it in an incomplete manner), how do you, as a web developer, even begin to build the next generation of cutting-edge XML applications?

Well, there's a simple solution: insert an intermediary layer between the client and the server to handle the processing of XML-encoded data. This intermediary layer can handle XML parsing, XSLT transformation, and other related tasks, serving as a translator between the server (which has XML data to transmit) and the client (which only understands a specific language like HTML or Wireless Markup Language (WML)).

That's where PHP fits in. PHP serves as the meat in the sandwich, acting as the intermediary layer through which all XML processing is handled. Although PHP does not (yet) support the entire family of XML technologies, the latest version does include a very capable XML parser with both DOM and SAX extensions, and an XSL processor, through its Sablotron extension.

PHP also supports Web Distributed Data Exchange (WDDX), a rapidly emerging XML-based standard for data transmission over the web and can be coaxed into working with XML-RPC and SOAP to issue XML-based procedure calls over the Internet. Finally, because PHP has support for a wide variety of databases, it's possible to use the language to build an XML document from a database or populate a database by parsing an XML document.

Some of the applications that arise as a result of this combination are

- **Data processing.** PHP's XML functions make it possible to parse XML data and carry out commands based on the type of data encountered. With some clever coding, this can be used to easily convert XML-encoded data into browser-compliant HTML output. You also can use PHP's XML functions to create a database from an XML document, or vice versa.

- **Data transformation.** PHP's XSLT extension brings the full power of XSLT processing to the language, making it possible to apply XSLT stylesheets to XML data. With support for a wide range of XSLT processing instructions, transforming data from one format to another becomes very simple.

- **Platform-independent information exchange.** PHP's WDDX functions make it possible to easily transfer information (including typed data like arrays) from one system to another using platform-neutral data structures. This capability is particularly useful for content publishers who need to disburse information to requesting clients on a periodic basis, yet have no control over the platform and operating environment of those clients—for example, news syndication services or stock market tickers. Because WDDX structures are platform-neutral, the PHP/WDDX combination encourages interoperability by making it possible to exchange data between programming languages in a simple and elegant manner.

- **Remote process execution.** Support for XML-RPC implies that PHP scripts can trigger processes on remote servers by sending them messages encoded in XML. This makes it possible to access different web services directly from your PHP script using standard client-server protocols and create new types of web applications based on these services. These processes/scripts might be written in other languages (such as Java, Python, Perl, and so on), again demonstrating how the XML/PHP combination can encourage greater interoperability between platforms and languages.

Summary

Clearly, PHP and XML are each powerful and flexible tools. Given the current state of the web, however, with browser support still evolving and many ancillary technologies yet to mature, you will need to use them together to gain the true measure of their capabilities.

Unlike the chapters yet to follow, this one contained almost no code; instead, it attempted to place both PHP and XML in context with a discussion of their individual capabilities and applications. It then proceeded to an explanation of how the two fit together and previewed some of the applications that become possible as a result. The subsequent chapters explore some of these applications in greater depth.

"I am not young enough to know everything."

~Oscar Wilde

2

PHP and the Simple API for XML (SAX)

I F YOU'RE NEW TO XML, SOMETHING BAD will happen to you right after you finish converting your little black book into XML-compliant format. You'll lean back in your swivel chair, sip a glass of wine, ponder the remnants of your shattered weekend, and ask yourself: "Now what?"

It's a question every XML newbie asks at least once, and it's not hard to understand why. When you're first learning XML, it's easy to get lost in the intricacies of name-spaces and entities, and to find satisfaction in the successful creation of valid XML documents and DTDs. As you gain experience, though, you'll find yourself wondering if there shouldn't be more to this than just tags and theory.

Well, you're right to wonder, and you're right in thinking that there's more here than meets the eye. Marking up data in XML is only the first step; the true value of the language becomes visible only when you try to do something useful with all that marked-up data. Because XML makes it possible for applications to easily recognize and operate on disparate pieces of data, it allows developers to do some complex things in very simple ways—which, when you get down to it, is what good program-ming is all about.

In this chapter, I will be attempting to answer that "Now what?" question by describing one of XML's simplest—yet most potent—applications: parsing and format-ting marked-up documents for greater readability and better presentation. My weapon of choice here will be the Simple API for XML (SAX), implemented via PHP. So keep reading!

SAX

There are two basic approaches to parsing an XML document:

- **The event-based approach.** Under this approach, an XML parser reads an XML document one chunk at a time, processing each tag as it finds it in the document. Each time the parser encounters an XML construct (an element start tag, a CDATA block, or a PI), it generates an event that can be intercepted and processed by the application layer. A Simple API for XML (SAX) parser uses this event-based approach to parsing an XML document.

- **The tree-based approach (DOM).** Here, an XML parser reads the entire document into memory at one time, and creates a hierarchical tree representation of it in memory. The parser also exposes a number of traversal methods, which developers can use to navigate between, and process, individual tree nodes. A Document Object Model (DOM) parser uses this tree-based approach to parsing an XML document.

This chapter focuses on the first approach. The second approach is dealt with in detail in Chapter 3, "PHP and the Document Object Model (DOM)."

In order to better understand the event-driven approach, consider Listing 2.1.

Listing 2.1 **Simple XML Document** (*fox.xml*)

```
<?xml version="1.0"?>
<sentence>The <animal color="blue">fox</animal> leaped over the <vegetable
➥color="green">cabbage</vegetable> patch and vanished into the darkness.</sentence>
```

Now, if a SAX parser processed this document, it would generate an event trail that would look something like this:

```
[tag opened] sentence
[cdata] The
[tag opened] animal
[attribute name] color
[attribute value] blue
[cdata] fox
[tag closed] animal
[cdata] leaped over the
[tag opened] vegetable
[attribute name] color
[attribute value] green
[cdata] cabbage
[tag closed] vegetable
[cdata] patch and vanished into the darkness.
[tag closed] sentence
```

Under the SAX approach, the parser has a very clear and defined role. Its function is merely to parse the XML data that's being fed to it and to call appropriate functions (also referred to as "handlers" or "callback functions") at the application layer to handle the different types of constructs it encounters. It's up to the developer to write the code necessary to handle each event, depending on the application requirements; the SAX parser itself is completely insulated from the internals of each handler function.

PHP and SAX

PHP 4.0 comes with a very capable SAX parser based on the expat library. Created by James Clark, the expat library is a fast, robust SAX implementation that provides XML parsing capabilities to a number of open-source projects, including the Mozilla browser (http://www.mozilla.org/).

If you're using a stock PHP binary, it's quite likely that you'll need to recompile PHP to add support for this library to your PHP build. Detailed instructions for accomplishing this are available in Appendix A, "Recompiling PHP to Add XML Support."

A Simple Example

You can do a number of complex things with a SAX parser; however, I'll begin with something simple to illustrate just how it all fits together. Let's go back to the previous XML document (see Listing 2.1), and write some PHP code to process this document and do something with the data inside it (see Listing 2.2).

Listing 2.2   **Generic PHP-Based XML Parser**

```
<html>
<head>
<basefont face="Arial">
</head>
<body>

<?php
// XML data file
$xml_file = "fox.xml";

// initialize parser
$xml_parser = xml_parser_create();

// set callback functions
xml_set_element_handler($xml_parser, "startElementHandler", "endElementHandler");
xml_set_character_data_handler($xml_parser, "characterDataHandler");

// read XML file
if (!($fp = fopen($xml_file, "r")))
{
     die("File I/O error: $xml_file");
}
```

continues

Listing 2.2 **Continued**

```
// parse XML
while ($data = fread($fp, 4096))
{
    // error handler
    if (!xml_parse($xml_parser, $data, feof($fp)))
    {
        die("XML parser error: " .
xml_error_string(xml_get_error_code($xml_parser)));
    }
}

// all done, clean up!
xml_parser_free($xml_parser);
?>
</body>
</html>
```

I'll explain Listing 2.2 in detail:

1. The first order of business is to initialize the SAX parser. This is accomplished via PHP's aptly named `xml_parser_create()` function, which returns a handle for use in successive operations involving the parser.

   ```
   $xml_parser = xml_parser_create();
   ```

2. With the parser created, it's time to let it know which events you would like it to monitor, and which user-defined functions (or *callback functions*) it should call when these events occur. For the moment, I'm going to restrict my activities to monitoring start tags, end tags, and the data embedded within them:

   ```
   xml_set_element_handler($xml_parser, "startElementHandler",
   ➡"endElementHandler");
   xml_set_character_data_handler($xml_parser, "characterDataHandler");
   ```

Speaking Different Tongues

It's possible to initialize the parser with a specific encoding. For example:

```
$xml_parser = xml_parser_create("UTF-8");
```

PHP's SAX parser currently supports the following encodings:

- ISO-8859-1

- US-ASCII

- UTF-8

An attempt to use an unsupported encoding will result in a slew of ugly error messages. Try it yourself to see what I mean.

What have I done here? Very simple. I've told the parser to call the function
`startElementHandler()` when it finds an opening tag, the function
`endElementHandler()` when it finds a closing tag, and the function
`characterDataHandler()` whenever it encounters character data within
the document.

When the parser calls these functions, it will automatically pass them all relevant
information as function arguments. Depending on the type of callback registered,
this information could include the element name, element attributes, character
data, processing instructions, or notation identifiers.

From Listing 2.2, you can see that I haven't defined these functions yet; I'll do
that a little later, and you'll see how this works in practice. Until these functions
have been defined, any attempt to run the code from Listing 2.2 as it is right
now will fail.

3. Now that the callback functions have been registered, all that remains is to actually parse the XML document. This is a simple exercise. First, create a file handle
for the document:

```
if (!($fp = fopen($xml_file, "r")))
{
        die("File I/O error: $xml_file");
}
```

Then, read in chunks of data with `fread()`, and parse each chunk using the
`xml_parse()` function:

```
while ($data = fread($fp, 4096))
{
    // error handler
      if (!xml_parse($xml_parser, $data, feof($fp)))
      {
            die("XML parser error: " .
xml_error_string(xml_get_error_code($xml_parser)));
      }
}
```

In the event that errors are encountered while parsing the document, the script
will automatically terminate via PHP's `die()` function. Detailed error information
can be obtained via the `xml_error_string()` and `xml_get_error_code()` functions
(for more information on how these work, see the "Handling Errors" section).

4. After the complete file has been processed, it's good programming practice to
clean up after yourself by destroying the XML parser you created:

```
xml_parser_free($xml_parser);
```

That said, in the event that you forget, PHP will automatically destroy the parser
for you when the script ends.

Endgame

You already know that SAX can process XML data in chunks, making it possible to parse XML documents larger than available memory. Ever wondered how it knows when to stop?

That's where the optional third parameter to xml_parse() comes in. As each chunk of data is read from the XML file, it is passed to the xml_parse() function for processing. When the end of the file is reached, the feof() function returns true, which tells the parser to stop and take a well-deserved break.

The preceding four steps make up a pretty standard process, and you'll find yourself using them over and over again when processing XML data with PHP's SAX parser. For this reason, you might find it more convenient to package them as a separate function, and call this function wherever required—a technique demonstrated in Listing 2.23.

With the generic XML processing code out of the way, let's move on to the callback functions defined near the top of the script. You'll remember that I registered the following three functions:

- startElementHandler()—Executed when an opening tag is encountered
- endElementHandler()—Executed when a closing tag is encountered
- characterDataHandler()—Executed when character data is encountered

Listing 2.3 is the revised script with these handlers included.

Listing 2.3 **Defining SAX Callback Functions**

```
<html>
<head>
<basefont face="Arial">
</head>
<body>
<?php

// run when start tag is found
function startElementHandler($parser, $name, $attributes)
{
    echo "Found opening tag of element: <b>$name</b> <br>";

    // process attributes
    while (list ($key, $value) = each ($attributes))
    {
        echo "Found attribute: <b>$key = $value</b> <br>";
    }
}

// run when end tag is found
function endElementHandler($parser, $name)
{
    echo "Found closing tag of element: <b>$name</b> <br>";
}
```

```
// run when cdata is found
function characterDataHandler($parser, $cdata)
{
        echo "Found CDATA: <i>$cdata</i> <br>";
}

// XML data file
$xml_file = "fox.xml";

// initialize parser
$xml_parser = xml_parser_create();

// set callback functions
xml_set_element_handler($xml_parser, "startElementHandler", "endElementHandler");
xml_set_character_data_handler($xml_parser, "characterDataHandler");

// read XML file
if (!($fp = fopen($xml_file, "r")))
{
        die("File I/O error: $xml_file");
}

// parse XML
while ($data = fread($fp, 4096))
{
    // error handler
        if (!xml_parse($xml_parser, $data, feof($fp)))
        {
                die("XML parser error: " .
xml_error_string(xml_get_error_code($xml_parser)));
        }
}

// all done, clean up!
xml_parser_free($xml_parser);

?>
</body>
</html>
```

Nothing too complex here. The tag handlers print the names of the tags they encounter, whereas the character data handler prints the data enclosed within the tags. Notice that the startElementHandler() function automatically receives the tag name and attributes as function arguments, whereas the characterDataHandler() gets the CDATA text.

And when you execute the script through a browser, here's what the end product looks like (and if you're wondering why all the element names are in uppercase, take a look at the "Controlling Parser Behavior" section):

```
Found opening tag of element: SENTENCE
Found CDATA: The
Found opening tag of element: ANIMAL
Found attribute: COLOR = blue
Found CDATA: fox
Found closing tag of element: ANIMAL
Found CDATA: leaped over the
Found opening tag of element: VEGETABLE
Found attribute: COLOR = green
Found CDATA: cabbage
Found closing tag of element: VEGETABLE
Found CDATA: patch and vanished into the darkness.
Found closing tag of element: SENTENCE
```

Not all that impressive, certainly—but then again, we're just getting started!

Handling SAX Events

Let's move on to a more focused discussion of the various event handlers you can register with the parser.

PHP includes handlers for elements and attributes, character data, processing instructions, external entities, and notations. Each of these is discussed in detail in the following sections.

Handling Elements

The `xml_set_element_handler()` function is used to identify the functions that handle elements encountered by the XML parser as it progresses through a document. This function accepts three arguments: the handle for the XML parser, the name of the function to call when it finds an opening tag, and the name of the function to call when it finds a closing tag, respectively.

Here's an example:

```
xml_set_element_handler($xml_parser, "startElementHandler", "endElementHandler");
```

In this case, I've told the parser to call the function `startElementHandler()` when it finds an opening tag and the function `endElementHandler()` when it finds a closing tag.

These handler functions must be set up to accept certain basic information about the element generating the event.

When PHP calls the start tag handler, it passes it the following three arguments:

- A handle representing the XML parser
- The name of the element
- A list of the element's attributes (as an associative array)

Because closing tags do not contain attributes, the end tag handler is only passed two arguments:

- A handle representing the XML parser
- The element name

In order to demonstrate this, consider Listing 2.4—a simple XML document.

Listing 2.4   **Letter Marked Up with XML (*letter.xml*)**

```xml
<?xml version="1.0"?>
<letter>
<date>10 January 2001</date>
<salutation>
     <para>
     Dear Aunt Hilda,
     </para>
</salutation>
<body>
     <para>
     Just writing to thank you for the wonderful train set you sent me for
     Christmas. I like it very much, and Sarah and I have both enjoyed playing
     with it over the long holidays.
     </para>
     <para>
     It has been a while since you visited us. How have you been? How are the
     dogs, and has the cat stopped playing with your knitting yet? We were hoping
     to come by for a short visit on New Year's Eve, but Sarah wasn't feeling
     well. However, I hope to see you next month when I will be home from school
     for the holidays.
     </para>
</body>
<conclusion>
     <para>Hugs and kisses -- Your nephew, Tom</para>
</conclusion>
</letter>
```

Listing 2.5 uses element handlers to create an indented list mirroring the hierarchical structure of the XML document in Listing 2.4.

Listing 2.5   **Representing an XML Document as a Hierarchical List**

```php
<html>
<head>
<basefont face="Arial">
</head>
<body>

<?php

// run when start tag is found
function startElementHandler($parser, $name, $attributes)
{
     echo "<ul><li>$name</li>";
}
```

continues

Listing 2.5 **Continued**

```php
function endElementHandler($parser, $name)
{
     echo "</ul>";
}

// XML data file
$xml_file = "letter.xml";

// initialize parser
$xml_parser = xml_parser_create();

// set element handler
xml_set_element_handler($xml_parser, "startElementHandler", "endElementHandler");

// read XML file
if (!($fp = fopen($xml_file, "r")))
{
     die("File I/O error: $xml_file");
}

// parse XML
while ($data = fread($fp, 4096))
{
     // error handler
     if (!xml_parse($xml_parser, $data, feof($fp)))
     {
          die("XML parser error: " .
xml_error_string(xml_get_error_code($xml_parser)));
     }
}

// all done, clean up!
xml_parser_free($xml_parser);
?>
</body>
</html>
```

Each time the parser finds an opening tag, it creates an unordered list and adds the tag name as the first item in that list; each time it finds an ending tag, it closes the list. The result is a hierarchical representation of the XML document's structure.

Handling Character Data

The xml_set_character_data_handler() registers event handlers for character data. It accepts two arguments: the handle for the XML parser and the name of the function to call when it finds character data.

For example:

```
xml_set_character_data_handler($xml_parser, "characterDataHandler");
```

This tells the SAX parser to use the function named `characterDataHandler()` to process character data.

When PHP calls this function, it automatically passes it the following two arguments:

- A handle representing the XML parser
- The character data found

Listing 2.6 demonstrates how this could be used.

Listing 2.6   **Stripping Out Tags from an XML Document**

```
<html>
<head>
<basefont face="Arial">
</head>
<body>

<?php

// cdata handler
function characterDataHandler($parser, $data)
{
      echo $data;
}

// XML data
$xml_data = <<<EOF
<?xml version="1.0"?>
<grammar>
      <noun type="proper">Mary</noun> <verb tense="past">had</verb> a
<adjective>little</adjective> <noun type="common">lamb.</noun>
</grammar>
EOF;

// initialize parser
$xml_parser = xml_parser_create();

// set cdata handler
xml_set_character_data_handler($xml_parser, "characterDataHandler");

if (!xml_parse($xml_parser, $xml_data))
{
      die("XML parser error: " .
xml_error_string(xml_get_error_code($xml_parser)));
}
```

continues

Listing 2.6   **Continued**

```
// all done, clean up!
xml_parser_free($xml_parser);

?>
</body>
</html>
```

In this case, the `characterDataHandler()` function works in much the same manner as PHP's built-in `strip_tags()` function—it scans through the XML and prints only the character data encountered. Because I haven't registered any element handlers, any tags found during this process are ignored.

You'll notice also that this example differs from the ones you've seen thus far, in that the XML data doesn't come from an external file, but has been defined via a variable in the script itself using "here document" syntax.

> **Here, Boy!**
>
> "Here-document" syntax provides a convenient way to create PHP strings that span multiple lines, or strings that retain their internal formatting (including tabs and line breaks).
>
> Consider the following example:
>
> ```
> <?php
> $str = <<<MARKER
> This is
>         a multi·
>    line
>                        string
> MARKER;
> ?>
> ```
>
> The <<< symbol indicates to PHP that what comes next is a multiline block, and should be stored "as is," right up to the specified marker. This marker must begin with an alphabetic or underscore character, can contain only alphanumeric and underscore characters, and when indicating the end of the block, must be flush with the left-hand margin of your code.

It should be noted that the character data handler is also invoked on CDATA blocks; Listing 2.7 is a variant of Listing 2.6 that demonstrates this.

Listing 2.7   **Parsing CDATA Blocks**

```
<html>
<head>
<basefont face="Arial">
</head>
<body>

<?php
```

```php
// cdata handler
function characterDataHandler($parser, $data)
{
    echo $data;
}

// XML data
$xml_string = <<<EOF
<?xml version="1.0"?>
<message>
    <from>Agent 5292</from>
    <to>Covert-Ops HQ</to>
    <encoded_message>
    <![CDATA[
    563247 !#9292 73%639 1^2736 @@6473 634292 930049 292$88 *7623&& 62367&
    ]]>
    </encoded_message>
</message>
EOF;

// initialize parser
$xml_parser = xml_parser_create();

// set cdata handler
xml_set_character_data_handler($xml_parser, "characterDataHandler");

if (!xml_parse($xml_parser, $xml_string))
{
    die("XML parser error: " .
xml_error_string(xml_get_error_code($xml_parser)));
}

// all done, clean up!
xml_parser_free($xml_parser);

?>
</body>
</html>
```

When Less Work Is More

There's an important caveat you should note when dealing with character data via PHP's SAX parser. If a character data section contains entity references, then PHP will not replace the entity reference with its actual value first and then call the handler. Rather, it will split the character data into segments around the reference and operate on each segment separately.

What does this mean? Well, here's the sequence of events:

1. PHP first calls the handler for the CDATA segment before the entity reference.

2. It then replaces the reference with its value, and calls the handler again.

continues

Continued

3. Finally, it calls the handler a third time for the segment following the entity reference.

Table 2.1 might help to make this clearer. The first column uses a basic XML document without entities; the second column uses a document containing an entity reference within the data block. Both examples use the same character data handler; however, as the output shows, the first example calls the handler once, whereas the second calls the handler thrice.

Table 2.1   **A Comparison of Parser Behavior in CDATA Sections Containing Entity References**

XML Document without Entity References	XML Document with Entity References
```<?xml version="1.0"?><message>Welcome to GenericCorp.We're just like everyone else.</message>```	```<?xml version="1.0"?><!DOCTYPE message[<!ENTITY company "GenericCorp">]><message>Welcome to &company;.We're just like everyoneelse.</message>```
THE HANDLER:`<?php// cdata handlerfunction characterDataHandler($parser, $data){ echo "	handler in	" .$data . "	handler out	";}?>`	`<?php// cdata handlerfunction characterDataHandler($parser, $data){ echo "	handler in	" .$data . "	handler out	";}?>`
THE OUTPUT:`| handler in	Welcome toGenericCorp. We're just likeeveryone else.	handler out |`	`| handler in	Welcome to	handlerout		handler in	GenericCorp |handler out		handler in	.We're just like everyone else. |handler out |`

Handling Processing Instructions

You can set up a handler for PIs with xml_set_processing_instruction_handler(), which operates just like the character data handler above.

This snippet designates the function PIHandler() as the handler for all PIs found in the document:

```
xml_set_processing_instruction_handler($xml_parser, "PIHandler");
```

The designated handler must accept three arguments:

- A handle representing the XML parser (you can see that this is standard for all event handlers)
- The PI *target* (an identifier for the application that is to process the instruction)
- The instruction itself

Listing 2.8 demonstrates how it works in practice. When the parser encounters the PHP code within the document, it calls the PI handler, which executes the code as a PHP statement and displays the result.

Listing 2.8   **Executing PIs within an XML Document**

```
<html>
<head>
<basefont face="Arial">
</head>
<body>

<?php

// cdata handler
function characterDataHandler($parser, $data)
{
      echo $data . "<p>";
}

// PI handler
function PIHandler($parser, $target, $data)
{
      // if php code, execute it
      if (strtolower($target) == "php")
      {
          eval($data);
      }
      // otherwise just print it
      else
      {
          echo "PI found: [$target] $data";
      }
}

// XML data
$xml_data = <<<EOF
<?xml version="1.0"?>
<article>
      <header>insert slug here</header>
      <body>insert body here</body>
      <footer><?php print "Copyright UNoHoo Inc," . date("Y", mktime()); ?></footer>
```

continues

Listing 2.8   **Continued**

```
</article>
EOF;

// initialize parser
$xml_parser = xml_parser_create();

// set cdata handler
xml_set_character_data_handler($xml_parser, "characterDataHandler");

// set PI handler
xml_set_processing_instruction_handler($xml_parser, "PIHandler");

if (!xml_parse($xml_parser, $xml_data))
{
     die("XML parser error: " .
xml_error_string(xml_get_error_code($xml_parser)));
}

// all done, clean up!
xml_parser_free($xml_parser);

?>
</body>
</html>
```

Listing 2.8 designates the function `PIHandler()` as the handler to be called for all PIs encountered within the document. As explained previously, this function is passed the PI target and instruction as function arguments.

When a PI is located within the document, `PIHandler()` first checks the PI target (`$target`) to see if is a PHP instruction. If it is, `eval()` is called to evaluate and execute the PHP code (`$data`) within the PI. If the target is any other application, PHP obviously cannot execute the instructions, and therefore resorts to merely displaying the PI to the user.

> **Careful `eval()`-uation**
>
> You may not know this (I didn't), but PHP—which is usually pretty rigid about ending every statement with a semicolon—allows you to omit the semicolon from the statement immediately preceding a closing PHP tag. For example, this is perfectly valid PHP code:
>
> ```
> <?php print "Copyright UNoHoo Inc," . date("Y", mktime()) ?>
> ```
>
> However, if you were to place this code in a PI, and pass it to `eval()`, as in Listing 2.8, `eval()` would generate an error. This is because the `eval()` function *requires* that all PHP statement(s) passed to it for evaluation must end with semicolons.

Handling External Entities

You already know that an entity provides a simple way to reuse frequently repeated text segments within an XML document. Most often, entities are defined and referenced within the same document. However, sometimes a need arises to separate entities that are common across multiple documents into a single external file. These entities, which are defined in one file and referenced in others, are known as *external entities*.

If a document contains references to external entities, PHP offers `xml_set_external_entity_ref_handler()`, which specifies how these entities are to be handled.

This snippet designates the function `externalEntityHandler()` as the handler for all external entities found in the document:

```
xml_set_external_entity_ref_handler($xml_parser, "externalEntityHandler");
```

The handler designated by `xml_set_external_entity_ref_handler()` must be set up to accept the following five arguments:

- A handle representing the XML parser
- The entity name
- The base URI for the SYSTEM identifier (PHP currently sets this to an empty string)
- The SYSTEM identifier itself (if available)
- The PUBLIC identifier (if available)

In order to illustrate this, consider the following XML document (see Listing 2.9), which contains an external entity reference (see Listing 2.10).

Listing 2.9   **XML Document Referencing an External Entity (*mission.xml*)**

```
<?xml version="1.0"?>
<!DOCTYPE mission
[
<!ENTITY warning SYSTEM "warning.txt">
]>
<mission>
        <objective>Find the nearest Starbucks</objective>
        <goal>Bring back two lattes, one espresso and one black coffee</goal>
        <priority>Critical</priority>
        <w>&warning;</w>
</mission>
```

True to You

The handler for external entities must explicitly return `true` if its actions are successful. If the handler returns `false` (or returns nothing at all, which works out to the same thing), the parser exits with error code 21 (see the "Handling Errors" section for more information on error codes).

Listing 2.10 **Referenced External Entity** (*warning.txt*)

```
This document will self-destruct in thirty seconds.
```

Listing 2.11 is a sample script that demonstrates how the entity resolver works.

Listing 2.11 **Resolving External Entities**

```php
<html>
<head>
<basefont face="Arial">
</head>
<body>
<?php

// external entity handler
function externalEntityHandler($parser, $name, $base, $systemId, $publicId)
{
        // read referenced file
        if (!readfile($systemId))
        {
            die("File I/O error: $systemId");
        }
        else
        {
            return true;
        }
}

// cdata handler
function characterDataHandler($parser, $data)
{
        echo $data . "<p>";
}

// XML data file
$xml_file = "mission.xml";

// initialize parser
$xml_parser = xml_parser_create();

// set cdata handler
xml_set_character_data_handler($xml_parser, "characterDataHandler");

// set external entity handler
xml_set_external_entity_ref_handler($xml_parser, "externalEntityHandler");

// read XML file
if (!($fp = fopen($xml_file, "r")))
{
```

```
        die("File I/O error: $xml_file");
}

// parse XML
while ($data = fread($fp, 4096))
{
        // error handler
        if (!xml_parse($xml_parser, $data, feof($fp)))
        {
                die("XML parser error: " .
xml_error_string(xml_get_error_code($xml_parser)));
        }
}

// all done, clean up!
xml_parser_free($xml_parser);

?>
</body>
</html>
```

When this script runs, the external entity handler finds and resolves the entity reference, and includes it in the main document. In this case, the external entity is merely
included, not parsed or processed in any way; however, if you want to see an example
in which the external entity is itself an XML document that needs to be parsed further, take a look at Listing 2.23 in the "A Composite Example" section.

Handling Notations and Unparsed Entities

You already know that notations and unparsed entities go together—and PHP
allows you to handle them, too, via its `xml_set_notation_decl_handler()` and
`xml_set_unparsed_entity_decl_handler()` functions. (If you don't know what notations and unparsed entities are, drop by Chapter 1, "XML and PHP Basics," and find
out what you missed.) Like all the other handlers discussed thus far, both these functions designate handlers to be called when the parser encounters either a notation
declaration or an unparsed entity.

The following snippet designates the functions `unparsedEntityHandler()` and
`notationHandler()` as the handlers for unparsed entities and notations found in
the document:

```
xml_set_unparsed_entity_decl_handler($xml_parser, "unparsedEntityHandler");
xml_set_notation_decl_handler($xml_parser, "notationHandler");
```

The handler designated by `xml_set_notation_decl_handler()` must be capable of
accepting the following five arguments:

- A handle representing the XML parser
- The notation name

- A base URI for the SYSTEM identifier
- The SYSTEM identifier itself (if available)
- The PUBLIC identifier (if available)

Similarly, the handler designated by xml_set_unparsed_entity_decl_handler() must be capable of accepting the following six arguments:

- A handle representing the XML parser
- The name of the unparsed entity
- A base for the SYSTEM identifier
- The SYSTEM identifier itself (if available)
- The PUBLIC identifier (if available)
- The notation name

In order to understand how these handlers work in practice, consider Listing 2.12, which sets up two unparsed entities representing directories on the system and a notation that tells the system what to do with them (run a script that calculates the disk space they're using, and mail the results to the administrator).

Listing 2.12 **XML Document Containing Unparsed Entities and Notations** (*list.xml*)

```
<?xml version="1.0"?>
<!DOCTYPE list
[
<!ELEMENT list (#PCDATA | dir)*>
<!ELEMENT dir EMPTY>
<!ATTLIST dir name ENTITY #REQUIRED>
<!NOTATION directory SYSTEM "/usr/local/bin/usage.pl">
<!ENTITY config SYSTEM "/etc" NDATA directory>
<!ENTITY temp SYSTEM "/tmp" NDATA directory>
]>
<list>
    <dir name="config" />
    <dir name="temp" />
</list>
```

Listing 2.13 is the PHP script that parses the XML document.

Listing 2.13 **Handling Unparsed Entities**

```
<html>
<head>
<basefont face="Arial">
</head>
<body>
```

```php
<?php

// cdata handler
function characterDataHandler($parser, $data)
{
 echo $data . "<p>";
}

// unparsed entity handler
function unparsedEntityHandler($parser, $entity, $base, $systemId, $publicId,
$notation)
{
     global $notationsArray;
     if ($systemId)
     {
          exec("$notationsArray[$notation] $systemId");
     }
}

// notation handler
function notationHandler($parser, $notation, $base, $systemId, $publicId)
{
     global $notationsArray;
     if ($systemId)
     {
          $notationsArray[$notation] = $systemId;
     }
}

// XML data file
$xml_file = "list.xml";

// initialize array to hold notation declarations
$notationsArray = array();

// initialize parser
$xml_parser = xml_parser_create();

// set cdata handler
xml_set_character_data_handler($xml_parser, "characterDataHandler");

// set entity and notation handlers
xml_set_unparsed_entity_decl_handler($xml_parser, "unparsedEntityHandler");
xml_set_notation_decl_handler($xml_parser, "notationHandler");

// read XML file
if (!($fp = fopen($xml_file, "r")))
{
     die("File I/O error: $xml_file");
}
```

continues

Listing 2.13 **Continued**

```php
// parse XML
while ($data = fread($fp, 4096))
{
    // error handler
    if (!xml_parse($xml_parser, $data, feof($fp)))
    {
        die("XML parser error: " .
xml_error_string(xml_get_error_code($xml_parser)));
    }
}

// all done, clean up!
xml_parser_free($xml_parser);

?>
</body>
</html>
```

This is a little different from the scripts you've seen so far, so an explanation is in order.

The `notationHandler()` function, called whenever the parser encounters a notation declaration, simply adds the notation and its associated system identifier to a global associative array, `$notationsArray`. Now, whenever an unparsed entity is encountered, the `unparsedEntityHandler()` function matches the notation name within the entity declaration to the keys of the associative array, and launches the appropriate script with the entity as parameter.

Obviously, how you use these two handlers depends a great deal on how your notation declarations and unparsed entities are set up. In this case, I use the notation to specify the location of the application and the entity handler to launch the application whenever required. You also can use these handlers to display binary data within the page itself (assuming that your target environment is a browser), to process it further, or to ignore it altogether.

Rapid "exec()-ution"

The PHP `exec()` function provides a handy way to execute any command on the system. That's why it's so perfect for a situation like the one shown in Listing 2.13. With the `usage.pl` script and directory name both available to the parser, it's a simple matter to put them together and then have `exec()` automatically run the disk usage checker every time a directory name is encountered within the XML document.

The convenience of `exec()` comes at a price, however. Using `exec()` can pose significant security risks, and can even cause your system to slow down or crash if the program you are "exec()-uting" fails to exit properly. The PHP manual documents this in greater detail.

If you prefer to have the output from the command displayed (or processed further), you should consider the `passthru()` function, designed for just that purpose.

Handling Everything Else

Finally, PHP also offers the `xml_set_default_handler()` function for all those situations not covered by the preceding handlers. In the event that no other handlers are defined for the document, all events generated will be trapped and resolved by this handler.

This snippet designates the function `defaultHandler()` as the default handler for the document:

```
xml_set_default_handler($xml_parser, "defaultHandler");
```

The function designated by `xml_set_default_handler()` must be set up to accept the following two arguments:

- A handle representing the XML parser
- The data encountered

In Listing 2.14, every event generated by the parser is passed to the default handler (because no other handlers are defined), which simply prints the data received. The final output? An exact mirror of the input!

Listing 2.14   **Demonstrating the Default Handler**

```php
<html>
<head>
<basefont face="Arial">
</head>
<body>

<?php

// default handler
function defaultHandler($parser, $data)
{
      echo "<pre>" . htmlspecialchars($data) . "</pre>";
}

// XML data
$xml_data = <<<EOF
<?xml version="1.0"?>
<element>carbon <!-- did you know that diamond is a form of carbon? -Ed -->
</element>
EOF;

// initialize parser
$xml_parser = xml_parser_create();

// set default handler
xml_set_default_handler($xml_parser, "defaultHandler");

if (!xml_parse($xml_parser, $xml_data))
```

continues

Listing 2.14 **Continued**

```
{
      die("XML parser error: " .
xml_error_string(xml_get_error_code($xml_parser)));
}

// all done, clean up!
xml_parser_free($xml_parser);

?>
</body>
</html>
```

Controlling Parser Behavior

Currently, PHP's XML parser allows you to control the following:

- Case folding
- Target encoding
- Whitespace processing

All these attributes can be controlled via the `xml_set_option()` function, which accepts three parameters:

- A handle for the parser to be modified
- The attribute name
- The attribute value (either string or Boolean)

The sections that follow describe each of these parameters in greater detail with examples.

Case Folding

Within the context of an XML document, *case folding* simply involves replacing lower-case characters in element names with their uppercase equivalents. XML element names are case-sensitive; typically, you use case folding to impose consistency on mixed-case element names so that they can be handled in a predictable manner.

This option is controlled via the `XML_OPTION_CASE_FOLDING` attribute and is set to true by default.

In order to see how this works, take a look at Listing 2.15, which modifies Listing 2.3 to turn off case folding (element names will no longer be uppercase).

Listing 2.15   **Demonstration of Case Folding**

```
...

// initialize parser
$xml_parser = xml_parser_create();

// turn off case folding
xml_parser_set_option($xml_parser, XML_OPTION_CASE_FOLDING, FALSE);

// set callback functions
xml_set_element_handler($xml_parser, "startElementHandler", "endElementHandler");
xml_set_character_data_handler($xml_parser, "characterDataHandler");

...
```

Here's the output:

```
Found opening tag of element: sentence
Found CDATA: The
Found opening tag of element: animal
Found attribute: color = blue
Found CDATA: fox
Found closing tag of element: animal
Found CDATA: leaped over the
Found opening tag of element: vegetable
Found attribute: color = green
Found CDATA: cabbage
Found closing tag of element: vegetable
Found CDATA: patch and vanished into the darkness.
Found closing tag of element: sentence
```

Target Encoding

You already know that it's possible to specify a character set for document encoding when an XML parser is created with the xml_parser_create() function. (Refer to the "Speaking Different Tongues" sidebar at the beginning of this chapter.) In geek lingo, this is referred to as *source encoding*.

In addition, PHP also allows you to specify *target encoding*, which is the encoding to use when the parser passes data to a handler function.

By default, this encoding is the same as the source encoding; however, you can alter it via the XML_OPTION_TARGET_ENCODING attributes, which supports any one of the following encodings: ISO-8859-1, US-ASCII, and UTF-8.

The following example sets the target encoding for the parser to UTF-8:

```
xml_parser_set_option($xml_parser, XML_OPTION_TARGET_ENCODING, "UTF-8");
```

Whitespace Processing

You can tell the parser to skip the whitespace it encounters by setting the XML_OPTION_SKIP_WHITE attribute to true. This attribute can come in handy if your XML document contains tabs or spaces that could interfere with your program logic.

The following example turns whitespace processing off:

```
xml_parser_set_option($xml_parser, XML_OPTION_SKIP_WHITE, 1);
```

You can obtain the current value of any of the parser's attributes with the xml_parser_get_option() function, which returns the value of the specified attribute. For example:

```
xml_parser_get_option($xml_parser, XML_OPTION_CASE_FOLDING);
```

Using Native Data Structures

You may sometimes come across a situation that requires you to convert raw XML markup into native data structures such as variables, arrays, or custom objects. For these situations, PHP offers a very specialized little function named xml_parse_into_struct(). The xml_parse_into_struct() function requires four arguments:

- A reference to the XML parser
- The raw XML data to be processed
- Two arrays to hold the data in structured form

After xml_parse_into_struct() has processed the XML document, it populates the two arrays with detailed information on the structure of the XML document. One array holds a list of all the elements encountered by the parser in its journey through the XML document; the other contains information on the frequency of occurrence of each element.

An example might help to make this clearer. Consider the XML document shown in Listing 2.16.

Listing 2.16 **XML-Compliant Bookmark List (*links.xml*)**

```
<?xml version="1.0"?>
<bookmarks category="News">
    <link id="15696">
        <title>CNN</title>
        <url>http://www.cnn.com/</url>
        <last_access>2000-09-08</last_access>
    </link>

    <link id="3763">
        <title>Freshmeat</title>
        <url>http://www.freshmeat.net/</url>
```

```
                <last_access>2001-04-23</last_access>
        </link>

        <link id="84574">
                <title>Slashdot</title>
                <url>http://www.slashdot.com/</url>
                <last_access>2001-12-30</last_access>
        </link>
</bookmarks>
```

Then take a look at the script in Listing 2.17, which parses the preceding XML data and creates native PHP arrays representing the document structure (you can view these arrays with the print_r() function).

Listing 2.17   **Converting XML Data Structures into PHP Arrays**

```php
<?php
// XML data
$xml_file = "links.xml";

// read XML file
if (!($fp = fopen($xml_file, "r")))
{
        die("File I/O error: $xml_file");
}

// create string containing XML data
while ($chunk = fread($fp, 4096))
{
        $data .= $chunk;
}

// initialize parser
$xml_parser = xml_parser_create();

// turn off whitespace processing
xml_parser_set_option($xml_parser,XML_OPTION_SKIP_WHITE, TRUE);

// read file
if (!xml_parse_into_struct($xml_parser, $data, $elementArray, $frequencyArray))
{
        die("XML parser error: " .
xml_error_string(xml_get_error_code($xml_parser)));
}

// all done, clean up!
xml_parser_free($xml_parser);
?>
```

Quick Experiment

In Listing 2.17, comment out the line that turns off whitespace processing, and see what happens to the generated arrays.

After the script has finished processing, the individual elements of $elementArray correspond to the elements within the XML document. Each of these elements is itself an array containing information such as the element name, attributes, type, and depth within the XML tree. Take a look:

```
Array
(
    [0] => Array
        (
            [tag] => BOOKMARKS
            [type] => open
            [level] => 1
            [attributes] => Array
                (
                    [CATEGORY] => News
                )

        )

    [1] => Array
        (
            [tag] => LINK
            [type] => open
            [level] => 2
            [attributes] => Array
                (
                    [ID] => 15696
                )

        )

    [2] => Array
        (
            [tag] => TITLE
            [type] => complete
            [level] => 3
            [value] => CNN
        )

    [3] => Array
        (
            [tag] => URL
            [type] => complete
            [level] => 3
            [value] => http://www.cnn.com/
        )
```

```
    [4] => Array
        (
            [tag] => LAST_ACCESS
            [type] => complete
            [level] => 3
            [value] => 2000-09-08
        )

    [5] => Array
        (
            [tag] => LINK
            [type] => close
            [level] => 2
        )

    [6] => Array
        (
            [tag] => LINK
            [type] => open
            [level] => 2
            [attributes] => Array
                (
                    [ID] => 3763
                )

        )


... and so on ...

)
```

The second array, $frequencyArray, is a more compact associative array, with keys corresponding to the element names found within the document. Each key of this array is linked to a list of indexes, which points to the locations within $elementArray holding information on the corresponding element. Take a look:

```
Array
(
    [BOOKMARKS] => Array
        (
            [0] => 0
            [1] => 11
        )

    [LINK] => Array
        (
            [0] => 1
            [1] => 5
            [2] => 6
            [3] => 10
        )
```

```
[TITLE] => Array
    (
        [0] => 2
        [1] => 7
    )

[URL] => Array
    (
        [0] => 3
        [1] => 8
    )

[LAST_ACCESS] => Array
    (
        [0] => 4
        [1] => 9
    )
)
```

By studying the elements of $frequencyArray, it's easy to do the following:

- Determine the frequency with which particular elements occur within the XML document
- Identify individual element occurrences, and obtain their corresponding value or attributes from the $elementArray array via the specified index

After the raw XML has been converted into this structured (albeit complex) representation and stored in memory, it's possible to manipulate it or perform tree-type traversal on it. It's possible, for example, to convert this structured representation into a tree object, and write an API to travel between the different branches of the tree, thereby replicating much of the functionality offered by PHP's DOM library. (I say "possible" instead of "advisable" for obvious reasons: Using PHP's native DOM functions to build an XML tree would be faster than simulating the same with SAX.)

Nevertheless, it might be instructive to see how this structured representation can be used to extract specific information from the document. Consider Listing 2.18, which is an enhancement to Listing 2.17. It manipulates the structured representation to create a third array containing only the URLs from each link.

Listing 2.18 **Creating Custom Structures from Raw XML Data**

```php
<?php

// XML data
$xml_file = "links.xml";

// read XML file
```

```php
if (!($fp = fopen($xml_file, "r")))
{
    die("File I/O error: $xml_file");
}

// create string containing XML data
while ($chunk = fread($fp, 4096))
{
    $data .= $chunk;
}

// initialize parser
$xml_parser = xml_parser_create();

// turn off whitespace processing
xml_parser_set_option($xml_parser,XML_OPTION_SKIP_WHITE,1);

// read file
if (!xml_parse_into_struct($xml_parser, $data, $elementArray, $frequencyArray))
{
    die("XML parser error: " .
xml_error_string(xml_get_error_code($xml_parser)));
}

// all done, clean up!
xml_parser_free($xml_parser);

// create array to hold URLs
$urls = array();

// look up $frequencyArray for <url> element
// this element is itself an array, so iterate through it
foreach($frequencyArray["URL"] as $element)
{
    // for each value found, look up $elementsArray and retrieve the value
    // add this to the URLs array
    $urls[] = $elementArray[$element]["value"];
}

?>
```

You're probably thinking that this might be easier using a character data handler and an element handler. You're right—it would be. Listing 2.18 is shown merely to demonstrate an alternative approach to the event-based approach you've become familiar with. Personally, I haven't ever used this function; I prefer to use the DOM for XML tree generation and traversal where required. (The DOM approach to XML processing is covered in Chapter 3.)

Handling Errors

During the initial stages of application development, it's possible to get by without using error handlers in your code; however, as an application is being packaged for release, graceful error handling and recovery becomes a must.

PHP allows developers to accomplish this error handling via its `xml_get_error_code()` function (which prints the error code returned by the parser when it hits a bump) and its `xml_error_string()` function, (which returns a short, human-readable error message corresponding to the error code). Table 2.2 is a list of error codes and their corresponding named constants, together with what they mean.

Table 2.2 **SAX Parser Error Codes**

Error Code	Error Constant	Meaning
1	XML_ERROR_NO_MEMORY	Parser out of memory
2	XML_ERROR_SYNTAX	Syntax error
3	XML_ERROR_NO_ELEMENTS	No element found
4	XML_ERROR_INVALID_TOKEN	Document not well-formed
5	XML_ERROR_UNCLOSED_TOKEN	Unclosed token
6	XML_ERROR_PARTIAL_CHAR	Unclosed token
7	XML_ERROR_TAG_MISMATCH	Mismatched tag
8	XML_ERROR_DUPLICATE_ATTRIBUTE	Duplicate attribute
9	XML_ERROR_JUNK_AFTER_DOC_ELEMENT	Junk after document element
10	XML_ERROR_PARAM_ENTITY_REF	Illegal parameter entity reference found
11	XML_ERROR_UNDEFINED_ENTITY	Undefined entity
12	XML_ERROR_RECURSIVE_ENTITY_REF	Recursive entity reference
13	XML_ERROR_ASYNC_ENTITY	Asynchronous entity
14	XML_ERROR_BAD_CHAR_REF	Reference to invalid character number found
15	XML_ERROR_BINARY_ENTITY_REF	Reference to binary entity found
16	XML_ERROR_ATTRIBUTE_EXTERNAL_ENTITY_REF	Reference to external entity found within attribute
17	XML_ERROR_MISPLACED_XML_PI	XML processing instruction not found at start of external entity
18	XML_ERROR_UNKNOWN_ENCODING	Unknown document encoding
19	XML_ERROR_INCORRECT_ENCODING	Incorrect document encoding specified

Error Code	Error Constant	Meaning
20	. `XML_ERROR_UNCLOSED_CDATA_SECTION`	CDATA section not closed correctly
21	`XML_ERROR_EXTERNAL_ENTITY_HANDLING`	Error in processing external entity reference

In order to illustrate how this error-handling works, consider Listing 2.19, which contains a badly formed XML document. (There's a duplicate attribute within the element <circle>.) Note that the `xml_error_string()` function has been used to return a more helpful description of the error.

Listing 2.19 **Better Error Handling**

```
<html>
<head>
<basefont face="Arial">
</head>
<body>

<?php

// XML data
$xml_data = <<<EOF
<?xml version="1.0"?>
<shape>
      <circle color="red" radius="5" x="14" y="574" color="red" />
</shape>
EOF;

// define handlers
function startElementHandler($parser, $name, $attributes)
{
      // code snipped out
}

function endElementHandler($parser, $name)
{
      // code snipped out
}

// initialize parser
$xml_parser = xml_parser_create();

// set callback functions
xml_set_element_handler($xml_parser, "startElementHandler", "endElementHandler");
```

continues

Listing 2.19 **Continued**

```
if (!xml_parse($xml_parser, $xml_data))
{
     $ec = xml_get_error_code($xml_parser);
     die("XML parser error (error code $ec): " . xml_error_string($ec));
}


// all done, clean up!
xml_parser_free($xml_parser);

?>
</body>
</html>
```

Why stop there? It's also possible to include information on where exactly the error occurred within the document, with these three built-in functions:

- `xml_get_current_line_number()`—Returns the current line number
- `xml_get_current_column_number()`—Returns the current column number
- `xml_get_current_byte_index()`—Returns the current byte offset

Listing 2.20 is the revised script that incorporates this information.

Listing 2.20 **Adding Line and Column Information to Error Messages**

```
<html>
<head>
<basefont face="Arial">
</head>
<body>

<?php

// XML data
$xml_data = <<<EOF
<?xml version="1.0"?>
<shape>
     <circle color="red" radius="5" x="14" y="574" color="red" />
</shape>
EOF;

// define handlers
function startElementHandler($parser, $name, $attributes)
{
     // code snipped out
}
```

```
function endElementHandler($parser, $name)
{
     // code snipped out
}

// initialize parser
$xml_parser = xml_parser_create();

// set callback functions
xml_set_element_handler($xml_parser, "startElementHandler", "endElementHandler");

if (!xml_parse($xml_parser, $xml_data))
{
     $ec = xml_get_error_code($xml_parser);
     die("XML parser error (error code $ec): " . xml_error_string($ec) .
➥"<br>Error occurred at line " .
➥xml_get_current_line_number($xml_parser) . ",
➥column " . xml_get_current_column_number($xml_parser) . ",
➥byte offset " . xml_get_current_byte_index($xml_parser));
}

// all done, clean up!
xml_parser_free($xml_parser);

?>
</body>
</html>
```

And here's the output:

```
XML parser error (error code 8): duplicate attribute
Error occurred at line 3, column 46, byte offset 78
```

There! Isn't that much more helpful?

A Few Examples

Now that you know the theory, let's see how it works in some real-life examples. The following sections illustrate how PHP's SAX parser can be used to "do something useful" with XML data.

Formatting an XML Invoice for Display in a Web Browser

Consider the XML document in Listing 2.21, which contains an invoice for material delivered by Sammy's Sports Store.

Listing 2.21   **XML Invoice (*invoice.xml*)**

```xml
<?xml version="1.0"?>
<!DOCTYPE invoice
[
<!ENTITY message "Thank you for your purchases!">
<!ENTITY terms SYSTEM "terms.xml">
]>

<invoice>

        <customer>
                <name>Joe Wannabe</name>
                <address>
                        <line>23, Great Bridge Road</line>
                        <line>Bombay, MH</line>
                        <line>India</line>
                </address>
        </customer>

        <date>2001-09-15</date>

        <reference>75-848478-98</reference>

        <items>
                <item cid="AS633225">
                        <desc>Oversize tennis racquet</desc>
                        <price>235.00</price>
                        <quantity>1</quantity>
                        <subtotal>235.00</subtotal>
                </item>

                <item cid="GT645">
                        <desc>Championship tennis balls (can)</desc>
                        <price>9.99</price>
                        <quantity>4</quantity>
                        <subtotal>39.96</subtotal>
                </item>

                <item cid="U73472">
                        <desc>Designer gym bag</desc>
                        <price>139.99</price>
                        <quantity>1</quantity>
                        <subtotal>139.99</subtotal>
                </item>

                <item cid="AD848383">
                        <desc>Custom-fitted sneakers</desc>
                        <price>349.99</price>
                        <quantity>1</quantity>
                        <subtotal>349.99</subtotal>
```

```
        </item>
    </items>

    <?php displayTotal(); ?>

    <delivery>Next-day air</delivery>

    &terms;

    &message;

</invoice>
```

The entity &terms references the file "terms.xml", which is shown in Listing 2.22.

Listing 2.22   **Payment Terms and Conditions in XML (*terms.xml*)**

```
<?xml version="1.0"?>
<terms>
        <term>Visa, Mastercard, American Express accepted. Checks will be accepted
for orders totalling more than USD 5000.00</term>
        <term>All payments must be made in US currency</term>
        <term>Returns within 15 days</term>
        <term>International orders may be subject to additional customs duties and
levies</term>
</terms>
```

This invoice contains many of the constructs you've just studied: PIs, external entities, and plain-vanilla elements and data. It therefore serves as a good proving ground to demonstrate how PHP, combined with SAX, can be used to format XML data for greater readability. The script in Listing 2.23 parses the previous XML data to create an HTML page that is suitable for printing or viewing in a browser.

Listing 2.23   **Generating HTML Output from XML Data with SAX**

```
<html>
<head>
<basefont face="Arial">
</head>
<body bgcolor="white">

<font size="+3">Sammy's Sports Store</font>
<br>
<font size="-2">14, Ocean View, CA 12345, USA http://www.sammysportstore.com/</font>
<p>
<hr>
```

continues

Listing 2.23 **Continued**

```php
<center>INVOICE</center>
<hr>
<?php

// element handlers
// these look up the element in the associative arrays
// and print the equivalent HTML code
function startElementHandler($parser, $name, $attribs)
{
    global $startTagsArray;

    // expose element being processed
    global $currentTag;
    $currentTag = $name;

    // look up element in array and print corresponding HTML
    if ($startTagsArray[$name])
    {
        echo $startTagsArray[$name];
    }
}

function endElementHandler($parser, $name)
{
    global $endTagsArray;
    if ($endTagsArray[$name])
    {
        echo $endTagsArray[$name];
    }
}

// character data handler
// this prints CDATA as it is found
function characterDataHandler($parser, $data)
{
    global $currentTag;
    global $subTotals;

    echo $data;

    // record subtotals for calculation of grand total
    if ($currentTag == "SUBTOTAL")
    {
        $subTotals[] = $data;
    }
}

// external entity handler
// if SYSTEM-type entity, this function looks up the entity and parses it
```

```
function externalEntityHandler($parser, $name, $base, $systemId, $publicId)
{
      if ($systemId)
      {
            parse($systemId);
            // explicitly return true
            return true;
      }
      else
      {
            return false;
      }


}


// PI handler
// this function processes PHP code if it finds any
function PIHandler($parser, $target, $data)
{
   .  // if php code, execute it
      if (strtolower($target) == "php")
      {
            eval($data);
      }
}


// this function adds up all the subtotals
// and prints a grand total
function displayTotal()
{
      global $subTotals;
      foreach($subTotals as $element)
      {
            $total += $element;
      }
      echo "<p> <b>Total payable: </b> " . $total;
}


// function to actually perform parsing
function parse($xml_file)
{
      // initialize parser
      $xml_parser = xml_parser_create();

      // set callback functions
      xml_set_element_handler($xml_parser, "startElementHandler",
➥"endElementHandler");
xml_set_character_data_handler($xml_parser, "characterDataHandler");
xml_set_processing_instruction_handler($xml_parser, "PIHandler");
```

continues

Listing 2.23   **Continued**

```php
xml_set_external_entity_ref_handler($xml_parser, "externalEntityHandler");

    // read XML file
    if (!($fp = fopen($xml_file, "r")))
    {
        die("File I/O error: $xml_file");
    }

    // parse XML
    while ($data = fread($fp, 4096))
    {
        // error handler
        if (!xml_parse($xml_parser, $data, feof($fp)))
        {
            $ec = xml_get_error_code($xml_parser);
            die("XML parser error (error code " . $ec . "): " .
➥xml_error_string($ec) . "<br>Error occurred at line " .
xml_get_current_line_number($xml_parser));
        }
    }

// all done, clean up!
xml_parser_free($xml_parser);
}

// arrays to associate XML elements with HTML output
$startTagsArray = array(
'CUSTOMER' => '<p> <b>Customer: </b>',
'ADDRESS' => '<p> <b>Billing address: </b>',
'DATE' => '<p> <b>Invoice date: </b>',
'REFERENCE' => '<p> <b>Invoice number: </b>',
'ITEMS' => '<p> <b>Details: </b> <table width="100%" border="1" cellspacing="0"
➥cellpadding="3"><tr><td><b>Item
description</b></td><td><b>Price</b></td><td><b>Quantity</b></td><td><b>Sub-
➥total</b></td></tr>',
'ITEM' => '<tr>',
'DESC' => '<td>',
'PRICE' => '<td>',
'QUANTITY' => '<td>',
'SUBTOTAL' => '<td>',
'DELIVERY' => '<p> <b>Shipping option:</b> ',
'TERMS' => '<p> <b>Terms and conditions: </b> <ul>',
'TERM' => '<li>'
);

$endTagsArray = array(
'LINE' => ',',
```

```
'ITEMS' => '</table>',
'ITEM' => '</tr>',
'DESC' => '</td>',
'PRICE' => '</td>',
'QUANTITY' => '</td>',
'SUBTOTAL' => '</td>',
'TERMS' => '</ul>',
'TERM' => '</li>'
);

// create array to hold subtotals
$subTotals = array();

// begin parsing
$xml_file = "invoice.xml";
parse($xml_file);

?>
</body>
</html>
```

Figure 2.1 shows what the end result looks like.

Figure 2.1   Results of converting the XML invoice into HTML with SAX.

How did I accomplish this? Quite easily by using the various event handlers exposed by SAX. As the script in Listing 2.23 demonstrates, I defined handlers for elements, character data, PIs, and external entities. I also created two associative arrays, which map XML element names to HTML constructs; each time one of those XML elements is encountered, PHP replaces it with the corresponding HTML output, and prints it. PIs and external entities are handled in the normal manner; note that this time around, my external entity handler is not merely displaying the content of the referenced entity, but it is also parsing its contents.

Listing 2.23 demonstrates how easy it is to take marked-up XML data and "do something useful" with it—in this case, render it in a format capable of display in a standard web browser. You could just as easily format the XML as ASCII text, WML pages, or (in combination with PHP's PDF generation functions) PDF documents.

A technique such as the one described previously is suitable for simple, short XML documents; however, it can prove to be tedious when dealing with larger, more complex documents. For documents like these, you might want to consider using the Document Object Model (DOM), discussed in the next chapter; or a more powerful stylesheet language such as XSLT, discussed in Chapter 4, "PHP and Extensible Stylesheet Language Transformations (XSLT)."

Parsing and Displaying RSS Data on a Web Site

Another fairly common application of PHP's SAX parser involves using it to parse RDF Site Summary (RSS) documents and extract data from them for display on a web site.

In case you didn't already know, RSS 1.0 documents are well-formed XML documents that conform to the W3C's Resource Description Format (RDF) specification. RSS 1.0 documents typically contain a description of the content on a web site. Many popular portals publish these documents as an easy way to allow other web sites to syndicate and link to their content.

A Rich Resource

For more information on RSS and RDF, take a look at http://purl.org/rss/1.0/ for the RSS 1.0 specification, and also visit the W3C's web site for RDF at http://www.w3.org/RDF/. And then drop by this book's companion web site (http://www.xmlphp.com), which has links to tutorials on how to integrate RSS 1.0 content feeds into your own web site.

Listing 2.24 demonstrates what an RSS 1.0 document looks like.

Listing 2.24 **RSS 1.0 document (*fm-releases.rdf*)**

```
<?xml version="1.0" encoding="ISO-8859-1"?>
<rdf:RDF
  xmlns:rdf="http://www.w3.org/1999/02/22-rdf-syntax-ns#"
```

```
  xmlns="http://purl.org/rss/1.0/"
 xmlns:dc="http://purl.org/dc/elements/1.1/">
  <channel rdf:about="http://freshmeat.net/">
    <title>freshmeat.net</title>
    <link>http://freshmeat.net/</link>
    <description>freshmeat.net maintains the Web's largest index of Unix and
cross-platform open source software. Thousands of applications are meticulously
cataloged in the freshmeat.net database, and links to new code are added
daily.</description>
    <dc:language>en-us</dc:language>
    <dc:subject>Technology</dc:subject>
    <dc:publisher>freshmeat.net</dc:publisher>
    <dc:creator>freshmeat.net contributors</dc:creator>
    <dc:rights>Copyright (c) 1997-2002 OSDN</dc:rights>
    <dc:date>2002-02-11T10:20+00:00</dc:date>
    <items>
      <rdf:Seq>
        <rdf:li rdf:resource="http://freshmeat.net/releases/69583/" />
        <rdf:li rdf:resource="http://freshmeat.net/releases/69581/" />
        <!-- remaining items deleted -->
      </rdf:Seq>
    </items>
    <image rdf:resource="http://freshmeat.net/img/fmII-button.gif" />
    <textinput rdf:resource="http://freshmeat.net/search/" />
  </channel>

  <image rdf:about="http://freshmeat.net/img/fmII-button.gif">
    <title>freshmeat.net</title>
    <url>http://freshmeat.net/img/fmII-button.gif</url>
    <link>http://freshmeat.net/</link>
  </image>

  <item rdf:about="http://freshmeat.net/releases/69583/">
    <title>sloop.splitter 0.2.1</title>
    <link>http://freshmeat.net/releases/69583/</link>
    <description>A real time sound effects program.</description>
    <dc:date>2002-02-11T04:52-06:00</dc:date>
  </item>

  <item rdf:about="http://freshmeat.net/releases/69581/">
    <title>apacompile 1.9.9</title>
    <link>http://freshmeat.net/releases/69581/</link>
    <description>A full-featured Apache compilation HOWTO.</description>
    <dc:date>2002-02-11T04:52-06:00</dc:date>
  </item>

  <!-- remaining items deleted -->
</rdf:RDF>
```

The Scent of Fresh Meat

The RSS 1.0 document in Listing 2.24 describes the content appearing on the front page of the popular open-source software portal Freshmeat.net (http://www.freshmeat.net/).

Freshmeat.net's RSS content feed is updated on a frequent basis with a list of the latest software added to the site; visit the web site for a copy of the latest version.

Now, this is a well-formed XML document, with clearly defined blocks for <channel> and <item> information. All that's needed now is some code to parse this document and return a list of the <item>s within it, together with the title, URL, and description of each.

With PHP's SAX parser, this is easy to accomplish. Listing 2.25 contains the code for a PHP class designed to parse the RSS document in Listing 2.24 and return PHP arrays containing the information within it. This information can then be formatted and displayed on a web page.

Listing 2.25   **A PHP class to parse an RSS 1.0 document** (*rssparser.class.inc*)

```
<?
class RSSParser
{

    //
    // class variables
    //

    // holds name of element currently being parser
    var $tag = "";

    // location variable indicating whether parser is within
    // item or channel block
    var $location = 0;

    // array counter
    var $counter = 0;

    // name of RSS file
    var $file = "";

    // associative array for channel data
    var $channelData = array();

    // nested array of arrays for item data
    // every element of this array will represent
    // one item in the channel
    var $itemData = array();


    //
    // class methods
    //
```

```
// set the name of the RSS file to parse
// this is usually a local file
// set it to a remote file only
// if your PHP build supports fopen() over HTTP
function setRSS($file)
{
    $this->file = $file;
}


// element handlers
// these keep track of the element currently being parsed
// and adjust $location and $tag accordingly
function startElementHandler($parser, $name, $attributes)
{
    $this->tag = $name;

    if ($name == "ITEM")
    {
        // if entering item block
        // set location variable to 1
        $this->location = 1;
    }
    else if ($name == "CHANNEL")
    {
        // if entering channel block
        // set location variable to 2
        $this->location = 2;
    }
}

function endElementHandler($parser, $name)
{
    $this->tag = "";

    // if exiting channel or item block
    // reset location variable to 0
    if ($name == "ITEM")
    {
        $this->counter++;
        $this->location = 0;
    }
    else if ($name == "CHANNEL")
    {
        $this->location = 0;
    }
}
```

continues

Listing 2.25   **Continued**

```
// character data handler
// this function checks to see whether the parser is
// currently reading channel or item information
// and appends the information to the appropriate array
function characterDataHandler($parser, $data)
{
    $data = trim(htmlspecialchars($data));

    // only interested in these three elements...
    if ($this->tag == "TITLE" || $this->tag == "LINK" || $this->tag ==
➥"DESCRIPTION")
    {
        // if within an item block
        // add data to item array
        if ($this->location == 1)
        {
            $this->itemData[$this->counter][strtolower($this->tag)] .= $data;
        }
        else if ($this->location == 2)
        {
            // else add it to channel array
            $this->channelData[strtolower($this->tag)] .= $data;
        }
    }
}


// data retrieval methods

// this returns the array with channel information
function getChannelData()
{
    return $this->channelData;
}

// this returns the array with item information
function getItemData()
{
    return $this->itemData;
}

// all the work happens here

// parse the specified RSS file
// this populates the $channelData and $itemData arrays
function parseRSS()
{
    // create parser
    $this->xmlParser = xml_parser_create();
```

```
        // set object reference
        xml_set_object($this->xmlParser, $this);

        // configure parser behaviour
        xml_parser_set_option($this->xmlParser, XML_OPTION_CASE_FOLDING, TRUE);
        xml_parser_set_option($this->xmlParser, XML_OPTION_SKIP_WHITE, TRUE);

        // set up handlers
        xml_set_element_handler($this->xmlParser, "startElementHandler",
        ➥"endElementHandler");
        xml_set_character_data_handler($this->xmlParser, "characterDataHandler");

        // read RSS file
        if (!($fp = fopen($this->file, "r")))
        {
            die("Could not read $this->file");
        }

        // begin parsing...
        while ($data = fread($fp, 2048))
        {
            if (!xml_parse($this->xmlParser, $data, feof($fp)))
            {
                die("The following error occurred: " .
                ➥xml_error_string(xml_get_error_code($this->xmlParser)));
            }
        }

        // destroy parser
        xml_parser_free($this->xmlParser);
    }

// end of class
}
?>
```

This might look complicated, but it's actually pretty simple. The class above attempts
to simplify the task of parsing and using an RDF file by parsing it and extracting the
information within it into the following two arrays:

- The $channelData associative array, which contains information on the channel
  title, URL, and description
- The $itemData array, which is a two-dimensional array containing information
  (title, URL, and description) on the individual items in the channel list. The total
  number of elements in the $itemData array corresponds to the total number of
  <item> elements in the RSS document.

The class also exposes the following public methods:

- `setRSS()`—Set the name of the RSS file to parse
- `parseRSS()`—Actually parse the specified RSS file and place the information extracted from it into the two arrays
- `getChannelData()`—Retrieve the array containing channel information
- `getItemData()`—Retrieve the array containing the item list

When using this class (look at Listing 2.26 for a usage example), the first step is, obviously, to specify the name of the RSS file to parse. Once this has been specified and stored in a class variable, the `parseRSS()` method is invoked to actually parse the document.

This `parseRSS()` method does all the things you've become familiar with in this chapter: Create an XML parser, configure it, set up callback functions, and sequentially iterate through the document, calling appropriate handlers for each XML construct encountered. As the parser moves through the document, it uses the `$location` variable to identify its current location, and the `$tag` variable to identify the name of the element currently being parsed. Based on these two pieces of data, the character data handler knows which array to place the descriptive channel/item information into.

> **An Object Lesson**
>
> Special mention should be made of the `xml_set_object()` function used within the `parseRSS()` class method in Listing 2.25. You've probably not seen this function before, so I'll take the opportunity to explain it a little.
>
> The `xml_set_object()` function is designed specifically to associate an XML parser with a class, and to link class methods and parser callback functions together. Callback functions defined for the parser are assumed to be methods of the enveloping class.
>
> In order to better understand why `xml_set_object()` is necessary, try commenting out the call to the `xml_set_object()` function in Listing 2.25, and see what happens.

Listing 2.26 demonstrates how the class from Listing 2.25 can be combined with the RSS document in Listing 2.24 to generate PHP arrays representing the RSS content, and how those arrays can then be manipulated to display the information as browser-readable HTML.

Listing 2.26 **Parsing an RDF File and Formatting the Result as an HTML Document**

```php
<?php
// include class
include("rssparser.class.inc");

// instantiate a new RSSParser
```

```
$rp = new RSSParser();

// define the RSS 1.0 file to parse
$rp->setRSS("fm-releases.rdf");

// parse the file
$rp->parseRSS();

// get channel information
$channel = $rp->getChannelData();

// retrieve item list (array)
// every element of this array is itself an associative array
// with keys ('title', 'link', 'description')
$items = $rp->getItemData();

// uncomment the next line to see a list of object properties
// print_r($rp);
?>

<html>
<head><basefont face="Arial"></head>
<body>

<h2><? echo $channel['title']; ?></h2>
<ul>
<?
// iterate through item list
// print each item as a list item with hyperlink, title and description
foreach($items as $item)
{
    echo "<li>";
    echo "<a href=" . $item['link'] . ">" . $item['title'] . "</a>";
    echo "<br>" . $item['description'];
}
?>
</ul>

</body>
</html>
```

The script in Listing 2.26 creates an instance of the RSSParser class and parses the specified RSS file via the parseRSS() class method. It then iterates through the arrays returned by the class methods getChannelData() and getItemData(), and formats the elements of these arrays for display.

Figure 2.2 demonstrates what the output of Listing 2.26 looks like.

Figure 2.2   The results of converting an RDF file into HTML with SAX.

Summary

That concludes this tour of PHP's SAX functions. In this chapter, you got your first taste of PHP's XML functions by learning how to implement a generic XML processor in PHP and to use callback functions to handle the different events caught by the SAX parser. You also learned how to modify specific aspects of parser behavior, handle errors gracefully, and create native data structures from XML documents. Finally, you road-tested the XML processor with two composite examples, combining your knowledge of all these techniques to create simple XML applications to format and present XML data in HTML.

In the next chapter, I will be exploring an alternative technique of XML processing—using the tree-based model discussed at the beginning of this chapter.

*"A fool sees not the same tree
that a wise man sees."*

~WILLIAM BLAKE

3

PHP and the Document Object Model (DOM)

IF YOU'VE BEEN PAYING ATTENTION, YOU NOW know the basics of parsing XML with PHP. As Chapter 2, "PHP and the Simple API for XML (SAX)" demonstrated, it's pretty simple—whip up some XML data and mix in a few callback functions. It's a simple yet effective recipe, and one that can be used to great effect for the rapid development of XML-based applications.

That said, although the event-driven approach to XML parsing is certainly popular, it's not the only option available. PHP also allows you to parse XML using the *Document Object Model (DOM)*, an alternative technique that allows developers to create and manipulate a hierarchical tree representation of XML data for greater flexibility and ease of use.

In this chapter, this tree-based approach is explored in greater detail. First it is put under the microscope to see exactly how it works and then PHP's implementation of the DOM is introduced. The various methods exposed by PHP to simplify interaction with the DOM are also examined, together with examples and code listings that demonstrate its capabilities.

Both tree- and event-based approaches have significant advantages and disadvantages, and these can impact your choice of technique when implementing specific projects. To that end, this chapter also includes a brief discussion of the pros and cons of each approach in the hope that it will assist you in making the right choice for a particular project.

Let's get started!

Document Object Model (DOM)

The Document Object Model (DOM) is a standard interface to access and manipulate structured data.

As the name suggests, it does this by *modeling*, or representing, a *document* as a hierarchical tree of *objects*. A number of different object types are defined in the W3C's DOM specification; these objects expose methods and attributes that can be used by the application layer to navigate and process the DOM tree, exploit the relationships between the different branches of the tree, and extract information from it.

The W3C's DOM specification defines a number of different objects to represent the different structures that appear within an XML document. For example, elements are represented by an `Element` object, whereas attributes are represented by `Attr` objects.

Each of these different object types exposes specific methods and properties. `Element` objects expose a `tagName` property containing the element name and `getAttribute()` and `setAttribute()` methods for attribute manipulation, whereas `Attr` objects expose a `value` property containing the value of the particular attribute. These methods and properties can be used by the application layer to navigate and process the DOM tree, exploit the relationships between the different branches of the tree, and extract information from it.

The very first specification of the DOM (DOM Level 1) appeared on the W3C's web site in October 1998, and simply specified the "core" features of the DOM—the basic objects and the interfaces to them. The next major upgrade, DOM Level 2, appeared in November 2000; it examined the DOM from the perspective of core functions, event handling, and document traversal. DOM Level 3, which is currently under development, builds on past work, and incorporates additions and changes from other related technologies (XPath, abstract schemas, and so on).

As a standard interface to structured data, the DOM was designed from the get-go to be platform- and language-independent. It can be (and is) used to represent structured HTML and XML data, with DOM (or DOM-based) implementations currently available for Java, JavaScript, Python, C/C++, Visual Basic, Delphi, Perl, SMIL, SVG, and PHP. (The PHP implementation is discussed in detail in the next section.)

In order to better understand how the DOM works, consider Listing 3.1.

Listing 3.1 **A Simple XML Document**

```
<?xml version="1.0"?>
<sentence>What a wonderful profusion of colors and smells in the market -
<vegetable color='green'>cabbages</vegetable>, <vegetable
color='red'>tomatoes</vegetable>, <fruit color='green'>apples</fruit>,
<vegetable color='purple'>aubergines</vegetable>, <fruit
color='yellow'>bananas</fruit></sentence>
```

Once a DOM parser chewed on this document, it would spit out the tree structure shown in Figure 3.1.

```
<element>   "sentence"

    |  —   <text>   "What a wonderful profusion of colors and smells in the market - "
    |  —   <element> "vegetable"
    |      |  —   <attribute>  "color=green"
    |      |  —   <text>  "cabbages"
    |  —   <text> ",  "
    |  —   <element>  "vegetable"
    |      |  —   <attribute>  "color=red"
    |      |  —   <text>  "tomatoes"
    |  —   <text> ",  "
    |  —   <element>  "fruit"
    |      |  —   <attribute>  "color=green"
    |      |  —   <text>  "apples"
    |  —   <text> ",  "
    |  —   <element>  "vegetable"
    |      |  —   <attribute>  "color=purple"
    |      |  —   <text>  "aubergines"
    |  —   <text> ",  "
    |  —   <element>  "fruit"
    |      |  —   <attribute>  "color=yellow"
    |      |  —   <text>  "bananas"
```

Figure 3.1   A DOM tree.

As you can see, the parser returns a tree containing multiple nodes linked to each other by parent-child relationships. Developers can then write code to move around the tree, access node properties, and manipulate node content.

This approach is in stark contrast to the event driven approach you studied in Chapter 2, "PHP and the Simple API for XML (SAX)." A SAX parser progresses sequentially through a document, firing events based on the tags it encounters and leaving it to the application layer to decide how to process each event. A DOM parser, on the other hand, reads the entire document into memory, and builds a tree representation of its structure; the application layer can then use standard DOM interfaces to find and manipulate individual nodes on this tree, in a non-sequential manner.

PHP and the DOM

PHP 4.0 comes with a primitive, though effective, implementation of the DOM, based on the libxml library. Created by Daniel Veillard, libxml (http://www.xmlsoft.org/) is a modular, standards-compliant C library that provides XML parsing capabilities to the GNOME project (http://www.gnome.org/).

If you're using a stock PHP binary, it's quite likely that you'll need to recompile PHP to add support for this library to your PHP build. (Detailed instructions for accomplishing this are available in Appendix A, "Recompiling PHP to Add XML Support.")

Under Construction

If you're planning on using PHP's DOM extension in your development activities, be warned that this extension is still under development and is, therefore, subject to change without notice. Consequently, DOM code that works with one version of PHP may need to be rewritten or retested with subsequent versions.

Note also that the examples in this chapter have been tested with the DOM extension that ships with PHP 4.1.1, and are not likely to work with earlier versions because PHP's DOM implementation underwent some fairly radical changes between the release of PHP 4.0.6 and PHP 4.1.1. If you're using an earlier PHP build, you might want to upgrade to PHP 4.1.1 in order to try out the examples in this chapter.

A Simple Example

When PHP parses an XML document, it creates a hierarchical tree structure (mirroring the structure of the document) that is composed of objects. Each of these objects has standard properties and methods, and you can use these properties and methods to traverse the object tree and access specific elements, attributes, or character data.

The best way to understand how this works is with a simple example. Take a look at Listing 3.2, which demonstrates the basic concepts of this technique by traversing a DOM tree to locate a particular type of element, and print its value.

Listing 3.2 **Traversing a DOM Tree**

```php
<?php

// XML data
$xml_string = "<?xml version='1.0'?>
<sentence>What a wonderful profusion of colors and smells in the market -
     <vegetable color='green'>cabbages</vegetable>,
     <vegetable color='red'>tomatoes</vegetable>,
     <fruit color='green'>apples</fruit>,
     <vegetable color='purple'>aubergines</vegetable>,
     <fruit color='yellow'>bananas</fruit>
</sentence>";

// create a DOM object from the XML data
if(!$doc = xmldoc($xml_string))
{
     die("Error parsing XML");
}

// start at the root
$root = $doc->root();

// move down one level to the root's children
$children = $root->children();
```

```
// iterate through the list of children
foreach ($children as $child)
{
    // if <vegetable> element
    if ($child->tagname == "vegetable")
    {
        // go down one more level
        // get the text node
        $text = $child->children();
        // print the content of the text node
        echo "Found: " . $text[0]->content . "<br>";
    }
}

?>
```

Let's go through Listing 3.2 step-by-step:

1. The first order of business is to feed the parser the XML data, so that it can generate the DOM tree. This is accomplished via the `xmldoc()` function, which accepts a string of XML as argument, and creates a DOM object representing the XML data. (You can use `xmldocfile()` to parse an XML file instead of a string. Check out Listing 3.5 for an example.) The following line of code creates a DOM object, and assigns it to the PHP variable `$doc`:

   ```
   if(!$doc = xmldoc($xml_string))
   {
       die("Error parsing XML");
   }
   ```

2. This newly created DOM object has certain properties and methods. One of the most important ones is the `root()` method, which returns an object representing the document's root element.

   The following line of code returns an object representing the document element, and assigns it to the PHP variable `$root`:

   ```
   $root = $doc->root();
   ```

3. This returned node is itself an object, again with properties and methods of its own. These methods and properties provide information about the node, and its relationship to other nodes in the tree: its name and type, its parent, and its children. However, the elements I'm looking for aren't at this level—they're one level deeper. And so I used the root node's `children()` method to obtain a list of the nodes below it in the document hierarchy:

   ```
   $children = $root->children();
   ```

4. This list of child nodes is returned as an array containing both text and element nodes. All I need to do now is iterate through this node list, looking for vegetable elements. As and when I find these, I dive one level deeper into the tree to access the corresponding character data and print it (this is a snap, given that each text node has a content property).

```
foreach ($children as $child)
{
    // if <vegetable> element
    if ($child->tagname == "vegetable")
    {
        // go down one more level
        // get the text node
        $text = $child->children();
        // print the content of the text node
        echo "Found: " . $text[0]->content . "<br>";
    }
}
```

When this script runs, it produces the following output:

```
Found: cabbages
Found: tomatoes
Found: aubergines
```

As Listing 3.2 demonstrates, DOM tree traversal takes place primarily by exploiting the parent-child relationships that exist between the nodes of the tree. After traversal to a particular depth has been accomplished, node properties can be used to extract all required information from the tree.

Traversing the DOM with PHP's DOM Classes

Because PHP's DOM parser works by creating standard objects to represent XML structures, an understanding of these objects and their capabilities is essential to using this technique effectively. This section examines the classes that form the blueprint for these objects in greater detail.

DomDocument Class

A DomDocument object is typically the first object created by the DOM parser when it completes parsing an XML document. It may be created by a call to xmldoc():

```
$doc = xmldoc("<?xml version='1.0'?><element>potassium</element>");
```

Or, if your XML data is in a file (rather than a string), you can use the xmldocfile() function to create a DomDocument object:

```
$doc = xmldocfile("element.xml");
```

Treading the Right Path

If you're using Windows, you'll need to give `xmldocfile()` the full path to the XML file. Don't forget to include the drive letter!

When you examine the structure of the DomDocument object with `print_r()`, you can see that it contains basic information about the XML document—including the XML version, the encoding and character set, and the URL of the document:

```
DomDocument Object
(
    [name] =>
    [url] =>
    [version] => 1.0
    [standalone] => -1
    [type] => 9
    [compression] => -1
    [charset] => 1
)
```

Peekaboo!

You'll notice that many examples in this book (particularly in this chapter) use the `print_r()` function to display the structure of a particular PHP variable. In case you're not familiar with this function, you should know that it provides an easy way to investigate the innards of a particular variable, array, or object. Use it whenever you need to look inside an object to see what makes it tick; and, if you're feeling really adventurous, you might also want to take a look at the `var_dump()` and `var_export()` functions, which provide similar functionality.

Each of these properties provides information on some aspect of the XML document:

- `name`—Name of the XML document
- `url`—URL of the document
- `version`—XML version used
- `standalone`—Whether or not the document is a standalone document
- `type`—Integer corresponding to one of the DOM node types (see Table 3.1)
- `compression`—Whether or not the file was compressed
- charset—Character set used by the document

The application can use this information to make decisions about how to process the XML data—for example, as Listing 3.3 demonstrates, it may reject documents based on the version of XML being used.

Listing 3.3   **Using DomDocument Properties to Verify XML Version Information**

```php
<?php

// XML data
$xml_string = "<?xml version='1.0'?><element>potassium</element>";

// create a DOM object
if (!$doc = xmldoc($xml_string))
{
    die("Error in XML");
}
// version check
else if ($doc->version > 1.0)
{
    die("Unsupported XML version");
}
else
{
    // XML processing code here
}

?>
```

In addition to the properties described previously, the DomDocument object also comes with the following methods:

- root() — Returns a DomElement object representing the document element
- dtd() — Returns a DTD object containing information about the document's DTD
- add_root() — Creates a new document element, and returns a DomElement object representing that element
- dumpmem() — Dumps the XML structure into a string variable
- xpath_new_context() — Creates an XPathContext object for XPath evaluation

While parsing XML data, you'll find that the root() method is the one you use most often, whereas the add_root() and dumpmem() methods come in handy when you're creating or modifying an XML document tree in memory (discussed in detail in the "Manipulating DOM Trees" section).

X Marks the Spot

In case you're wondering, XPath, or the XML Path Language, provides an easy way to address specific parts of an XML document. The language uses directional axes, coupled with conditional tests, to create node collections matching a specific criterion, and also provides standard constructs to manipulate these collections.

PHP's XPath implementation is discussed in detail in the upcoming section titled "Traversing the DOM with PHP's XPath Classes."

In Listing 3.4, the variable `$fruit` contains the root node (the element named `fruit`).

Listing 3.4   **Accessing the Document Element via the DOM**

```php
<?php

// create a DomDocument object
$doc = xmldoc("<?xml version='1.0' encoding='UTF-8'
⇒standalone='yes'?><fruit>watermelon</fruit>");

// root node
$fruit = $doc->root();
?>
```

To DTD or Not to DTD

The dtd() method of the DomDocument object creates a DTD object, which contains basic information about the document's Document Type Definition. Here's what it looks like:

```
Dtd Object
(
    [systemId] => weather.dtd
    [name] => weather
)
```

This DTD object exposes two properties: the systemId property reveals the filename of the DTD document, whereas the name property contains the name of the document element.

DomElement Class

The PHP parser represents every element within the XML document as an instance of the DomElement class, which makes it one of the most important in this lineup. When you view the structure of a DomElement object, you see that it has two distinct properties that represent the element name and type, respectively. You'll remember from Listing 3.2 that these properties can be used to identify individual elements and extract their values. Here is an example:

```
DomElement Object
(
    [type] => 1
    [tagname] => vegetable
)
```

A special note should be made here of the **type** property, which indicates the type of node under discussion. This **type** property contains an integer value mapping to one of the parser's predefined node types. Table 3.1 lists the important types.

Table 3.1 **DOM Node Types**

Integer	Node type	Description
1	XML_ELEMENT_NODE	Element
2	XML_ATTRIBUTE_NODE	Attribute
3	XML_TEXT_NODE	Text
4	XML_CDATA_SECTION_NODE	CDATA section
5	XML_ENTITY_REF_NODE	Entity reference
7	XML_PI_NODE	Processing instruction
8	XML_COMMENT_NODE	Comment
9	XML_DOCUMENT_NODE	XML document
12	XML_NOTATION_NODE	Notation

If you plan to use the `type` property within a script to identify node types (as I will be doing shortly in Listing 3.5), you should note that it is considered preferable to use the named constants rather than their corresponding integer values, both for readability and to ensure stability across API changes.

The DomElement object also exposes a number of useful object methods:

- `children()`—Returns an array of DomElement objects representing the children of this node
- `parent()`—Returns a DomElement object representing the parent of this node
- `attributes()`—Returns an array of DomAttribute objects representing the attributes of this node
- `get_attribute()`—Returns the value of an attribute of this node
- `new_child()`—Creates a new DomElement object, and attaches it as a child of this node (note that this newly created node is placed at the end of the existing child list)
- `set_attribute()`—Sets the value of an attribute of this node
- `set_content()`—Sets the content of this node

Again, the two most commonly used ones are the `children()` and `attributes()` methods, which return an array of DomElement and DomAttribute objects, respectively. The `get_attribute()` method can be used to return the value of a specific attribute of an element (refer to Listing 3.8 for an example), whereas the `new_child()`, `set_attribute()`, and `set_content()` methods are used when creating or modifying XML trees in memory, and are discussed in detail in the section entitled "Manipulating DOM Trees."

Note that PHP's DOM implementation does not currently offer any way of removing an attribute previously set with the `set_attribute()` method.

Choices

Most of the object methods discussed in this chapter can also be invoked as functions by prefixing the method name with domxml and passing a reference to the object as the first function argument. The following snippets demonstrate this:

```php
<?php
// these two are equivalent
$root1 = $doc->root();
$root2 = domxml_root($doc);

// these two are equivalent
$children1 = $root1->children();
$children2 = domxml_children($root2);
?>
```

Listing 3.5 demonstrates one of these in action by combining the children() method of a DomElement object with a recursive function and HTML's unordered lists to create a hierarchical tree mirroring the document structure (similar in concept, though not in approach, to Listing 2.5). At the end of the process, a count of the total number of elements encountered is displayed.

Listing 3.5   **Representing an XML Document as a Hierarchical List**

```php
<?php

// XML file
$xml_file = "letter.xml";

// parse it
if (!$doc = xmldocfile($xml_file))
{
    die("Error in XML document");
}

// get the root node
$root = $doc->root();

// get its children
$children = get_children($root);

// element counter
// start with 1 so as to include document element
$elementCount = 1;

// start printing
print_tree($children);

// this recursive function accepts an array of nodes as argument,
// iterates through it and prints a list for each element found
function print_tree($nodeCollection)
{
```

continues

Listing 3.5 **Continued**

```php
        global $elementCount;

        // iterate through array
        echo "<ul>";

        for ($x=0; $x<sizeof($nodeCollection); $x++)
        {
            // add to element count
            $elementCount++;

            // print element as list item
            echo "<li>" . $nodeCollection[$x]->tagname;

            // go to the next level of the tree
            $nextCollection = get_children($nodeCollection[$x]);

            // recurse!
            print_tree($nextCollection);

        }

        echo "</ul>";
    }

    // function to return an array of children, given a parent node
    function get_children($node)
    {
        $temp = $node->children();
        $collection = array();

        // iterate through children array
        for ($x=0; $x<sizeof($temp); $x++)
        {
            // filter out all nodes except elements
            // and create a new array
            if ($temp[$x]->type == XML_ELEMENT_NODE)
            {
                $collection[] = $temp[$x];
            }
        }

        // return array containing child nodes
        return $collection;
    }

    echo "Total number of elements in document: $elementCount";
?>
```

Listing 3.5 is fairly easy to understand. The first step is to obtain a reference to the root of the document tree via the `root()` method; this reference serves as the starting point for the recursive `print_tree()` function. This function obtains a reference to the children of the root node, processes them, and then calls itself again to process the next level of nodes in the tree. The process continues until all the nodes in the tree have been exhausted. An element counter is used to track the number of elements found, and to display a total count of all the elements in the document.

DomText Class

Character data within an XML document is represented by the DomText class. Here's what it looks like:

```
DomText Object
(
     [type] => 3
     [content] => cabbages
)
```

The `type` property represents the node type (`XML_TEXT_NODE` in this case, as can be seen from Table 3.1), whereas the `content` property holds the character data itself. In order to illustrate this, consider Listing 3.6, which takes an XML-encoded list of country names, parses it, and puts that list into a PHP array.

Listing 3.6   **Using DomText Object Properties to Retrieve Character Data from an XML Document**

```php
<?php

// XML data
$xml_string = "<?xml version='1.0'?>
<earth>
     <country>Albania</country>
     <country>Argentina</country>
     <!-- and so on -->
     <country>Zimbabwe</country>
</earth>";

// create array to hold country names
$countries = array();

// create a DOM object from the XML data
if(!$doc = xmldoc($xml_string))
{
     die("Error parsing XML");
}

// start at the root
$root = $doc->root();
```

continues

Listing 3.6 **Continued**

```
// move down one level to the root's children
$nodes = $root->children();

// iterate through the list of children
foreach ($nodes as $n)
{
        // for each <country> element
        // get the text node under it
        // and add it to the $countries[] array
        $text = $n->children();
        if ($text[0]->content != "")
        {
                $countries[] = $text[0]->content;
        }
}

// uncomment this line to see the contents of the array
// print_r($countries);
?>
```

Fairly simple—a loop is used to iterate through all the <country> elements, adding the character data found within each to the global $countries array.

Taking up Space

It's important to remember that XML, unlike HTML, does not ignore whitespace, but treats it as literal character data. Consequently, if your XML document includes whitespace or line breaks, PHP's DOM parser identifies them as text nodes, and creates DomText objects to represent them. This is a common cause of confusion for DOM newbies, who are often stumped by the "extra" nodes that appear in their DOM tree.

DomAttribute Class

A call to the attributes() method of the DomElement object generates an array of DomAttribute objects, each of which looks like this:

```
DomAttribute Object
(
        [name] => color
        [value] => green
)
```

The attribute name can be accessed via the name property, and the corresponding attribute value can be accessed via the value property. Listing 3.7 demonstrates how this works by using the value of the color attribute to highlight each vegetable or fruit name in the corresponding color.

Listing 3.7   **Accessing Attribute Values with the DomAttribute Object**

```php
<?php

// XML data
$xml_string = "<?xml version='1.0'?>
<sentence>
What a wonderful profusion of colors and smells in the market - <vegetable
color='green'>cabbages</vegetable>, <vegetable color='red'>tomatoes</vegetable>,
<fruit color='green'>apples</fruit>, <vegetable
color='purple'>aubergines</vegetable>, <fruit color='yellow'>bananas</fruit>
</sentence>";

// parse it
if (!$doc = xmldoc($xml_string))
{
    die("Error in XML document");
}

// get the root node
$root = $doc->root();

// get its children
$children = $root->children();

// iterate through child list
for ($x=0; $x<sizeof($children); $x++)
{
    // if element node
    if ($children[$x]->type == XML_ELEMENT_NODE)
    {
        // get the text node under it
        $text = $children[$x]->children();
        $cdata = $text[0]->content;

        // check its attributes to see if "color" is present
        $attributes = $children[$x]->attributes();

        if (is_array($attributes) && ($index =
        ↪is_color_attribute_present($attributes)))
        {
            // if it is, colorize the element content
            echo "<font color=" . $index . ">" . $cdata . "</font>";
        }
        else
        {
            // else print it as is
            echo $cdata;
        }
    }
    // if text node
```

Listing 3.7 **Continued**

```php
    else if ($children[$x]->type == XML_TEXT_NODE)
    {
    // simply print the content
        echo $children[$x]->content;
    }

}

// function to iterate through attribute list
// and return the value of the "color" attribute if available
function is_color_attribute_present($attributeList)
{

    foreach($attributeList as $attrib)
    {
        if ($attrib->name == "color")
        {
            $color = $attrib->value;
            break;
        }
    }

    return $color;
}

?>
```

There is, of course, a simpler way to do this—just use the DomElement object's
get_attribute() method. Listing 3.8, which generates equivalent output to Listing
3.7, demonstrates this alternative (and much shorter) approach.

Listing 3.8 **Accessing Attribute Values (a Simpler Approach)**

```php
<?php

// XML data
$xml_string = "<?xml version='1.0'?>
<sentence>
What a wonderful profusion of colors and smells in the market - <vegetable
color='green'>cabbages</vegetable>, <vegetable color='red'>tomatoes</vegetable>,
<fruit color='green'>apples</fruit>, <vegetable
color='purple'>aubergines</vegetable>, <fruit color='yellow'>bananas</fruit>
</sentence>";

// parse it
if (!$doc = xmldoc($xml_string))
{
    die("Error in XML document");
}
```

```
// get the root node
$root = $doc->root();

// get its children
$children = $root->children();

// iterate through child list
for ($x=0; $x<sizeof($children); $x++)
{
    // if element node
    if ($children[$x]->type == XML_ELEMENT_NODE)
    {
        // get the text node under it
        $text = $children[$x]->children();
        $cdata = $text[0]->content;

        // check to see if element contains the "color" attribute
        if ($children[$x]->get_attribute("color"))
        {
            // "color" attribute is present, colorize text
            echo "<font color=" . $children[$x]->get_attribute("color") . ">" .
            ➥$cdata . "</font>";
        }
        else
        {
            // otherwise just print the text as is
            echo $cdata;
        }
    }
    // if text node
    else if ($children[$x]->type == XML_TEXT_NODE)
    {
        // print content as is
        echo $children[$x]->content;
    }
}

?>
```

A Composite Example

Now that you know how it works, how about seeing how it plays out in real life? This example takes everything you learned thus far, and uses that knowledge to construct an HTML file from an XML document.

I'll be using a variant of the XML invoice (Listing 2.21) from Chapter 2, adapting the SAX-based approach demonstrated there to the new DOM paradigm. As you'll see, although the two techniques are fundamentally different, they can nonetheless achieve a similar effect. Listing 3.9 is the marked-up invoice.

Listing 3.9 **An XML Invoice (*invoice.xml*)**

```xml
<?xml version="1.0"?>

<invoice>

    <customer>
        <name>Joe Wannabe</name>
        <address>
            <line>23, Great Bridge Road</line>
            <line>Bombay, MH</line>
            <line>India</line>
        </address>
    </customer>

    <date>2001-09-15</date>

    <reference>75-848478-98</reference>

    <items>
        <item cid="AS633225">
            <desc>Oversize tennis racquet</desc>
            <price>235.00</price>
            <quantity>1</quantity>
            <subtotal>235.00</subtotal>
        </item>

        <item cid="GT645">
            <desc>Championship tennis balls (can)</desc>
            <price>9.99</price>
            <quantity>4</quantity>
            <subtotal>39.96</subtotal>
        </item>

        <item cid="U73472">
            <desc>Designer gym bag</desc>
            <price>139.99</price>
            <quantity>1</quantity>
            <subtotal>139.99</subtotal>
        </item>

        <item cid="AD848383">
            <desc>Custom-fitted sneakers</desc>
            <price>349.99</price>
            <quantity>1</quantity>
            <subtotal>349.99</subtotal>
        </item>
    </items>

    <delivery>Next-day air</delivery>

</invoice>
```

Listing 3.10 parses the previous XML data to create an HTML page, suitable for printing or viewing in a browser.

Listing 3.10   **Formatting an XML Document with the DOM**

```
<html>
<head>
<basefont face="Arial">
</head>
<body bgcolor="white">

<font size="+3">Sammy's Sports Store</font>
<br>
<font size="-2">14, Ocean View, CA 12345, USA
➥http://www.sammysportstore.com/</font>
<p>
<hr>
<center>INVOICE</center>
<hr>
<?php

// arrays to associate XML elements with HTML output
$startTagsArray = array(
'CUSTOMER' => '<p> <b>Customer: </b>',
'ADDRESS' => '<p> <b>Billing address: </b>',
'DATE' => '<p> <b>Invoice date: </b>',
'REFERENCE' => '<p> <b>Invoice number: </b>',
'ITEMS' => '<p> <b>Details: </b> <table width="100%" border="1" cellspacing="0"
➥cellpadding="3"><tr><td><b>Item description</b></td><td><b>Price</b></td><td><b>
➥Quantity</b></td><td><b>Sub-total</b></td></tr>',
'ITEM' => '<tr>',
'DESC' => '<td>',
'PRICE' => '<td>',
'QUANTITY' => '<td>',
'SUBTOTAL' => '<td>',
'DELIVERY' => '<p> <b>Shipping option:</b> ',
'TERMS' => '<p> <b>Terms and conditions: </b> <ul>',
'TERM' => '<li>'
);

$endTagsArray = array(
'LINE' => ',',
'ITEMS' => '</table>',
'ITEM' => '</tr>',
'DESC' => '</td>',
'PRICE' => '</td>',
'QUANTITY' => '</td>',
'SUBTOTAL' => '</td>',
'TERMS' => '</ul>',
'TERM' => '</li>'
);
```

continues

Listing 3.10 **Continued**

```php
// array to hold sub-totals
$subTotals = array();

// XML file
$xml_file = "/home/sammy/invoices/invoice.xml";

// parse document
$doc = xmldocfile($xml_file);

// get the root node
$root = $doc->root();

// get its children
$children = $root->children();

// start printing
print_tree($children);

// this recursive function accepts an array of nodes as argument,
// iterates through it and:
//      - marks up elements with HTML
//      - prints text as is
function print_tree($nodeCollection)
{
    global $startTagsArray, $endTagsArray, $subTotals;

    foreach ($nodeCollection as $node)
    {
        // how to handle elements
        if ($node->type == XML_ELEMENT_NODE)
        {
            // print HTML opening tags
            echo $startTagsArray[strtoupper($node->tagname)];

            // recurse
            $nextCollection = $node->children();
            print_tree($nextCollection);

            // once done, print closing tags
            echo $endTagsArray[strtoupper($node->tagname)];
        }
        // how to handle text nodes
        if ($node->type == XML_TEXT_NODE)
        {
            // print text as is
            echo($node->content);
        }
```

```
            // PI handling code would come here
            // this doesn't work too well in PHP 4.1.1
            // see the sidebar entitled "Process Failure"
            // for more information
        }
    }


// this function gets the character data within an element
// it accepts an element node as argument
// and dives one level deeper into the DOM tree
// to retrieve the corresponding character data
function getNodeContent($node)
{
    $content = "";
    $children = $node->children();

    if ($children)
    {
        foreach ($children as $child)
        {
            $content .= $child->content;
        }
    }

    return $content;

}
?>
```

Figure 3.2 shows what the output looks like.

Sammy's Sports Store

14, Ocean View, CA 12345, USA http://www.sammysportstore.com/

INVOICE

Customer: Joe Wannabe

Billing address: 23, Great Bridge Road Bombay, MH India

Invoice date: 2001-09-15

Invoice number: 75-848478-98

Details:

Item description	Price	Quantity	Sub-total
Oversize tennis racquet	235.00	1	235.00
Championship tennis balls (can)	9.99	4	39.96
Designer gym bag	139.99	1	139.99
Custom-fitted sneakers	349.99	1	349.99

Total payable: 764.94

Shipping option: Next-day air

Figure 3.2   Sammy's Sports Store invoice.

As with the SAX example (refer to Listing 2.23), the first thing to do is define arrays to hold the HTML markup for specific tags; in Listing 3.10, this markup is stored in the `$startTagsArray` and `$endTagsArray` variables.

Next, the XML document is read by the parser, and an appropriate DOM tree is generated in memory. An array of objects representing the first level of the tree—the children of the root node—is obtained and the function `print_tree()` is called. This `print_tree()` function is a recursive function, and it forms the core of the script.

The `print_tree()` function accepts a node list as argument, and iterates through this list, examining each node and processing it appropriately. As you can see, the function is set up to perform specific tasks, depending on the type of node:

- If the node is an element, the function looks up the `$startTagsArray` and `$endTagsArray` variables, and prints the corresponding HTML markup.

- If the node is a text node, the function simply prints the contents of the text node as is.

Additionally, if the node is an element, the `print_tree()` function obtains a list of the element's children—if any exist—and proceeds to call itself with that node list as argument. And so the process repeats itself until the entire tree has been parsed.

As Listing 3.10 demonstrates, this technique provides a handy way to recursively scan through a DOM tree and perform different actions based on the type of node encountered. You can use this technique to count, classify, and process the different types of elements encountered (Listing 3.5 demonstrated a primitive element counter); or even construct a new tree from the existing one.

Process Failure

If you've been paying attention, you will have noticed that the XML invoice in Listing 3.9 is not exactly the same as the one shown in Listing 2.21. Listing 2.21 included an additional processing instruction (PI), a call to the PHP function `displayTotal()`, which is missing in Listing 3.9.

Why? Because the DOM extension that ships with PHP 4.1.1 has trouble with processing instructions, and tends to barf all over the screen when it encounters one. Later (beta) versions of the extension do, however, include a fix for the problem.

Traversing the DOM with PHP's XPath Classes

The DOM classes discussed in the previous section are more than adequate for most common tasks, but getting used to them can take awhile.

Additionally, for long and complex documents containing a large number of elements and/or levels, progressing from node to node in an iterative manner can often be tedious. You can use a recursive function to simplify the process, but you'll still have to write a fair amount of code to create and manipulate node collections, which are at different levels of the tree.

It's precisely to simplify this process that PHP also comes with a couple of XPath classes. XPath, as you may already know, is an addressing mechanism for XML documents, designed to allow XML document authors to quickly access node collections on the basis of both location and condition.

A discussion of XPath is beyond the scope of this book, so I'll assume that you already know the basics of axes, predicates, and node tests. In case you don't, you might want to brush up on the basics before proceeding with this section. Go to the companion web site for this book http://www.xmlphp.com/ or http://www.newriders.com) to find a list of reference material to get you started.

XPathContext and XPathObject Classes

PHP's XPath classes add flexibility to the DOM parser by freeing developers from the standard parent-child paradigm when constructing node collections. The XPath classes allow developers to quickly build node collections matching specific criteria—for example, every third element or every element containing the attribute shape=square—with scant regard for their position in the hierarchical document tree.

The XPathContext class is used to set up a context for all XPath evaluations, and is created by a call to the xpath_new_context() function. This function must be passed a reference to a DomDocument object. For example:

```php
<?php

// create a DomDocument object
$doc = xmldoc($xml_string);

// create an XPath context
$xpath = $doc->xpath_new_context();

?>
```

If you think this doesn't look very interesting, you're right—it's not. The XPathContext object merely sets up a context for all future XPath evaluations. These XPath evaluations usually result in instances of the XPathObject class, which are far more interesting.

An instance of the XPathObject class may be created with a call to the xpath_eval() method of the XPathContext object, which requires an XPath address for evaluation. If the XPath evaluates successfully, xpath_eval() returns an instance of the XPathObject

class containing a collection of nodes matching the specified XPath expression. Take a
look at Listing 3.11, which uses an XPath address to isolate all the `vegetable` elements
in the document:

Listing 3.11   **Creating Node Collections with XPath**

```php
<?php

// XML data
$xml_string = "<?xml version='1.0'?>
<sentence>What a wonderful profusion of colors and smells in the market -
    <vegetable color='green'>cabbages</vegetable>,
    <vegetable color='red'>tomatoes</vegetable>,
    <fruit color='green'>apples</fruit>,
    <vegetable color='purple'>aubergines</vegetable>,
    <fruit color='yellow'>bananas</fruit>
</sentence>";

$doc = xmldoc($xml_string);

// create an XPath context
$xpath = $doc->xpath_new_context();

// get all the "vegetable" elements
$vegetables = $xpath->xpath_eval("//vegetable");

// uncomment the next line to see the node collection
// print_r($vegetables);
?>
```

When you examine the structure of the XPathObject object instance with `print_r()`,
here's what you'll see:

```
XPathObject Object
(
    [type] => 1
    [nodeset] => Array
        (
            [0] => DomElement Object
                (
                    [type] => 1
                    [tagname] => vegetable
                )

            [1] => DomElement Object
                (
                    [type] => 1
                    [tagname] => vegetable
                )
```

```
            [2] => DomElement Object
                (
                    [type] => 1
                    [tagname] => vegetable
                )

        )

    )
```

As you can see, the object contains an array of DomElement objects, representing the element nodes matching the XPath expression. These DomElement objects can now be accessed and manipulated using standard class methods and properties.

A Composite Example

In order to demonstrate just how powerful XPath can be, consider the following situation. In a research project conducted to study the effect of temperature on bacterial culture growth, researchers publish their findings as XML data. Listing 3.12 contains a sample of this data.

Listing 3.12   **A Compilation of Experiment Readings (*data.xml*)**

```
<?xml version="1.0"?>
<project id="49">

    <!-- data for 3 cultures: Alpha, Beta and Gamma, tested at temperatures
    ranging from 10C to 50C -->
    <!-- readings indicate cell counts 4 hours after start of experiment -->

    <record>
        <culture>Alpha</culture>
        <temperature>10</temperature>
        <reading>25000</reading>
    </record>

    <record>
        <culture>Beta</culture>
        <temperature>10</temperature>
        <reading>4000</reading>
    </record>

    <record>
        <culture>Alpha</culture>
        <temperature>10</temperature>
        <reading>23494</reading>
    </record>
```

continues

Listing 3.12   **Continued**

```
    <record>
        <culture>Alpha</culture>
        <temperature>20</temperature>
        <reading>21099</reading>
    </record>

    <record>
        <culture>Gamma</culture>
        <temperature>40</temperature>
        <reading>768</reading>
    </record>

    <record>
        <culture>Gamma</culture>
        <temperature>10</temperature>
        <reading>900</reading>
    </record>

    <!-- snip -->
</project>
```

It now becomes necessary to compile this raw data into an easily understandable table so that the results can be analyzed. Ideally, what is required is a 2x2 table displaying the temperature scale on the Y-axis and the culture type on the X-axis. The intersection of the two axes should be an average of all readings made for that culture at that temperature.

With XPath, this is a snap to accomplish. Listing 3.13 demonstrates the script.

Listing 3.13   **Creating Node Collections with XPath**

```
<html>
<head>
<basefont face="Arial">
</head>
<body bgcolor="white">
<?php

// XML file
$xml_file = "data.xml";

// parse document
$doc = xmldocfile($xml_file) or die("Could not read file!");

// create arrays to hold culture/temperature list
$cultures = array();
$temperatures = array();

// create XPath context
$xpath = $doc->xpath_new_context();
```

```php
// get a list of "culture" nodes
$obj = $xpath->xpath_eval("//culture");
$nodeset = $obj->nodeset;

// ...and create an array containing
// the names of all available cultures
for ($x=0; $x<sizeof($nodeset); $x++)
{
    $children = $nodeset[$x]->children();
    $cultures[] = $children[0]->content;
}

// strip out duplicates
$cultures = array_unique($cultures);

// do the same thing for temperature points
$obj = $xpath->xpath_eval("//temperature");
$nodeset = $obj->nodeset;

for ($x=0; $x<sizeof($nodeset); $x++)
{
    $children = $nodeset[$x]->children();
    $temperatures[] = $children[0]->content;
}

$temperatures = array_unique($temperatures);

// sort both arrays
natsort($temperatures);
natsort($cultures);
?>
<table border="1" cellspacing="5" cellpadding="5">

<tr>
    <td> </td>
<?php
// first row of table, print culture names
foreach($cultures as $c)
{
    echo "<td>$c</td>";
}
?>
</tr>

<?php
foreach($temperatures as $t)
{
    // create as many rows as there are temperature points
    echo "<tr>";
    echo "<td>$t</td>";
```

continues

Listing 3.13   **Continued**

```php
        // for each intersection (culture, temperature)
        // print average of available readings
        foreach($cultures as $c)
        {
              echo "<td>" . intersection($t, $c) . "</td>";
        }

        echo "</tr>";
}
?>

</table>

<?php
// this function collects all readings for
// a particular culture/temperature
// totals them and averages them
function intersection($temperature, $culture)
{
        // get a reference to the XPath context
        global $xpath;

        // set up variables to hold total and frequency
        $total = 0;
        $count=0;

        // get a list of "reading" nodes
        // for records with culture c and temperature t
        $obj = $xpath->xpath_eval("//record[culture='" . $culture . "' and
        ↪temperature='" . $temperature . "']/reading");

        // if XPath evaluation successful
        if ($obj)
        {
              $nodeset = $obj->nodeset;

              // iterate through nodeset
              if (is_array($nodeset))
              {
              // add the readings
                 foreach ($nodeset as $reading)
                 {
                       $children = $reading->children();
                       $total += $children[0]->content;
                       $count++;
                 }
```

```
            }
      }

      // and then average them
      if ($count > 0)
      {
            return $total/$count;
      }

      return 0;
}

?>
</body>
</html>
```

I've used three different XPath expressions here. The first two are used to create a list of available cultures and temperature points; these are required for the row and column headings of the table. The third XPath returns a list of nodes matching a specific culture and temperature. Now, all I need to do is add the readings associated with each of these nodes to reach a total number, and divide that total number by the number of nodes (readings) to obtain an average cell count.

Figure 3.3 shows what the output looks like.

	Alpha	Beta	Gamma
10	24247	4000	900
20	21099	3672	2593
30	16484	2320	6738
40	6839	1949	9875
50	3402	300	19000

Figure 3.3   Statistical analysis with Xpath.

This kind of thing comes in particularly handy when you need to perform statistical analysis of sampling data; it provides a simple and easy way to bring together different elements of each sample, perform calculations on these elements, and relate them to each other in two or three dimensions. XPath's conditional expressions are a boon here—although you can certainly do the same thing without XPath (and I encourage you to try, just so you have a better understanding of the difference), the process would be far more tedious.

Manipulating DOM Trees

The preceding section discussed traversing an already-extant DOM tree, demonstrating how the nodes of the tree can be processed in a recursive manner. That's not all you can do with the DOM, though; it's also possible to programmatically construct DOM trees from scratch, or modify existing tree structures, and save the result as one or more XML documents. This section discusses the details.

Creating New DOM Trees

If you go back to the section dealing with PHP's DOM classes, you'll see that both the DomDocument and DomElement objects include functions to create new documents, nodes, and attributes. The first of these is the `new_xmldoc()` method of the DomDocument object, which constructs and returns a new instance of the DomDocument object.

After a DomDocument instance is available, it becomes possible to add new element and text nodes with the `add_root()` and `new_child()` methods. And why stop at elements? The `set_attribute()` method allows you to define and add attributes to specific elements as well. The following code snippet (see Listing 3.14) demonstrates this by creating a complete XML document tree on the fly with the `add_root()` and `new_child()` methods:

Listing 3.14 **Creating an XML Document Tree**

```php
<?php

// create DomDocument object
$doc = new_xmldoc("1.0");

// add root node
$root = $doc->add_root("article");

// set attribute for root node
$root->set_attribute("id", "567");

// add children to the root
$title = $root->new_child("title", "Goat milk for dinner can cause insomnia");
$author = $root->new_child("author", "K. Kittle");
```

```
// note how I can programatically generate node values!
$date = $root->new_child("date", date("d-M-Y", mktime()));

// dump the tree as a string
echo $doc->dumpmem();
?>
```

After the tree is constructed to your satisfaction, you need to output it, either for display or storage. The DomDocument object's dumpmem() method returns a representation of the current tree as a string. You can then format it for printing, save it to a file, or transmit it to another agent.

Here, Pretty!

Note that if you intend to print the dynamically generated DOM tree, it might be a good idea to run your own formatting functions on it first to pretty it up a little. This is because dumpmem() outputs the document tree as a single string, without formatting or indenting it; in the case of long and/or complex XML documents, it can be fairly difficult to read.

The ability to construct new DOM trees on the fly comes in particularly handy if you need to build a customized DOM tree from another data source. This data source may be a text file that needs to be parsed, a database that needs to be queried, or even another XML document tree that needs to be pruned or combined with other data. Consider Listing 3.15, which uses MySQL database records to construct an XML book catalog and display it to the user.

Listing 3.15   **Constructing a DOM Tree from a MySQL Resultset**

```
<?php

// create DomDocument object
$doc = new_xmldoc("1.0");

// add root node
$root = $doc->add_root("collection");

// query database for records
$connection = mysql_connect("localhost", "us8749", "secret") or die ("Unable to
↪connect!");
mysql_select_db("db633") or die ("Unable to select database!");
$query = "SELECT id, title, author, price FROM books";

$result = mysql_query($query) or die ("Error in query: $query. " . mysql_error());
```

continues

Listing 3.15   **Continued**

```
// iterate through resultset
while($row = mysql_fetch_object($result))
{
    $record = $root->new_child("record", "");
    $record->set_attribute("id", $row->id);

    $record->new_child("title", $row->title);
    $record->new_child("author", $row->author);
    $record->new_child("price", $row->price);
}

// close connection
mysql_close($connection);

// dump the tree as a string
echo $doc->dumpmem();
?>
```

Nothing too complicated here—I'm connecting to the database, extracting a list of titles and authors, and creating an XML document from the result. After the document tree has been created in memory, I can either display it (which is what I've done) or save it to a file (demonstrated in Listing 3.17).

Manipulating Existing DOM Trees

It's also possible to use the functions described previously to modify an existing DOM tree. Consider the XML document in Listing 3.16, which contains the outline for a book chapter.

Listing 3.16   **A Book Chapter Marked up in XML (*ch9.xml*)**

```
<?xml version="1.0"?>

<chapter id="9">

    <!-- chapter 9 of a really bad pulp fiction novel -->

    <title>Luke Gets Angry</title>

    <para>As the black-suited warriors swarmed off the HUMVEE, Luke turned to Jo
    ➥and said quietly, "Don't go anywhere. I'll just be a minute."</para>

    <para>The first warrior reached Luke and aimed a roundhouse kick at his head.
    ➥Luke ducked easily, twisting under the leg and breaking with a sharp crack.
    ➥The warrior moaned and tumbled backwards. Luke grinned. "Bring it on, " he
    ➥hollered.</para>
```

```
<para>The second soldier approached more cautiously. Moving carefully, he
↪crept up behind Luke and leaped at him. Sensing movement, Luke moved aside
↪at the last moment, knocked the soldier unconscious with a well-placed
↪punch and stripped him of his portable grenade launcher. A few seconds
↪later, the HUMVEE was in flames, and the soldiers had fled in panic.</para>

    <para>Luke laughed crazily. He was just beginning to enjoy himself.</para>
</chapter>
```

Now, let's suppose the author decides that "Luke" is actually a pretty wimpy name for the lead character. Instead, he decides to go with "Crazy Dan," which has a much more macho ring to it. Because he's already nine chapters into the book, he needs to change every previous occurrence of "Luke" to "Crazy Dan." All he needs to do is write a PHP program to construct a DOM tree from the XML file, scan through it for every occurrence of "Luke," alter it to "Crazy Dan," and save the result to a new file (see Listing 3.17).

Search and Destroy

I know, I know, he could use any text editor's search-and-replace function. But this chapter's about the DOM, smart guy.

Listing 3.17 **Performing a Search-and-Replace Operation on a DOM Tree**

```php
<?php
// XML file
$xml_file = "/tmp/ch9.xml";

// parse document
if(!$doc = xmldocfile($xml_file))
{
    die("Error in XML document");
}

// get the root
$root = $doc->root();

// children of the root
$children = $root->children();

// start traversing the tree
search_and_replace($children, "Luke", "Crazy Dan");

// all done, save the new tree to a file
// or display it if file write not possible
if (is_writable(dirname($xml_file)))
{
```

continues

Listing 3.17 **Continued**

```php
        $filename = dirname($xml_file) . "/_new_" . basename($xml_file);
        $fp = fopen($filename,"w+");
        fputs($fp,$doc->dumpmem());
        fclose($fp);
}
else
{
        echo $doc->dumpmem();
}


// this is a recursive function to traverse the DOM tree
// when it finds a text node, it will look for the search string and replace with
// the replacement string
function search_and_replace($nodeCollection, $search, $replace)
{
        for ($x=0; $x<sizeof($nodeCollection); $x++)
        {

                if ($nodeCollection[$x]->type == XML_ELEMENT_NODE)
                {
                        // if element, it may contain child text nodes
                        // go one level deeper
                        $nextCollection = $nodeCollection[$x]->children();
                        search_and_replace($nextCollection, $search, $replace);
                }
                else if ($nodeCollection[$x]->type == XML_TEXT_NODE)
                {
                        // if text node, perform replacement
                        $str = str_replace($search, $replace, $nodeCollection[$x]-
                        ->content);
                        // remember to write the value of the text node back to the tree!
                        $nodeCollection[$x]->set_content($str);
                }

        }
}
?>
```

This example is similar to Listing 3.10, in that it too uses a recursive function to process the DOM tree. In this case, though, the recursive function limits its activities to two types of nodes: element nodes and text nodes. If the node is an element node, I ignore it, and call the recursive function again to move one level deeper into the tree; if it's a text node, I scan it for a match to the search string, substitute the replacement text, and write the new string back to the tree.

After the process has concluded, the new DOM tree is written to a file (or, in the event that the directory is not accessible, displayed to the user).

If you examine the resulting output, you'll notice one interesting thing about the set_content() method—it automatically replaces special characters (such as the double quotation marks in Listing 3.16) with the corresponding XML entities (in this case, ").

Going Native

You may sometimes come across situations that require you to convert raw XML markup into native data structures such as variables, arrays, or custom objects. For these situations, PHP's DOM parser includes a very specialized little function named xmltree().

The xmltree() function parses an XML string, and constructs a hierarchical tree of PHP objects representing the structured markup. This tree includes many of the same objects you've become familiar with—instances of the DomDocument, DomElement, DomText, and DomAttribute objects.

xmltree() provides an easy way to quickly see the structure of a complete XML document. For the moment, though, that's all it's useful for; it's not possible to write the tree back to a file, or to memory, after manipulating it.

Note also that, as of this writing, xmltree() only accepts an XML string. You cannot pass it a file name or file reference.

DOM or SAX?

Now that you've seen (and hopefully understood) the two most common approaches to parsing XML with PHP, you're probably wondering: Which one do I use?

It's a good question, and one that doesn't have a one-size-fits-all answer. Both DOM and SAX approaches have advantages and disadvantages, and your choice of technique must depend on the type of data being parsed, the requirements of your application, and the constraints under which you are operating.

The SAX approach is linear: It processes XML structures as it finds them, generating events and leaving the event handlers to decide what to do with each structure. The advantage of this approach is that it is resource-friendly; because SAX does not build a tree representation of the document in memory, it can parse XML data in chunks, processing large amounts of data with very little impact on memory. This also translates into better performance; if your document structure is simple, and the event handlers don't have anything too complicated to do, SAX-based applications will generally offer a speed advantage over DOM-based ones.

The downside, though, is an inability to move around the document in a non-linear manner. SAX does not maintain any internal record of the relationships between the different nodes of an XML document (as the DOM does), making it difficult to create customized node collections or to traverse the document in a non-sequential manner. The only way around this with SAX is to create your own custom object model, and map the document elements into your own custom structures—a process that adds to complexity and can possibly degrade performance.

Where SAX flounders, though, the DOM shines. The DOM creates a tree representation of the document in memory, making it possible to easily travel from one node to another, or even access the same node repeatedly (again, not something you can do easily in SAX). This tree representation is based on a standard, easy-to-understand model, making it easier to write code to interact with it.

This flexibility does, however, come with an important caveat. Because the DOM builds a tree in memory, DOM processing cannot begin until the document has been fully parsed (SAX, on the other hand, can begin parsing a document even if it's not all available immediately). This reduces a developer's ability to "manage" the parsing process by feeding data to the parser in chunks, and also implies greater memory consumption and consequent performance degradation.

Consequently, the choice of technique depends significantly on the type of constraints the application will be performing under, and the type of processing it will be expected to carry out. For systems with limited memory, SAX is a far more efficient approach. On the other hand, complex data-processing requirements can benefit from the standard object model and API of the DOM.

Summary

This chapter demonstrated an alternative approach to the event-based method of parsing XML data. The Document Object Model (DOM) builds a representation of the document structure in memory, and provides the application layer with a standard API to traverse and manipulate this tree.

PHP implements the DOM via a number of standard classes; this chapter examined these classes in detail, together with examples of how they can be used to format XML data, construct XML documents on the fly, and create customized representations of XML data.

Finally, the concluding section of this chapter examined the pros and cons of the SAX and DOM approaches, discussing them vis-a-vis with each other, in an attempt to help developers with the correct approach for their specific requirements.

In the next chapter, I will be discussing Extensible Stylesheet Language Transformations (XSLT), which provides developers with yet another option when it comes to formatting and processing XML data.

"Out of intense complexities, intense simplicities emerge."

~WINSTON CHURCHILL

4

PHP and Extensible Stylesheet Language Transformations (XSLT)

DATA MARKED UP IN XML CAN BE put to a variety of different uses. It can be tagged for identification by search engines, transmitted from one location to another, or formatted for rendering in a web browser or other display agent. The preceding chapters have focused primarily on this last application, using DOM and SAX to process and format XML data for simple user-friendly display.

For mere information formatting and display, using the DOM or SAX approach is a snap. The process is simple and, once you've figured out how it works, adapting it to your particular requirements is a piece of cake. When it comes to longer, more complex transformations, though, using either of these two approaches can be a lot like using a water pistol to put out a forest fire—tedious and, in the long run, not very efficient. For these complex conversions, it's far more effective to use XSL Transformations (XSLT), a stylesheet language designed expressly for the purpose of converting, or "transforming," XML documents into other formats (XML, HTML, WML, ASCII, and so on).

This chapter examines PHP's XSLT extension, reprising examples from earlier chapters to demonstrate how XSLT can be used to quickly and easily create and format different types of documents from a single XML source.

XSLT

As you know, XML, by itself, merely provides the constructs necessary to describe data; it offers no information about how that data is to be presented to a user. Hence, a requirement arises for a separate stylesheet language to handle the presentation aspects of an XML application. This stylesheet language is the Extensible Stylesheet Language (XSL), and it consists of the following three components:

- XML Path Language (XPath), which provides constructs to locate specific nodes or node collections in an XML document tree

- XSL Transformations (XSLT), which is responsible for restructuring, or transforming, XML data into a different format

- XSL Formatting Objects (XSL-FO), which is responsible for the formatting and presentation of the result.

The very first Working Draft of XSL appeared on the W3C's web site in August 1998. At that time, the specification combined XSLT, XPath, and XSL-FO into a single document; the three were later separated into independent entities. The XSLT and XPath specifications were approved by the W3C as W3C Recommendations in November 1999, with the XSL 1.0 specification achieving Recommendation status in October 2001. The W3C's XSL Working Group is currently working to develop the next versions of these specifications in order to address new XML technologies and develop new extensions to the language.

By separating the layout and presentation of data from the data itself, the XSL family of technologies makes it possible to create different representations and views of the same data, simply by applying a different stylesheet to the same XML source. For example, a single inventory statement that is marked up in XML could be combined with different stylesheets to create views customized to the requirements of a purchase manager (who needs to view stock quantities), an accountant (who needs to view costs), and a customer (who needs to view unit availability). In a similar vein, a separate presentation layer also makes it easier to export data into a variety of different formats—the same XML source could therefore be used to generate ASCII documents, HTML web pages, and WML content.

This chapter focuses primarily on XSLT, which provides high-level constructs to transform a source XML document (referred to in the official specification as a *source tree*) into a new document (the *result tree*). It does this by using a *stylesheet* containing *template rules* to locate and match structures in the source tree, and transform them into new structures in the corresponding result tree.

Perhaps the best way to understand this is with a simple example. Consider the XML document in Listing 4.1, which contains a (fictional) list of best-selling books.

Listing 4.1 **Simple XML Book List** (*list.xml*)

```xml
<?xml version="1.0"?>

<list>
        <item>
                <title>Waking Up With The Red-Eyed Bed Monster</title>
                <author>J. I. M. Somniac</author>
                <blurb>The blood-chillingly true story of one man's fight against
                ⇒the monsters under his bed.</blurb>
        </item>

        <item>
                <title>The Case Of The Hungry Hippopotamus</title>
                <author>P. I. Hardhat</author>
                <blurb>A tough private eye is hired to solve the most challenging
                ⇒case of his career.</blurb>
        </item>

        <item>
                <title>Making Money, Losing Friends</title>
                <author>T. Backstabber</author>
                <blurb>The bestselling self-help book for corporate executives on
                ⇒the fast track.</blurb>
        </item>

        <item>
                <title>The Idiot's Guide to Sandwiches</title>
                <author>B. L. Tuhmatto</author>
                <blurb>Making tasty sandwiches has never been so easy!</blurb>
        </item>

</list>
```

Listing 4.2 is its associated XSLT stylesheet.

Listing 4.2 **XSLT Stylesheet** (*list.xsl*)

```xml
<?xml version="1.0"?>
<xsl:stylesheet version="1.0" xmlns:xsl="http://www.w3.org/1999/XSL/Transform">

<!-- set up the main page container -->
<xsl:template match="/">
        <html>
        <head>
```

continues

Listing 4.2   **Continued**

```
          </head>
          <body>
          <xsl:apply-templates />
          </body>
          </html>
</xsl:template>

<!-- look for the list node -->
<xsl:template match="/list" xml:space="preserve">
          <h3><font face="Arial">Bestsellers</font></h3>

          <!-- iterate through the item nodes under the list node -->
          <ul>
          <xsl:for-each select="item">
                <li>
                <font face="Arial"><b><xsl:value-of select="title" /></b> -
                ➥<xsl:value-of select="author" /></font>
                <br />
                <font face="Arial"><i><xsl:value-of select="blurb" /></i></font>
                <p />
                </li>
          </xsl:for-each>
          </ul>

</xsl:template>

</xsl:stylesheet>
```

When I put the two together and run them through an XSLT processor, Figure 4.1 is what I get.

The rules in the stylesheet are matched against the XML markup to create new HTML structures; the resulting HTML output is viewable in any web browser. If, for example, I decided to output WML rather than HTML, I would need merely to modify the presentation layer (the stylesheet) to reflect the new formatting required in the result tree with no modifications required to the original XML data source. (Take a look at Listing 4.20 for an example of how this works.)

This is a very simple example—XSLT allows for a much greater level of complexity, both in creating template rules and in manipulating the result tree. I won't get into the details here—this chapter assumes a familiarity with the basics of XSLT—although you can find links to a number of interesting articles and tutorials (for both novices and experts) on this book's companion web site.

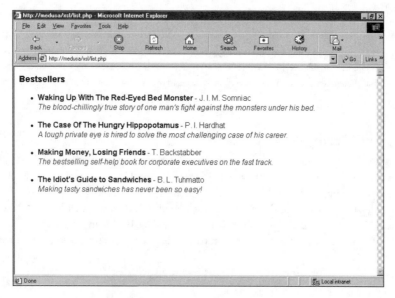

Figure 4.1 An HTML page created via an XSL Transformation.

PHP and XSLT

Although there is nothing to stop you from creating an XML document and a corresponding XSLT stylesheet, you typically need to rely on a third-party XSLT processor (such as Sablotron) to combine the two. Web browsers today have limited XML parsing capabilities, and even less support for XSLT stylesheet processing; this implies that an intermediary layer, such as PHP, is required to perform the task of formatting XML data per XSLT-specified template rules.

PHP 4.0.6 (and later) comes with an XSLT extension designed specifically to provide a consistent interface to different XSLT processors (Sablotron, Xalan, and so on). Created by Sterling Hughes, this XSLT extension works much like an abstraction layer, exposing a generic API that can be used to interact with any compatible XSLT processor. Because the functions defined in this API are common to most XSLT engines, it allows developers to switch between different processors without requiring any changes to the PHP code or application layer.

If you're using a stock PHP binary, it's quite likely that you'll need to recompile PHP to add support for this extension to your PHP build (detailed instructions for accomplishing this are available in Appendix A, "Recompiling PHP to Add XML Support").

As of PHP 4.1.1, the XSLT extension supports only the Sablotron XSLT engine, although you can expect to see support for other XSLT engines in future PHP releases.

Out with the Old . . .

Earlier versions of PHP supported a different Sablotron-specific extension that was activated by adding the `--with-sablot` option during the build process. That extension has now been superseded by the newer, more generic API described in the "PHP and XSLT" section. If you're using a PHP build earlier than 4.0.6, you should upgrade to the latest version in order to use the functions discussed in this chapter.

A Simple Example

PHP's XSLT extension exposes a number of functions to easily transform XML documents into other formats. Together, these functions can be organized into a standard process that is applicable to all XSL Transformations performed with PHP.

In order to demonstrate this process, consider the PHP script in Listing 4.3, which uses the XML and XSLT documents from Listing 4.1 and Listing 4.2 to carry out an XSL Transformation on the server and return the generated result tree to the browser.

Listing 4.3 **Performing an XSL Transformation with PHP**

```php
<?php

// set the filenames
$xml_file = "list.xml";
$xslt_file = "list.xsl";

// create the XSLT processor
$xp = xslt_create() or die("Could not create XSLT processor");

// process the two files to get the desired output
if($result = xslt_process($xp, $xml_file, $xslt_file))
{
        // print output
        echo $result;
}
else
{
        // else display error
        echo "An error occurred: " . xslt_error($xp) . "(error code " .
        ⇒xslt_errno($xp) . ")";
}

// free the resources occupied by the handler
xslt_free($xp);
?>
```

This is much simpler than it looks. Let's go through it step by step:

1. The first order of business is to create an instance of the XSLT processor, which is accomplished via PHP's `xslt_create()` function.

```
$xp = xslt_create() or die("Could not create XSLT processor");
```

The resulting handle is assigned to a variable, and it is used in calls to subsequent XSLT functions.

2. Next, the stylesheet and XML source need to be processed. PHP offers the `xslt_process()` function for this purpose, which accepts three arguments: a handle for the XSLT processor, the name of the file containing the XML data, and the name of the file containing the XSLT template rules.

```
if($result = xslt_process($xp, $xml_file, $xslt_file))
{
        echo $result;
}
else
{
        echo "An error occurred: " . xslt_error($xp) . "(error code " .
        ↦xslt_errno($xp) . ")";
}
```

The `xslt_process()` function is the real workhorse here—it reads the XML source tree, matches it against the rules in the XSLT stylesheet, and outputs a new result tree. The results of the transformation are assigned to a variable (`$result` in the previous example). Note that for large or complex transformations, the process can take awhile.

Windows on the World

If you're using Windows, you'll need to specify the full path to the XML and XSL files for these examples to work correctly.

Most often, you want to store and display the results of the transformation to the user. If, however, you prefer to write the result tree to a file, you can specify the filename as an optional fourth argument to `xslt_process()`. For an example, check out Listing 4.20.

If the processing is successful, all that remains is to output the result. If it is not successful, however, the `xslt_error()` and `xslt_errno()` functions can be used to obtain error information (see the "Handling Errors" section for more on these functions).

3. After the processing is complete, the final task is to clean things up by freeing all memory occupied by the handle:

```
xslt_free($xp);
```

And that's it. XSLT processing in three easy steps!

A Closer Look at `xslt_process()`

If you take a look at the documented API for PHP's XSLT extension, you see that I told a little white lie in my explanation of Listing 4.3. The `xslt_process()` function is actually capable of accepting six different arguments, not just the three described after Listing 4.3.

These arguments are the following, in order:

- Handle representing the XSLT processor

- Name of the file or buffer containing XML data

- Name of the file or buffer containing XSLT data

- Name of the file to which to save the result tree (optional)

- Associative array of argument buffers (optional)

- Associative array of XSLT parameters (optional)

Named buffers are discussed in the "Using Named Buffers" section.

XSLT parameters are discussed in the "Passing Parameters to an XSLT Stylesheet" section.

Handling Errors

PHP's XSLT API includes some functions designed specifically to assist in tracking and displaying errors. Depending on your requirements, you can set up a primitive error handler to display error codes and messages with the `xslt_errno()` and `xslt_error()` functions, or define a custom error handler with the `xslt_set_error_handler()` function.

Primitive Error Handling with *xslt_errno()* and *xslt_error()*

The `xslt_errno()` function returns the error code of the last error encountered by the XSLT processor, whereas the `xslt_error()` function generates a corresponding human-readable error message. Both functions require, as argument, a handle representing the current XSLT processor, as defined by `xslt_create()`. If no argument is provided, the last XSLT error number/error string that occurred is returned.

To illustrate how this error handling works, let's take another look at our first example (see Listing 4.4), which demonstrates this technique.

Listing 4.4   **Basic Error Handling**

```php
<?php

// set the filenames
$xml_file = "list.xml";
$xslt_file = "list.xsl";

// create the XSLT processor
$xp = xslt_create() or die("Could not create XSLT processor");

// process the two files to get the desired output
if($result = xslt_process($xp, $xml_file, $xslt_file))
{
      // print output
      echo $result;
}
else
{
      // else display error
      echo "An error occurred: " . xslt_error($xp) . "(error code " .
      ↝xslt_errno($xp) . ")";
}

// free the resources occupied by the handler
xslt_free($xp);
?>
```

As you can see, this is pretty basic. If an error is encountered while `xslt_process()` is performing the transformation, PHP will merely display an error code and message. You can verify this by deliberately introducing an error into your XML or XSLT document (mismatched tags are always a favorite) and watching how PHP reacts.

Defining a Custom Error Handler with *xslt_set_error_handler()*

A more professional approach to error handling would be to define a custom error handler to resolve all errors that occur during the transformation process. And PHP allows you to do just that with its `xslt_set_error_handler()` function, which lets you define and use your own exception handling mechanism.

The `xslt_set_error_handler()` function accepts two arguments: a handle representing the current XSLT processor, as returned by `xslt_create()`, and the name of the function to pass all errors to.

The following code snippet illustrates this by setting the user-defined function `myHandler()` as the handler for all errors generated during the transformation process:

```php
xslt_set_error_handler($xp, "myHandler");
```

The user-defined error handler specified as the second argument to `xslt_set_error_handler()` must be set up to accept the following four arguments:

- Handle representing the XSLT processor
- Error level (whether notice, warning, or fatal error)
- Error code
- Array containing information on the error

Of these, the last is perhaps the most interesting. It's an associative array containing detailed information on the error, such as the type of error, the line on which it occurred, and the name of the file containing the broken code. Take a look at the following sidebar (titled "Under the Microscope") for a closer look at the contents of this array.

> **Under the Microscope**
>
> The associative array passed to the user-defined error handler contains error information in the form of key-value pairs. If you examine this array with `print_r()`, here's what you see:
>
> ```
> Array
> (
>     [msgtype] => error
>
>     [code] => 2
>
>     [module] => Sablotron
>
>     [URI] =>  file:/usr/local/apache/htdocs/list.xml
>
>     [line] => 7
>
>     [msg] => XML parser error 7: mismatched tag
> )
> ```
>
> As Listing 4.5 demonstrates, most of this information is quite useful, and it can be combined into a fairly descriptive error message.

Listing 4.5 updates the example in Listing 4.4 to use the function `customErrorHandler()` as the handler for any and all errors encountered during the transformation process. A `while()` loop is used to iterate through the array to produce a more useful and descriptive error message.

Listing 4.5 **Using a Custom Error Handler**

```php
<?php

// set the filenames
$xml_file = "list.xml";
$xslt_file = "list.xsl";
```

```
// create the XSLT processor
$xp = xslt_create() or die("Could not create XSLT processor");

// set an error handler
xslt_set_error_handler($xp, "customErrorHandler");

// process the two files to get the desired output
$result = xslt_process($xp, $xml_file, $xslt_file);

// print output
echo $result;

// free the resources occupied by the handler
xslt_free($xp);

// custom error handler
function customErrorHandler($processor, $level, $ecode, $einfo)
{
        echo "<html><head></head><body>Something bad just happened.
        ⇒Here's some more information: <br>";

        // iterate through error array
        while(list($key, $value) = each($einfo))
        {
                echo "$key --> $value <br>";
        }

echo "</body></html>";
}

?>
```

If you prefer, you can have the error handler return only the error message and the line number on which it occurred simply by accessing the relevant keys of the associative array. In Listing 4.5, this information is stored within the associative array $einfo, in the keys line and msg respectively (take a look at the sidebar entitled "Under The Microscope" for details).

Logging Processor Messages

It's also possible to log XSLT activity and then send this information to a log file for later analysis. The function that lets you accomplish this is named xslt_set_log(), and it needs to be invoked twice: first to enable XSLT logging and then to set the name of the log file to write processor messages to.

The first time xslt_set_log() is called, it requires two parameters: a handle representing the XSLT processor to track, and a Boolean value to enable logging:

```
xslt_set_log($xp, true);
```

The second time the function is invoked, the first parameter remains the same; however, the second parameter is now the name of the file to write log messages to:

```
xslt_set_log($xp, "/tmp/xslt.log");
```

This is very simple and works like a charm. Listing 4.6 puts it in context.

Listing 4.6   **Logging XSLT Processor Messages**

```php
<?php

// set the filenames
$xml_file = "list.xml";
$xslt_file = "list.xsl";

// create the XSLT processor
$xp = xslt_create() or die("Could not create XSLT processor");

// set a log file for processor messages
xslt_set_log($xp, true);
xslt_set_log($xp, "/tmp/xslt.log");

// process the two files to get the desired output
$result = xslt_process($xp, $xml_file, $xslt_file);

// print output
echo $result;

// free the resources occupied by the handler
xslt_free($xp);
?>
```

And here's an excerpt from the resulting log file:

```
Sablotron Message on line none, level log: Parsing
➥'file:/usr/local/apache/htdocs/list.xml'...
Sablotron Message on line none, level log: Parse done in 0.003 seconds
Sablotron Message on line none, level log: Executing stylesheet
➥'file:/usr/local/apache/htdocs/list.xsl'...
Sablotron Message on line none, level log: Execution done in 0.006 seconds
```

This excerpt is not very useful at the moment, but expect the log messages to get more descriptive as the API evolves.

If the second argument to xslt_set_log()—the name of the log file—is absent (or NULL), errors are written to the standard error display (usually the browser running the script). If the specified log file already exists, new messages are appended to the end of the log.

> **The Professional Touch**
>
> In a production environment, it's more professional to log processor messages to a file rather than display them to the user via the browser. Consequently, you should make it a point to add the second argument to `xslt_set_log()` after you've finished debugging your code and are preparing to roll it out for release.

It should be noted that `xslt_set_log()` merely provides a mechanism to log processor messages. It does not catch or log errors in syntax; in order to catch these, you need to use one of the error-handling mechanisms described in the "Handling Errors" section.

Using Named Buffers

Thus far, all the examples you've seen have assumed the XML and XSLT data to be stored in static files. This assumption is true in most cases; however, some occasions do arise when your XML is dynamically generated, either from a database, by combining two or more files, or from some other dynamic data source. In such cases, saving this dynamically generated XML to a file and then processing it with `xslt_process()` can be a needlessly long and tedious process.

This is where named buffers come in. *Named buffers* allow you to store your XML and XSLT data in memory and then pass these variables on to `xslt_process()` for normal XSLT transformation.

As discussed in the "A Closer Look at `xslt_process()`" sidebar, the `xslt_process()` function can actually accept up to six arguments. Typically, the second and third arguments are references to the XML and XSLT files; however, they can also be the names of buffers containing the XML and XSLT data.

The following snippet might make this clearer:

```
$arg_buffer = array("/xml" => $xml_string, "/xslt" => $xslt_string);

$xp = xslt_create();

$result = xslt_process($xp, "arg:/xml", "arg:/xslt", NULL, $arg_buffer);
```

As you can see, I first defined an associative array named `$arg_buffer`, and set it up with two keys representing the XML and XSL data, respectively. Next, I've used these keys (with the `arg:` prefix) as arguments to `xslt_process()`, which reads the data in the corresponding buffer and uses it to perform the transformation.

It should be noted at the outset that this capability is available only if your PHP build uses the Sablotron engine. This is because the `arg:` URI scheme is a Sablotron-specific extension, and it is not likely to work with other XSLT processors.

When using this technique, it is mandatory to specify the name of the variable containing the buffers as the (otherwise optional) fifth argument to `xslt_process()`.

Listing 4.7 is a detailed example to put it all in context.

Listing 4.7   **Using Named Buffers**

```php
<?php

// set the filenames
$xml_file = "list.xml";
$xslt_file = "list.xsl";

// convert to strings
$xml_string = join('', file($xml_file));
$xslt_string = join('', file($xslt_file));

// set up buffers
$arg_buffer = array("/xml" => $xml_string, "/xslt" => $xslt_string);

// create the XSLT processor
$xp = xslt_create() or die("Could not create XSLT processor");

// process the two strings to get the desired output
if($result = xslt_process($xp, "arg:/xml", "arg:/xslt", NULL, $arg_buffer))
{
    echo $result;
}
else
{
    echo "An error occurred: " . xslt_error($xp) . "(error code " .
    ↦xslt_errno($xp) . ")";
}

// free the resources occupied by the handler
xslt_free($xp);
?>
```

You should also take a look at Listing 4.12, which demonstrates how named buffers can be used with dynamically generated XML data from a database.

Passing Parameters to an XSLT Stylesheet

If you need to pass data from the PHP script to the XSLT stylesheet, PHP's `xslt_process()` function can be used to pass an associative arrays of parameters to the XSLT stylesheet.

You'll remember that the `xslt_process()` function can accept an array containing parameter-value pairs as an optional sixth argument. These parameters can be passed on to the stylesheet and used within template rules.

Consider Listing 4.8, which creates an associative array named `$params`, and stores two elements containing the page title and current date in it. This associative array is then passed on to the stylesheet via the `xslt_process()` function.

Listing 4.8   **Passing Parameters to an XSLT Stylesheet**

```php
<?php

// set the filenames
$xml_file = "aloha.xml";
$xslt_file = "aloha.xsl";

// set up the parameters
$params = array("today" => date("d M Y", mktime()), "page_title" => "Aloha!");

// include an empty array for arguments (otherwise XSLT tends to break - hopefully
⇒corrected in next release)
$arg_buffer = array();

// create the XSLT processor
$xp = xslt_create() or die("Could not create XSLT processor");

// process the two files to get the desired output
if($result = xslt_process($xp, $xml_file, $xslt_file, NULL, $arg_buffer, $params))
{
    echo $result;
}
else
{
    echo "An error occurred: " . xslt_error($xp) . "(error code " .
    ⇒xslt_errno($xp) . ")";
}

// free the resources occupied by the handler
xslt_free($xp);
?>
```

These parameters are now available to the stylesheet and can be used within a template rule via the <xsl:param /> element (see Listing 4.9).

Listing 4.9   **Using Passed Parameters in an XSLT Stylesheet**

```xml
<?xml version="1.0"?>
<xsl:stylesheet version="1.0" xmlns:xsl="http://www.w3.org/1999/XSL/Transform">

<!-- define the parameter -->
<xsl:param name="page_title"/>
<xsl:param name="today"/>

<xsl:template match="/">
    <html>
    <head>
```

continues

Listing 4.9 **Continued**

```
        <!-- use the parameter -->
        <title><xsl:value-of select="$page_title" /> Today is <xsl:value-of
        ➥select="$today" /> </title>
        </head>
        <body>
        <!-- other templates - snip! -->
        </body>
        </html>
</xsl:template>

</xsl:stylesheet>
```

A Few Examples

Now that you understand the theory, let's look at a few examples that put it all in context. This section illustrates some common examples of XSLT usage, including using it to generate documents in multiple formats and transforming a dynamically generated XML document.

Transforming a Dynamically Generated XML Document

The standard transformation approach I've been using through this chapter involves reading XML and XSLT data from static files, converting this data into a single string, and processing it all at once with xslt_process(). Most of the time, this process works well; however, as discussed previously, there is an alternative approach that makes it possible to use dynamically generated XML (that is, XML built using data stored in a database, rather than a static file) in the transformation.

In order to illustrate this alternative approach, consider Listing 4.10, an XML file.

Listing 4.10 **An XML Bookmark List (*bookmarks.xml*)**

```
<?xml version="1.0"?>

<bookmarks>
    <category name="News">
        <record>
            <name>CNN.com</name>
            <url>http://www.cnn.com/</url>
        </record>
        <record>
            <name>Slashdot</name>
            <url>http://www.slashdot.org/</url>
        </record>
    </category>
```

```
    <category name="Shopping">
        <record>
            <name>Amazon.com</name>
            <url>http://www.amazon.com/</url>
        </record>
    </category>

    <category name="Technical Articles">
        <record>
            <name>Melonfire</name>
            <url>http://www.melonfire.com/</url>
        </record>
    </category>
</bookmarks>
```

Now, let's suppose that I want to generate this XML document dynamically from a database (in a manner similar to that used in Listing 3.15) and transform it into an HTML page using the stylesheet in Listing 4.11.

Listing 4.11 **An XLST Stylesheet to Convert the Bookmark List into HTML** (*bookmarks.xsl*)

```
<?xml version="1.0"?>
<xsl:stylesheet version="1.0" xmlns:xsl="http://www.w3.org/1999/XSL/Transform">

<!-- set up the main page container -->
<xsl:template match="/">
    <html>
    <head>
    </head>
    <body>
    <h3><font face="Arial">My Bookmarks</font></h3>
    <xsl:apply-templates />
    </body>
    </html>
</xsl:template>

<!-- look for the category node -->
<xsl:template match="//category">

    <font face="Arial"><b><xsl:value-of select="@name" /></b></font>

    <!-- iterate through the record nodes under it -->
    <ul>
    <xsl:for-each select="record">
        <!-- print each record as a list item with a label and hyperlink -->
        <li>
            <a>
```

continues

Listing 4.11 **Continued**

```
                    <xsl:attribute name="href"><xsl:value-of
                    ➥select="url"/></xsl:attribute>
                    <font face="Arial"><xsl:value-of select="name" /></font>
                    </a>
                    <p />
            </li>
        </xsl:for-each>
        </ul>

    </xsl:template>

    </xsl:stylesheet>
```

Listing 4.12 contains the PHP script to accomplish this.

Listing 4.12 **Performing an XSLT Transformation on a Dynamically Generated XML Document with PHP**

```php
<?php

$xslt_file = "bookmarks.xsl";

// create the XSLT processor
$xslt_processor = xslt_create();

// read in the data
$xslt_string = join("", file($xslt_file));

// create DomDocument object
$doc = new_xmldoc("1.0");

// add root node
$root = $doc->add_root("bookmarks");

// query database for records
$connection = mysql_connect("localhost", "us7584", "secret") or die ("Unable to
➥connect!");
mysql_select_db("bm") or die ("Unable to select database!");
$query = "SELECT DISTINCT category FROM bookmarks";
$result = mysql_query($query) or die ("Error in query: $query. " . mysql_error());

// iterate through resultset
while(list($category) = mysql_fetch_row($result))
{
    $c = $root->new_child("category", "");
    $c->set_attribute("name", $category);

    $query2 = "SELECT name, url FROM bookmarks WHERE category = '$category'";
    $result2 = mysql_query($query2) or die ("Error in query: $query2. " .
    ➥mysql_error());
```

```
        while(list($name, $url) = mysql_fetch_row($result2))
        {
                $record = $c->new_child("record", "");
                $record->new_child("name", $name);
                $record->new_child("url", $url);
        }
}

// close connection
mysql_close($connection);

// dump the tree as a string
$xml_string = $doc->dumpmem();

// set up buffers
$arg_buffer = array("/xml" => $xml_string, "/xslt" => $xslt_string);

// create the XSLT processor
$xp = xslt_create() or die("Could not create XSLT processor");

// process the two strings to get the desired output
if($result = xslt_process($xp, "arg:/xml", "arg:/xslt", NULL, $arg_buffer))
{
        echo $result;
}
else
{
        echo "An error occurred: " . xslt_error($xp) . "(error code " .
        ➥xslt_errno($xp) . ")";
}

// free the resources occupied by the handler
xslt_free($xp);
?>
```

As you can see, I started off by reading the XSLT file into a string variable. (I'll use this string a little later.) Next, I proceeded to dynamically construct an XML document, in the format described in Listing 4.10, querying a MySQL database for records and inserting them into the XML source tree using the DOM functions discussed in Chapter 3, "PHP and the Document Object Model (DOM)." After the document was fully constructed, I dumped it with the dumpmem() function and created an associative array to hold both the XML and XSLT strings in named buffers.

Finally, I instantiated an XSLT processor and passed the named buffers to the xslt_process() function for processing. At this stage, the XSLT engine took over and transformed the XML data per the template rules in the stylesheet.

Figure 4.2 shows what the output looks like.

Figure 4.2   Transforming a dynamically generated XML document into a web page with XSLT.

Averaging and Tabulating Data with XSLT

In Chapter 3, I demonstrated how the DOM's XPath classes could be used to build a 2×2 table of experiment readings (refer to Listing 3.12). That listing used the DOM API to traverse the document tree; this one uses a stylesheet to demonstrate how much simpler the process is with XSLT.

Listing 4.13 is the XML document containing the sample readings.

Listing 4.13   **A Compilation of Experiment Readings (*data.xml*)**

```
<?xml version="1.0"?>
<project id="49">

    <!-- data for 3 cultures: Alpha, Beta and Gamma, tested at temperatures
    ⇒ranging from 10C to 50C -->
    <!-- readings indicate cell counts 4 hours after start of experiment -->

    <record>
        <culture>Alpha</culture>
        <temperature>10</temperature>
        <reading>25000</reading>
    </record>

    <record>
        <culture>Beta</culture>
        <temperature>10</temperature>
        <reading>4000</reading>
    </record>
```

```
<record>
    <culture>Alpha</culture>
    <temperature>10</temperature>
    <reading>23494</reading>
</record>

<record>
    <culture>Alpha</culture>
    <temperature>20</temperature>
    <reading>21099</reading>
</record>

<record>
    <culture>Gamma</culture>
    <temperature>40</temperature>
    <reading>768</reading>
</record>

<record>
    <culture>Gamma</culture>
    <temperature>10</temperature>
    <reading>900</reading>
</record>

    <!-- snip -->
</project>
```

Listing 4.14 has the XSLT stylesheet I plan to use.

Listing 4.14 **An XSLT Stylesheet to Group and Average Readings (*data.xsl*)**

```
<?xml version="1.0"?>
<xsl:stylesheet version="1.0" xmlns:xsl="http://www.w3.org/1999/XSL/Transform">

<!-- define a custom number format so that non-numbers are displayed as 0 -->
<xsl:decimal-format name="NaNFixFormat" NaN="0" zero-digit="0"/>

<!-- start -->
<xsl:template match="/">
    <html>
    <head>
    </head>
    <body>
    <table border="1" cellspacing="5" cellpadding="5">

    <!-- first row -->
    <tr>
    <td> </td>
    <!-- this returns a list of unique culture names, which are printed in the
    ➥first row -->
```

continues

Listing 4.14 **Continued**

```
        <xsl:for-each select="//culture[not(.=preceding::culture)]">
        <td><xsl:value-of select="."/></td>
        </xsl:for-each>
        </tr>

        <!-- next, we need a list of available temperatures, printed as the first
        ↪column (so put into a loop) -->
        <xsl:for-each select="//temperature[not(.=preceding::temperature)]">
        <tr>
        <td><xsl:value-of select="."/></td>
        <!-- assign the current temperature value to $t-->
        <xsl:variable name="t" select="." />

                    <!-- iterate through the culture list for this temperature
                    ↪value -->
                    <xsl:for-each select="//culture[not(.=preceding::culture)]">

                    <!-- assign the current culture name to $c-->
                    <xsl:variable name="c" select="." />

                    <!-- average all readings corresponding to the intersection
                    ↪($t, $c), format and display -->
                    <td><xsl:value-of select="format-number(sum(//record[culture=$c
                    ↪and temperature=$t]/reading) div count(//record[culture=$c and
                    ↪temperature=$t]/reading), '0', 'NaNFixFormat')"/></td>
                    </xsl:for-each>

        </tr>
        <!-- iterate to next row-->
        </xsl:for-each>
        </table>
        </body>
        </html>
    </xsl:template>

</xsl:stylesheet>
```

In case you're wondering, I used XPath expressions to obtain a list of unique culture names and temperature points from the XML document; these are then used to construct the first row and column of the grid. Next, I used standard XSLT sum() and count() expressions, in combination with a loop, to add and average all the readings belonging to a particular (culture, temperature) combination.

Combinations for which no readings exist are normally represented by the string NaN (Not a Number); I used the <xsl: decimal-format> instruction and the format-number() function to replace this unsightly acronym with a zero.

Version Control

Note that some of the XSLT functions used in Listing 4.14 are supported only in Sablotron 0.71 and higher. If you encounter errors while running this script, you should upgrade to the latest version of Sablotron.

Listing 4.15 transforms the XML document in Listing 4.13 using the XSLT stylesheet in Listing 4.14.

Listing 4.15   **PHP Script to Perform XSL Transformation (*data.php*)**

```php
<?php

// set the filenames
$xml_file = "data.xml";
$xslt_file = "data.xsl";

// create the XSLT processor
$xp = xslt_create() or die("Could not create XSLT processor");

// define the error handler
xslt_set_error_handler($xp, "errHandler");

// process the two files to get the desired output
$result = xslt_process($xp, $xml_file, $xslt_file);

// print output
echo $result;

// free the resources occupied by the handler
xslt_free($xp);

// custom error handler
function errHandler($processor, $level, $ecode, $einfo)
{
    echo "<html><head></head><body>Something bad just happened. Here's some
    ➥more information: <br>";

    // iterate through error array
    while(list($key, $value) = each($einfo))
    {
        echo "$key --> $value <br>";
    }

echo "</body></html>";
}

?>
```

Figure 4.3 shows the output.

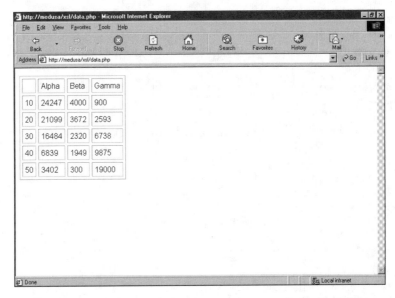

Figure 4.3 Tabulating and averaging experiment readings with XSLT.

Using XSLT to Generate Output in Different Formats from a Single XML Source

Although XSLT is certainly exciting, there's an important caveat: Using PHP to perform XSLT can degrade performance on a web site quite substantially. So, it's a very bad idea to use this technique on a high-traffic web server. It's preferable, therefore, to use transformation simply as a one-time publishing mechanism to generate static HTML or XML files on the server, which can be parsed and returned to the client faster than code-intensive PHP scripts. Yes, you need to regenerate, or republish, the static documents each time your stylesheet or XML source changes, but the extra effort pays dividends in terms of better web server performance and faster response times.

With this in mind, my final example demonstrates an extremely primitive publishing system. I use a single XML document and multiple XSLT stylesheets to output data in three different formats: HTML, WML, and comma-separated ASCII text (CSV). Listing 4.16 is the sample XML document, which lists elements from the periodic table.

Listing 4.16   **The Periodic Table in XML** (*ptable.xml*)

```
<?xml version="1.0"?>
<ptable>

    <element>
        <name>Hydrogen</name>
        <symbol>H</symbol>
        <number>1</number>
    </element>

    <element>
        <name>Lithium</name>
        <symbol>Li</symbol>
        <number>3</number>
    </element>

    <element>
        <name>Sodium</name>
        <symbol>Na</symbol>
        <number>11</number>
    </element>
    <!-- snip -->
</ptable>
```

Next, I need three different stylesheets, one for each format (see Listings 4.17, 4.18, and 4.19).

Listing 4.17   **XSLT Stylesheet to Generate HTML Output** (*ptable_html.xsl*)

```
<?xml version="1.0"?>

<xsl:stylesheet version="1.0" xmlns:xsl="http://www.w3.org/1999/XSL/Transform">

<xsl:template match="/">
    <html>
    <head>
    </head>
    <body>
    <h3>Periodic table of elements</h3>
    <table border="1" cellspacing="5" cellpadding="5">
    <tr>
    <td align="center">Element name</td>
    <td align="center">Symbol</td>
    <td align="center">Atomic number</td>
    </tr>
    <xsl:apply-templates />
    </table>
    </body>
```

continues

Listing 4.17 **Continued**

```
        </html>
</xsl:template>

<xsl:template match="//element">
        <tr>
        <td align="center"><xsl:value-of select="name" /></td>
        <td align="center"><xsl:value-of select="symbol" /></td>
        <td align="center"><xsl:value-of select="number" /></td>
        </tr>
</xsl:template>


</xsl:stylesheet>
```

Listing 4.18 **XSLT Stylesheet to Generate CSV Output** (*ptable_csv.xsl*)

```
<?xml version="1.0"?>

<xsl:stylesheet version="1.0" xmlns:xsl="http://www.w3.org/1999/XSL/Transform">
<xsl:output method="text" omit-xml-declaration="yes" />

<xsl:template match="//element">
<!-- separate the values with commas, put a carriage return at the end of
➥the line -->
<xsl:value-of select="concat(name, ', ', symbol, ',', number, '&#xD;')" />
</xsl:template>

</xsl:stylesheet>
```

Listing 4.19 **XSLT Stylesheet to Generate WML Output** (*ptable_wml.xsl*)

```
<?xml version="1.0"?>

<xsl:stylesheet version="1.0" xmlns:xsl="http://www.w3.org/1999/XSL/Transform">

<xsl:template match="/">
        <wml>
        <card id="ptable" title="Periodic table">
        <p align="center">
        Periodic table
        </p>
        <xsl:apply-templates />
        </card>
        </wml>
</xsl:template>
```

```
<xsl:template match="//element">
    * <xsl:value-of select="name" /> (<xsl:value-of select="symbol" />) ·
    ↩<xsl:value-of select="number" />
    <br />
</xsl:template>

</xsl:stylesheet>
```

Finally, I need a PHP script that accepts the file format as argument, picks up the correct stylesheet, and combines it with the XML document to generate appropriate output (see Listing 4.20).

Listing 4.20   **Generating Output in Different Formats Using XSLT and PHP**

```php
<?php

// alter this to see other formats
$format = "csv";

// set the filenames
$xml_file = "ptable.xml";

// pick the XSLT sheet based on the $format variable
$xslt_file = "ptable_" . $format . ".xsl";

// set the name for the output file
$out_file = "/www/ptable." . $format;

// create the XSLT processor
$xp = xslt_create() or die("Could not create XSLT processor");

// log messages
xslt_set_log($xp, "/tmp/xslt.log");

// define the error handler
xslt_set_error_handler($xp, "errHandler");

// process the files and write the output to $out_file
if(xslt_process($xp, $xml_file, $xslt_file, $out_file))
{
    echo "Success!";
}

// free the resources occupied by the handler
xslt_free($xp);

// custom error handler
function errHandler($processor, $level, $ecode, $einfo)
```

continues

Listing 4.20 **Continued**

```
{
        echo "<html><head></head><body>Something bad just happened. Here's some
    ➥more information: <br>";

        // iterate through error array
        while(list($key, $value) = each($einfo))
        {
                echo "$key --> $value <br>";
        }

echo "</body></html>";
}

?>
```

Nothing too complicated here. The `$format` variable specifies the file format required, and may be passed to the script either on the command line or as a form variable. Depending on the value of this variable, the appropriate stylesheet is used to generate corresponding output. This output may be displayed or saved to disk for later use (which is what Listing 4.20 does).

In this case, I specified a filename as the fourth argument to `xslt_process()`—this is the file to which the results of the transformation are written. If I'd omitted this file, the output would have been returned as a string.

Summary

This chapter offered a brief explanation of XSL Transformations, moving on rapidly to a description of PHP's XSLT support via its generic XSLT API. It demonstrated the standard process of performing XSLT transformations with PHP, explained the API's error-handling capabilities, and showed you how to use named buffers and parameters to add greater flexibility to the transformation process. Finally, it used three fairly complex examples to demonstrate the power inherent in the XSLT/PHP combination.

This chapter concludes our ongoing discussion of the different techniques of formatting and presenting XML markup. In the next chapter, I will move on to a discussion of using XML as the vehicle for data transmission and exchange over the web with Web Distributed Data Exchange (WDDX).

"Beam me up, Scotty!"

~Captain James T. Kirk, "Star Trek"

5

PHP and Web Distributed Data eXchange (WDDX)

THE PRECEDING CHAPTERS HAVE FOCUSED PRIMARILY on parsing XML documents with a strong emphasis on producing content for web browsers. Although accomplishing this is no mean feat—in fact, it's one of the most popular ways to use the XML/PHP combo—it's just the tip of the XML iceberg.

You'll remember from my opening remarks that XML provides constructs to encode any type of information in a standard, machine-readable format. This makes XML the ideal vehicle for information exchange over the web. All that's needed is an encoding format that is understandable to both sender and receiver and that can piggyback over standard Internet protocols (HTTP, SMTP, FTP, and so on).

That's where the Web Distributed Data eXchange (WDDX) comes in. WDDX provides a standard format for creating XML-based data structures designed for easy transmission across the Internet. These WDDX data structures are largely platform-independent, and they can be decoded and used by any application that understands the WDDX format.

Over the next few pages, I will be examining WDDX in greater detail, demonstrating how it can be combined with PHP to encode and exchange data across different systems and platforms.

This chapter marks the transition from merely parsing XML data to actually using XML as the vehicle for other applications. In addition to detailed descriptions of how PHP can be used to create WDDX structures, I'll also be demonstrating some real-life applications of the technology to illustrate its usefulness and versatility.

WDDX

Invented by Allaire Corp. (makers of the HomeSite HTML editor and the ColdFusion application development environment), WDDX is " . . . an XML-based technology that enables the exchange of complex data between web programming languages . . . "[1] It was created in 1998 as an open standard designed specifically to simplify data exchange across different platforms, and it has quickly gained popularity with web developers for its elegance and ease of use.

WDDX works by converting language-specific data structures into their corresponding XML representations. These XML data structures are text-based, platform-independent entities, and, as such, can be transmitted between different systems over standard HTTP protocols with minimal difficulty. Any WDDX-friendly application can read these WDDX *packets*, and convert them back into their original form. For example, a Python list could be encoded into WDDX and transmitted across HTTP to a PHP script, which could decode it into a PHP array. Or a PHP associative array could be translated into WDDX, sent to a Perl script, and decoded into a Perl-compliant hash, for use within a Perl script.

Perhaps an example would make this clearer. Consider Listing 5.1, a single-line PHP script that defines a variable and assigns it a value.

Listing 5.1   **A Simple PHP Variable**

```
<?php
$str = "amoeba";
?>
```

If this variable were to be converted (or, as the geeks say, "serialized" or "pickled") into its WDDX representation, it would look something like Listing 5.2.

Listing 5.2   **A WDDX Representation of a PHP Variable**

```
<wddxPacket version='1.0'>
      <header/>
      <data>
            <string>amoeba</string>
      </data>
</wddxPacket>
```

As you can see, this is regular XML markup, with both the variable type and its value embedded within it. The document element here is the `<wddxPacket>` element; it can

---

1. OpenWDDX.org: The Web Distributed Data Exchange. "Web Distributed Data Exchange FAQ." Available from the Internet: http://www.openwddx.org/faq/

be separated into distinct header and data areas. The header contains a human-readable comment, whereas the data block contains an XML-encoded structure representing the data to be transmitted.

This WDDX representation can be decoded (or "deserialized" or "unpickled") and used by any application that understands WDDX. And so, by creating a standard framework for representing common data structures and by expressing this framework in XML, WDDX makes it possible to easily exchange information over the standard Internet backbone.

WDDX consists of two parts: the WDDX specification that defines basic WDDX structures, and a set of WDDX components for different languages that handles the translation of language-specific data structures into platform-independent XML representations. As of this writing, the WDDX specification supports most commonly used data structures (see the "Not My Type" sidebar for a list), and WDDX components are available for PHP, Perl, ASP, Java, Python, JavaScript, and COM. This immediately makes the technology attractive to developers whose work involves exchanging bits and bytes in multiplatform environments.

It's important to note that WDDX is not an "official" specification per se; rather, it's an open standard created and supported by one company. Despite this, it's fairly popular, primarily for use in client-server or server-server content publishing systems, or as a wrapper for data exchange between multiple programming languages. By allowing applications written in different languages to easily communicate with each other, it also opens the door to new B2B applications, particularly in the areas of streamlining business processes and transactions.

For more information on WDDX, you should refer to the official web site at `http://www.openwddx.org/`, which contains the WDDX Document Type Definition (DTD), an SDK (if you need to implement WDDX on an unsupported platform), and usage examples.

Not My Type

The WDDX specification currently defines the following data types:

- Boolean values, represented by the `<boolean>` element

- Numbers, represented by the `<number>` element

- Strings, represented by the `<string>` element

- Date/time values, encoded in ISO8601 format, represented by the `<dateTime>` element

- Integer-indexed arrays, represented by the `<array>` element

- Structures, or string-indexed arrays, represented by the `<struct>` element;

- Recordsets, or two-dimensional (rows versus columns) data collections, represented by the `<recordset>` element

PHP and WDDX

As previously stated, a WDDX module has been available for PHP since version 4.0 of the language. Created by Andrei Zmievski, this WDDX module includes standard serialization and deserialization functions to convert PHP variables and arrays into WDDX-compatible data structures.

If you're using a stock PHP binary, it's quite likely that you'll need to recompile PHP to add support for this library to your PHP build (detailed instructions for accomplishing this are available in Appendix A, "Recompiling PHP to Add XML Support").

Encoding Data with WDDX

PHP's WDDX module offers a number of different ways to encode data into WDDX. The following sections demonstrate this by using the following:

- The wddx_serialize_value() function
- The wddx_serialize_vars() function
- The wddx_add_vars() function

The *wddx_serialize_value()* Function

The simplest way to encode data into WDDX (and the one I will use most frequently in this chapter) is via the wddx_serialize_value() function, which is used to encode a single variable into WDDX. Listing 5.3 demonstrates its application.

Listing 5.3   **Serializing a Single Variable with *wddx_serialize_value()***

```php
<?php
$flavor = "strawberry";

print wddx_serialize_value($flavor);
?>
```

Listing 5.4 demonstrates the result.

Listing 5.4   **A WDDX Packet Generated via *wddx_serialize_value()***

```xml
<wddxPacket version='1.0'>
      <header/>
      <data>
            <string>strawberry</string>
      </data>
</wddxPacket>
```

Manual Labor

Note that PHP typically generates the WDDX packet as one long string. This can sometimes get confusing, so I manually indented and spaced out some of the output listings in this chapter for greater readability. Whitespace within a WDDX packet, but outside WDDX elements, is ignored by the WDDX deserializer; whitespace embedded within a WDDX element is, obviously, preserved.

As Listings 5.5 and 5.6 demonstrate, this works with arrays, too.

Listing 5.5 **Serializing a PHP Array with** *wddx_serialize_value()*

```
<?php
$flavors = array("strawberry", "chocolate", "raspberry", "peach");

print wddx_serialize_value($flavors);
?>
```

Listing 5.6 **A WDDX Packet Representing an Array**

```
<wddxPacket version='1.0'>
     <header/>
     <data>
          <array length='4'>
               <string>strawberry</string>
               <string>chocolate</string>
               <string>raspberry</string>
               <string>peach</string>
          </array>
     </data>
</wddxPacket>
```

An optional second parameter to wddx_serialize_value() lets you add a human-readable comment to the resulting packet. Listing 5.7 is a variant of Listing 5.5 that demonstrates this, with the output shown in Listing 5.8.

Going to the Source

If you're using your web browser to view the examples in the section, you may wonder why the output you see on your screen doesn't match the output shown here. Well, that's because web browsers tend to hide tags that they don't know about; consequently, the WDDX tags generated during the serialization process are not displayed in the rendered web page.

The solution is fairly simple: use the browser's View Source command to view the raw source for the web page, and you should see the full uncensored output.

Listing 5.7   **Adding a Comment to a WDDX Packet**

```php
<?php
$flavors = array("strawberry", "chocolate", "raspberry", "peach");

print wddx_serialize_value($flavors, "A WDDX representation of my favorite
↪icecream flavors");
?>
```

Listing 5.8   **A WDDX Packet with a Human-Readable Comment in the Header**

```xml
<wddxPacket version='1.0'>
    <header>
        <comment>A WDDX representation of my favorite icecream
flavors</comment>
    </header>
     <data>
        <array length='4'>
            <string>strawberry</string>
            <string>chocolate</string>
            <string>raspberry</string>
            <string>peach</string>
        </array>
    </data>
</wddxPacket>
```

The *wddx_serialize_vars()* Function

The wddx_serialize_value() function cannot accept more than a single variable.
However, it's also possible to serialize more than one variable at a time with the
wddx_serialize_vars() function, which can accept multiple variables for serialization
as function arguments. Listing 5.9 demonstrates how this works.

Listing 5.9   **Serializing Multiple Values with *wddx_serialize_vars()***

```php
<?php
$phrase = "The game's afoot";
$animals = array("parrot" => "Polly", "hippo" => "Hal", "dog" => "Rover",
↪"squirrel" => "Sparky");

print wddx_serialize_vars("phrase", "animals");
?>
```

Note that wddx_serialize_vars() requires the names of the variables to be serialized
as string arguments.
Listing 5.10 displays the result of a wddx_serialize_vars() run.

Listing 5.10 **A WDDX Packet Generated via** *wddx_serialize_vars()*

```
<wddxPacket version='1.0'>
<header/>
      <data>
            <struct>
                  <var name='phrase'>
                        <string>The game's afoot</string>
                  </var>
                  <var name='animals'>
                        <struct>
                              <var name='parrot'>
                                    <string>Polly</string>
                              </var>
                              <var name='hippo'>
                                    <string>Hal</string>
                              </var>
                              <var name='dog'>
                                    <string>Rover</string>
                              </var>
                              <var name='squirrel'>
                                    <string>Sparky</string>
                              </var>
                        </struct>
                  </var>
            </struct>
      </data>
</wddxPacket>
```

It's interesting to note, also, that wddx_serialize_value() and wddx_serialize_vars() generate significantly different (though valid) WDDX packets. Consider Listing 5.11, which creates a WDDX packet containing the same variable-value pair as Listing 5.3, and compare the resulting output in Listing 5.12 with that in Listing 5.4.

Listing 5.11 **Serializing a Single Variable with** *wddx_serialize_vars()*

```
<?php
$flavor = "strawberry";

print wddx_serialize_vars("flavor");
?>
```

Listing 5.12 **A WDDX Packet Generated via** *wddx_serialize_vars()*

```
<wddxPacket version='1.0'>
      <header/>
      <data>
```

Listing 5.12 **Continued**

```
            <struct>
                <var name='flavor'>
                        <string>strawberry</string>
                </var>
            </struct>
        </data>
</wddxPacket>
```

The *wddx_add_vars()* Function

PHP also allows you to build a WDDX packet incrementally, adding variables to it as they become available, with the wddx_add_vars() function. Listing 5.13 demonstrates this approach, building a WDDX packet from the results of a form POST operation.

Listing 5.13 **Building a WDDX Packet Incrementally with *wddx_add_vars()***

```php
<?php

// create a packet handle
// the argument here is an optional comment
$wp = wddx_packet_start("A packet containing a list of form fields with values");

// iterate through POSTed fields
// add variables to packet
wddx_add_vars($wp, "HTTP_POST_VARS");

// end the packet
// you can now assign the generated packet to a variable
// and print it
wddx_packet_end($wp);
?>
```

This is a slightly more complicated technique than the ones described previously. Let's go through it step by step:

1. The first order of business is to create an empty WDDX packet to hold the data; this is accomplished with the aptly named wddx_packet_start() function, which returns a handle for the newly minted packet.

   ```
   $wp = wddx_packet_start("A packet containing a list of form fields with
   ⮑values");
   ```

   This handle is used in all subsequent operations. Note that the wddx_packet_start() function can be passed an optional comment string, which is used to add a comment to the header of the generated packet.

2. With the packet created, the next step is to add data to it. In Listing 5.13, the data is generated dynamically from a form submission, and each value is then added to the packet via the `wddx_add_vars()` function.

```
wddx_add_vars($wp, "HTTP_POST_VARS");
```

This function works in much the same way as `wddx_serialize_vars()` — it accepts multiple variable names as argument (although I've only used one here), serializes these variables into WDDX structures, and adds them to the packet. Note, however, that `wddx_add_vars()` requires, as first argument, the handle representing the packet to which the data is to be added.

3. After all the required data has been inserted into the packet, the final step is to close the packet, accomplished via the `wddx_packet_end()` function. Again, the packet handle is used to identify the packet to be closed.

```
wddx_packet_end($wp);
```

Note that the `wddx_packet_end()` function returns the contents of the newly minted packet; this return value can be assigned to a variable and used in subsequent lines of the PHP script.

This approach comes in particularly handy if you're dealing with dynamically generated data, either from a database or elsewhere.

With your data now safely encoded into WDDX, let's now look at how you can convert it back into usable PHP data structures.

Decoding Data with WDDX

Although there are five different functions available to encode data into WDDX, PHP has only a single function to perform the deserialization of WDDX packets. This function is named `wddx_deserialize()`, and it accepts a string containing a WDDX packet as its only argument.

Listing 5.14 demonstrates how a PHP variable encoded in WDDX can be deserialized by `wddx_deserialize()`.

Listing 5.14 **Deserializing a WDDX Packet into a Native PHP Structure**

```
<?php

$flavor = "blueberry";

// print value before converting to WDDX
echo "Before serialization, \$flavor = $flavor <br>";

// serialize into WDDX packet
$packet = wddx_serialize_value($flavor);
```

continues

Listing 5.14 **Continued**

```
// deserialize generated packet and display value
echo "After serialization, \$flavor = " . wddx_deserialize($packet);
?>
```

This works with arrays, too—in Listing 5.15, the deserialized result $output is an array containing the same elements as the original array $stooges.

Listing 5.15 **Deserializing a WDDX Packet into a PHP Array**

```
<?php

$stooges = array("larry", "curly", "moe");

// serialize into WDDX packet
$packet = wddx_serialize_value($stooges);

// deserialize generated packet
$output = wddx_deserialize($packet);

// view it
print_r($output);
?>
```

Buyer Beware!

There's an important caveat to keep in mind when using PHP's WDDX module. As shown in Listings 5.4 and 5.12, the wddx_serialize_vars() and wddx_add_vars() functions work in a slightly different manner from the wddx_serialize_value() function. Both wddx_serialize_vars() and wddx_add_vars() use WDDX *structures* (represented by <struct> elements) to store variables and their values, regardless of whether the variable is a string, number, or array. On the other hand, wddx_serialize_value() uses a <struct> only if the variable is an associative array.

This variation in the serialization process can significantly impact the deserialization process because PHP's wddx_deserialize() function automatically converts <struct>s into associative arrays. Consequently, the manner in which you access the original value of the variable will change, depending on how it was originally serialized.

Consider Table 5.1, which demonstrates the difference.

Table 5.1 **A Comparison of Serialization with *wddx_serialize_value()* and *wddx_serialize_vars()***

wddx_serialize_value()	wddx_serialize_vars()
```<?php```	```<?php```
```$lang = array("PHP", "Perl", "Python", "XML", "JSP");```	```$lang = array("PHP", "Perl", "Python", "XML", "JSP");```

wddx_serialize_value()	*wddx_serialize_vars()*
| ```
$alpha =
wddx_serialize_value($lang);

$beta =
wddx_deserialize($alpha)


// returns "PHP"
print $beta[0];



// returns "Python"
print $beta[2];
?>
``` | ```
$alpha =
wddx_serialize_vars("lang");

$beta =
wddx_deserialize($alpha);


// returns "PHP"
print $beta["lang"][0];



// returns "Python"
print $beta["lang"][2];
?>
``` |

A Few Examples

So that's the theory. There wasn't much of it, but don't let that discourage you—it's possible to build some fairly powerful distributed applications using the simple functions described in the previous sections.

Information Delivery with WDDX and HTTP

This section discusses one of the most popular applications of this technology, using it to build a primitive push/pull engine for information delivery over the web. I'll be using a MySQL database as the data source, WDDX to represent the data, and PHP to perform the actual mechanics of the transaction.

Requirements

Let's assume the existence of a fictional corporation—XTI Inc.—that plans to start up an online subscription service offering access to share market data. XTI already has access to this information via an independent source, and its database of stocks and their prices is automatically updated every few minutes with the latest market data. XTI's plan is to offer customers access to this data, allowing them to use it on their own web sites in exchange for a monthly subscription fee.

Listing 5.16 has a slice of the MySQL table that holds the data we're interested in.

Listing 5.16 **A Sample Recordset from the MySQL Table Holding Stock Market Information**

```
+---------+---------+----------------------+
| symbol  | price   | timestamp            |
+---------+---------+----------------------+
| DTSJ    |   78.46 | 2001-11-22 12:20:57  |
| DNDS    |    5.89 | 2001-11-22 12:32:12  |
| MDNC    |   12.94 | 2001-11-22 12:21:34  |
| CAJD    |  543.89 | 2001-11-22 12:29:01  |
| WXYZ    |  123.67 | 2001-11-22 12:28:32  |
+---------+---------+----------------------+
```

All that is required is an interface to this database so that subscribers to the service can connect to the system and obtain prices for all or some stocks (keyed against each stock's unique four-character symbol).

Implementing these requirements via WDDX is fairly simple and can be accomplished via two simple scripts—one for each end of the connection. A WDDX server can be used at the XTI end of the connection to accept incoming client requests and deliver formatted WDDX packets to them. At the other end of the connection, WDDX-friendly clients can read these packets, decode them, and use them in whatever manner they desire.

Server

Let's implement the server first. Listing 5.17 has the complete code.

Listing 5.17 **A Simple WDDX Server**

```php
<?php
// server.php - creates WDDX packet containing symbol, price and timestamp of
➥all/selected stock(s)

// this script will run at the URL http://caesar.xtidomain.com/customers/server.php

// open connection to database
$connection = mysql_connect("mysql.xtidomain.com", "wddx", "secret") or die
➥("Unable to connect!");
mysql_select_db("db7643") or die ("Unable to select database!");

// get data
$query = "SELECT symbol, price, timestamp FROM stocks";

// if a symbol is specified, modify query to get only that record
if ($_GET['symbol']);
{
    $symbol = $_GET['symbol'];
    $query .= " WHERE symbol = '$symbol'";
}
```

```
$query .= " ORDER BY timestamp";

$result = mysql_query($query) or die ("Error in query: $query. " . mysql_error());

// if a result is returned
if (mysql_num_rows($result) > 0)
{

    // iterate through resultset
    while($row = mysql_fetch_row($result))
    {

        // add data to $sPackage[] associative array
        // $sPackage is an array of the form ($symbol => array($price,
        ⇒$timestamp), ... )

        $sPackage[$row[0]] = array($row[1], $row[2]);
    }
}

// close database connection
mysql_close($connection);

// create WDDX packet
echo wddx_serialize_value($sPackage);
?>
```

This may appear complex, but it's actually pretty simple. Because the data is stored in a database, the first task must be to extract it using standard MySQL query functions. The returned resultset may contain either a complete list of all stocks currently in the database with their prices or a single record corresponding to a client-specified stock symbol.

Next, this data must be packaged into a form that can be used by the client. For this example, I packaged the data into an associative array named $sPackage, whose every key corresponds to a stock symbol in the table. Every key is linked to a value, which is itself a two-element array containing the price and timestamp.

After all the records in the resultset are processed, the $sPackage array is serialized into a WDDX packet with wddx_serialize_value() and then printed as output.

Client

So, you now have a server that is capable of creating a WDDX packet from the results of a database query. All you need now is a client to connect to this server, retrieve the packet, and decode it into a native PHP array for use on an HTML page. Listing 5.18 contains the code for this client.

Listing 5.18   **A Simple WDDX Client**

```php
<?php
// client.php - read and decode WDDX packet

// this script runs at http://brutus.clientdomain.com/client.php

// url of server page
$url = "http://caesar.xtidomain.com/customers/server.php";

// probably implement some sort of authentication mechanism here
// proceed further only if client is successfully authenticated

// read WDDX packet into string
$output = join ('', file($url));

// deserialize
$cPackage = wddx_deserialize($output);

?>
<html>
<head>
<basefont face="Arial">
<!-- reload page every two minutes for latest data -->
<meta http-equiv="refresh" content="120; URL=
http://brutus.clientdomain.com/client.php">
</head>
<body>

<?
// if array contains data
if (sizeof($cPackage) > 0)
{
    // format and display
?>

    <table border="1" cellspacing="5" cellpadding="5">

    <tr>
    <td><b>Symbol</b></td>
    <td><b>Price (USD)</b></td>
    <td><b>Timestamp</b></td>
    </tr>

    <?php
    // iterate through array
    // key => symbol
    // value = array(price, timestamp)
    while (list($key, $value) = each($cPackage))
    {
```

```
            echo "<tr>\n";
            echo "<td>$key</td>\n";
            echo "<td>$value[0]</td>\n";
            echo "<td>$value[1]</td>\n";
            echo "</tr>\n";
        }

    ?>

    </table>
<?
}
else
{
    echo "No data available";
}
?>
</body>
</html>
```

The client is even simpler than the server. It connects to the specified server URL and authenticates itself. (I didn't go into the details of the authentication mechanism to be used, but it would probably be a host-username-password combination to be validated against XTI's customer database.) It then reads the WDDX packet printed by the server into an array with the `file()` function. This array is then converted into a string and deserialized into a native PHP associative array with `wddx_deserialize()`.

After the data is decoded into a PHP associative array, a `while` loop can be used to iterate through it, identifying and displaying the important elements as a table.

Figure 5.1 shows what the resulting output looks like.

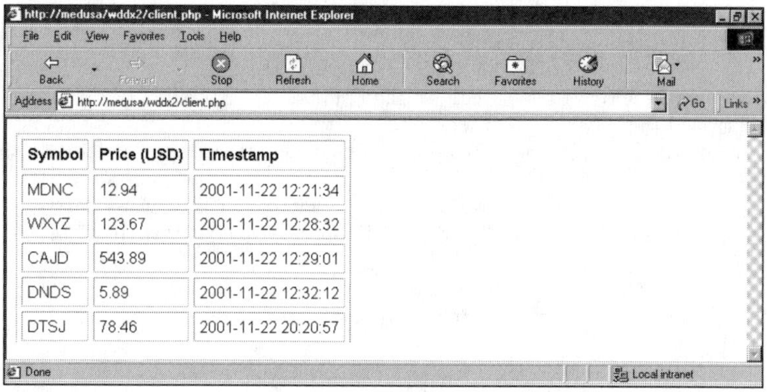

Figure 5.1   Retrieving stock prices from a database via a WDDX-based client-server system.

The beauty of this system is that the server and connecting clients are relatively independent of each other. As long as a client has the relevant permissions, and understands how to connect to the server and read the WDDX packet returned by it, it can massage and format the data per its own special requirements. To illustrate this, consider Listing 5.19, which demonstrates an alternative client—this one performing a "search" on the server for a user-specified stock symbol.

Listing 5.19 **An Alternative WDDX Client**

```php
<?php
// client.php - read and decode WDDX packet

// this script runs at http://brutus.clientdomain.com/client.php

if(!$_POST['submit'])
{
?>

        <!-- search page -->
        <!-- lots of HTML layout code - snipped out -->

        <form action="<? echo $_SERVER['PHP_SELF']; ?>" method="post">
        Enter stock symbol:
        <input type="text" name="symbol" size="4" maxlength="4">
        <input type="submit" name="submit" value="Search">

        </form>
<?
}
else
{
        // perform a few error checks

        // sanitize search term

        // query server with symbol as parameter
        $symbol = $_POST['symbol'];
        $url = "http://caesar.xtidomain.com/customers/server.php?symbol=$symbol";

        // probably implement some sort of authentication mechanism here
        // proceed further only if client is successfully authenticated

        // read WDDX packet into string
        $output = join ('', file($url));

        // deserialize
        $cPackage = wddx_deserialize($output);

        // if any data in array
        if (sizeof($cPackage) > 0)
        {
```

```
            // format and display
            list($key, $value) = each($cPackage);
            echo "Current price for symbol $key is $value[0]";
        }
        else
        {
            echo "No data available";
        }
    }
    ?>
```

This script consists of two parts:

- The search form itself, which contains a text box for user input
- The form processor, which connects to the content server with the user-specified stock symbol as parameter and massages the resulting WDDX output into easily readable HTML

Again, even though the two clients operate in two different ways (one displays a complete list of items, whereas the other uses a search term to filter down to one specific item), no change was required to the server or to the formatting of the WDDX packet.

Perl of Wisdom

It's not necessary that the WDDX clients described in Listings 5.18 and 5.19 be written in PHP. As discussed previously in this chapter, WDDX creates platform-independent data structures that can then be deserialized into native structures on the target platform. Consequently, it's possible for a WDDX client written in Perl or Python to connect to a WDDX server written in PHP, receive WDDX-compliant data packets, and use them within a script or program.

As an illustration, consider the following Perl port (see Listing 5.20) of the client described in Listing 5.18.

Listing 5.20   **A Perl WDDX Client**

```perl
#!/usr/bin/perl

# need this to read HTTP response
use LWP::UserAgent;

# need this to deserialize WDDX packets
use WDDX;

# instantiate client, connect and read response
$client = LWP::UserAgent->new;
my $req = HTTP::Request->new(GET => 'http://caesar.xtidomain.com/
⇒customers/server.php');
my $res = $client->request($req);
```

continues

Listing 5.20 **Continued**

```perl
# response is good...
if ($res->is_success)
{
        # deserialize resulting packet as hash and get reference
        my $wddx = new WDDX;
        $packet = $wddx->deserialize($res->content);
        $hashref = $packet->as_hashref;

        # get a list of keys (stock symbols) within the hash
        @keys = $packet->keys();

        # iterate through hash
        foreach $key (@keys)
        {
                # get a reference to the array [price, timestamp] for each key
                $arrayref = $$hashref{$key};

                # print data in colon-separated format
                print "$key:$$arrayref[0]:$$arrayref[1]\n";
        }
}
# response is bad...
else
{
        print "Error: bad connection!\n";
}
```

In this case, I used Perl's libwww module to connect to the WDDX server and read the resulting packet, and the WDDX module to deserialize it into a Perl hash reference. After the data is converted into a Perl-compliant structure, accessing and displaying the various elements is a snap.

Perl's WDDX.pm module is far more powerful than the WDDX module that ships with PHP 4.0, offering a wide array of different methods to simplify access to arrays, hashes, and recordsets. (Recordsets are not supported by PHP's WDDX module as of this writing, although support might become available in future versions.)

More information on Perl's WDDX.pm module is available at `http://www.scripted.com/wddx/`.

Remote Software Updates with WDDX and Socket Communication

The preceding section, "Information Delivery with WDDX and HTTP," demonstrated a WDDX client and server running over HTTP. As you might imagine, though, that's not the only way to use WDDX; this next example demonstrates WDDX-based data exchange using socket communication between a PHP server and client.

Requirements

In order to set the tone, let's again consider a fictional organization, Generic Corp (GCorp), which provides its customers with Linux-based software widgets. GCorp updates these widgets on a regular basis, and makes them available to paying customers via an online repository.

Now, GCorp has no fixed update schedule for these widgets—they're handled by different development teams, and are released to the online repository as installable files in RedHat Package Manager (RPM) format at irregular intervals. What GCorp wants is a way for every customer to automatically receive notification of software updates as and when they're released.

Most companies would send out email notification every time an update happened. But this is GCorp, and they like to make things complicated.

What GCorp has planned, therefore, is to have a WDDX server running on its web site, which automatically scans the repository and creates a WDDX packet containing information on the latest software versions available. This information can then be provided to any requesting client.

The client at the other end should have the necessary intelligence built into it to compare the version numbers received from the server with the version numbers of software currently installed on the local system. It may then automatically download and install the latest versions, or simply send notification to the system administrator about the update.

This is easily accomplished with WDDX; for variety, I'll perform the data exchange over TCP/IP sockets rather than HTTP.

Server

Let's begin with the server (see Listing 5.21), which opens up a socket and waits for connections from requesting clients.

Listing 5.21   **A WDDX Server to Read and Communicate Version Information Over a TCP/IP Socket**

```php
<?php

// IMPORTANT! This script should not be run via your Web server!
// You will need to run it from the command line,
// or as a service from inetd.conf

// set up some socket parameters
$ip = "127.0.0.1";
$port = 7890;

// area to look for updated files
$repository = "/tmp/updates/";
```

continues

Listing 5.21 **Continued**

```php
// start with socket creation
// get a handler
if (($socket = socket_create (AF_INET, SOCK_STREAM, 0)) < 0)
{
    // this is fairly primitive error handling
    echo "Could not create socket\n";
}

// bind to the port
if (($ret = socket_bind ($socket, $ip, $port)) < 0)
{
    echo "Could not bind to socket\n";
}

// start listening for connections
if (($ret = socket_listen ($socket, 7)) < 0)
{
    echo "Could not create socket listener\n";
}

// if incoming connection, accept and spawn another socket
// for data transfer
if (($child = socket_accept($socket)) < 0)
{
    echo "Could not accept incoming connection\n";
}

if (!$input = socket_read ($child, 2))
{
    echo "Could not read input\n";
}
else
{
    // at this stage, GCorp might want to perform authentication
    // using the input received by the client

    // assuming authentication succeeds...

    // look in the updates directory
    $dir = opendir($repository);
    while($file = readdir($dir))
    {
        // omit the "." and ".." directories
        if($file != "." && $file != "..")
        {
            $info = explode("-", $file);
            // create an array of associative arrays, one for each
            ➥file found
            // each associative array has the keys "name", "version"
            ➥and "size"
```

```
                    $filelist[] = array("name" => $info[0], "version" => $info[1],
                    ⇒"size" => filesize($repository . $file));
            }
        }
        closedir($dir);

        // serialize the array
        $output = wddx_serialize_value($filelist);

        // and send it to the client
        if(socket_write ($child, $output, strlen ($output)) < 0)
        {
            echo "Could not write WDDX packet";
        }

        // clean up
        socket_close ($child);
    }
    socket_close ($socket);
    ?>
```

I will not get into the details of how the socket server is actually created—if you're interested, the PHP manual has extensive information on this—but instead focus on how the server obtains information on the updates available and serializes it into a WDDX packet.

The variable $repository sets up the location of the online software repository maintained by GCorp's QA team. When the socket server receives an incoming connection, it obtains a file list from the repository and creates an array whose every element corresponds to a file in the repository.

Every element of the array is itself an associative array that contains the keys name, version, and size, corresponding to the package name, version, and size, respectively. (Some of this information is obtained by parsing the filename with PHP's string functions.) This entire array is serialized with wddx_serialize_value() and written to the requesting client via the open socket.

I used PHP to implement the server here for convenience; however, it's just as easy to use Perl, Python, or Java (as discussed in the "Perl Of Wisdom" sidebar). Note also that socket programming support was added to PHP fairly recently and is, therefore, not yet completely stable.

Client

At the other end of the connection, a WDDX-compliant client has to deserialize the packet received from the server and then compare the information within it against the information it has on locally installed versions of the software. Listing 5.22 demonstrates one implementation of such a client.

Listing 5.22   **A WDDX Client to Retrieve Version Information Over a TCP/
IP Socket**

```php
<?php


// IMPORTANT!  This script should not be run via your Web server!
// You will need to run it manually from the command line, or via crontab

// set up some socket parameters
// this is the IP address of the socket server
$ip = "234.56.789.1";
$port = 7890;

// open a socket connection
$socket = fsockopen($ip, $port);

if (!$socket)
{
    echo "Could not open connection\n";
}
else
{
    // send a carriage return
    fwrite($socket, "\n");
    $packet = fgets($socket, 4096);
    // get and deserialize list of server packages
    $remote_packages = wddx_deserialize($packet);
    // close the socket
    fclose($socket);

    // make sure that the deserialized packet is an array
    if(!is_array($remote_packages))
    {
        $message= "Bad/unsupported data format received\n";
    }
    else
    {
        // now, start processing the received data
        for ($x=0; $x<sizeof($remote_packages); $x++)
        {
            // for each item in the array
            // check to see if a corresponding package is installed on
            ➥the local system
            $local_package = exec("rpm -qa | grep " .
            ➥$remote_packages[$x]['name']);

            // not there? that means it's a new package
            // dump it into the $new_packages[] array
            if ($local_package == "")
            {
```

```
                $new_packages[] = $remote_packages[$x];
        }
        else
        {
                // present? check version
                // if a new version is available,
                // dump it into the $updated_packages[] array
                $arr = explode("-", $local_package);
                if ($arr[1] < $remote_packages[$x]['version'])
                {
                        $updated_packages[] = $remote_packages[$x];
                }
        }
}


// finally, put together a notification for the sysop
// list of updates, with file size and version

// an option here might be to initiate an automatic
// download of the updates
// RPM can be used to auto-install the downloaded updates
if (sizeof($updated_packages) > 0)
{
        $message .= "The following updates are available on our
        ➥server:\n";
        for ($x=0; $x<sizeof($updated_packages); $x++)
        {
                $message .= "Package: ". $updated_packages[$x]['name']
                ➥. "\n";
                $message .= "Version: " . $updated_packages[$x]['version']
                ➥. "\n";
                $message .= "Size: " . $updated_packages[$x]['size']
                ➥. " bytes\n\n";
        }
}


// ...and list of new packages, with file size and version
if (sizeof($new_packages) > 0)
{
        $message .= "The following new packages have been added to our
        ➥server (may require purchase):\n";
        for ($x=0; $x<sizeof($new_packages); $x++)
        {
                $message .= "Package: ". $new_packages[$x]['name'] . "\n";
                $message .= "Version: " . $new_packages[$x]['version']
                ➥. "\n";
                $message .= "Size: " . $new_packages[$x]['size']
                ➥. " bytes\n\n";
        }
}
```

continues

Listing 5.22 **Continued**

```
                // mail it out
                if(mail("root@localhost", "GCorp package updates for this week",
                ➥$message))
                {
                      echo "Operation successfully completed";
                }
                else
                {
                      echo "Error processing mail message";
                }
        }
}
?>
```

In this case, the client uses PHP's `fsockopen()` function to connect to the server and retrieve the WDDX packet. It then deserializes this packet into an array, and proceeds to iterate through it.

Because all GCorp packages are distributed in RPM format, it's fairly simple to obtain information on the currently installed versions of the files listed in the array with the `rpm` utility (standard on most Linux systems). These version numbers are compared with the version numbers of files on GCorp's server (remember the `version` key of each associative array?), and two new arrays are created:

- `$updated_packages`, which contains a list of updated packages
- `$new_packages`, which contains a list of packages available on the server but not installed locally

This information is then emailed to the system administrator via PHP's `mail()` function.

This isn't the only option, obviously; a variant of this might be for the client to automatically download and install the new software automatically. A more sophisticated client might even identify the new packages and send advertisements for, or information on, new software available, on a per-customer basis.

Command and Control

It's not advisable to run Listings 5.21 and 5.22 via your web server; rather, they should be run from the command line using the PHP binary.

For example, if you have a PHP binary located in /usr/local/bin/php, you would run the server script as the following:

```
$ /usr/local/bin/php -q /usr/local/work/bin/socket_server.php
```

> The additional -q (quiet) parameter forces PHP to omit the Content-Type: text/html header that it usually sends prior to executing a script.
>
> In case you don't have a PHP binary available, it's pretty easy to compile one. Just follow the instructions in Appendix A.
>
> Although the socket server should always be active—which is why I suggest running it as a service managed by the inet daemon—the client should be set up to instantiate connections on a more irregular basis, either via manual intervention or UNIX cron.

Other Applications for WDDX

As the preceding examples demonstrated, WDDX makes it possible to exchange data between different sites and systems in a simple and elegant manner. Consequently, one of its more common applications involves acting as the vehicle for the syndication of frequently updated content over the web. Examples of areas in which WDDX can be used include the following:

- News syndication services, which "push" the latest headlines, sports scores, stock and currency market information, and weather forecasts to connecting clients from a news database (for an example, check out http://www.moreover.com/, which offers news headlines in WDDX)

- Ad-rotation services, which accept demographic data from requesting clients and return links to appropriate banner ads for display on the resulting web page

- E-commerce agents, which browse different sites and return comparative pricing information for selected items

- Software-update services, which automatically update remote systems with new software versions

Summary

This chapter discussed WDDX, a method of creating platform-neutral data structures for information exchange over the web. It discussed PHP's WDDX support, explaining how to serialize and deserialize WDDX packets, and demonstrated how PHP and WDDX could be used to create a content distribution server for financial information updates and a software distribution network for web-based software updates. It also briefly discussed other applications of this technology for content dissemination over the web.

*"Any sufficiently advanced technology
is indistinguishable from magic."*

~ARTHUR C. CLARKE

6

PHP and XML–Based Remote Procedure Calls (RPC)

IT'S QUITE LIKELY, IF YOU'RE COMING at this from a non-C/C++ background, that you've never heard of Remote Procedure Calls (RPC). This is a shame, because not only has RPC been around for a while, it's also a fairly interesting idea that opens the door to a whole new generation of cutting-edge, network-based services.

Stripped down to its bare bones, RPC defines a client-server framework for distributed computing, allowing procedures on a server to be remotely executed by a client. The existing network layer is used for communication between the client and server; this implies that the client invoking the procedure may be on either the same physical machine or a completely different machine on the network (hence the term *remote procedure call*).

Now, the Internet is the biggest, baddest network of them all; and when it comes to implementing RPC over the web, it makes sense to use HTTP as the transport layer and XML as the encoding toolkit. All that's required is a formal specification to handle the nitty-gritty details: the format of RPC requests and responses, data types, error handling, and so on. And so we have XML-RPC, a specification for encoding remote procedure calls in XML; and Simple Object Access Protocol (SOAP), an emerging W3C standard for encoding and packaging data for distribution across a peer-to-peer network. Both are XML-based technologies, both are fairly simple to use, and both are supported in PHP 4.1.0.

In the preceding chapter, you saw how potent the XML/PHP combination can be, and how much it simplifies information exchange over the web. This chapter takes things a step further by examining, through examples and code listings, how PHP's implementation of XML-based RPC can be used to enable new types of distributed, web-based applications and services.

RPC

For users new to RPC, this section will provide a broad overview of what it is, and of the different components involved in the process. If you're already familiar with how RPC works, feel free to skip this section.

Speaking generically, RPC is a toolkit designed for distributed computing. It provides a framework for executing procedures on one system from another, completely independent system in a secure, reliable, and efficient manner.

The best way to understand the RPC programming model is perhaps by comparing it to the "regular" programming model, in which procedures, or functions, are invoked on the same system or within the same program. Figure 6.1 and Figure 6.2 illustrate the difference.

As you can see from Figure 6.2, the RPC programming model is built completely around a client-server framework and consists of the following components:

- An API to handle procedure registration and execution on the server, and procedure invocation on the client
- A set of rules for encoding and decoding RPC requests and responses
- A network transmission layer to actually perform communication between the client and server, and carry data packets back and forth (HTTP works well here, although other protocols may also be used)

Function definition

```
getRandomQuote(author)
{
    connect_to_database();
    construct_query(author);
    retrieve_result_set();
    return_result_set();
}
```

Function invocation

```
getRandomQuote("Shakespeare");
```

Figure 6.1 A local function call.

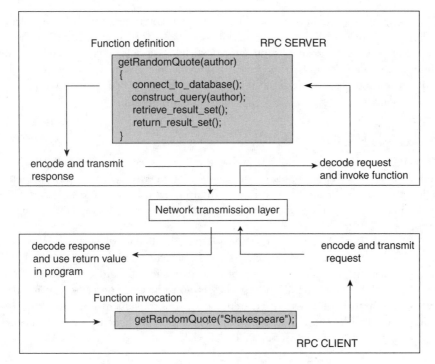

Figure 6.2 A remote function call.

Here's how it all comes together:

1. A remote procedure is invoked by an RPC client.

2. The procedure call, together with arguments (if any), is encoded into a request packet suitable for transmission across a network.

3. The request packet is transmitted to the RPC server.

4. The RPC server receives the packet and extracts the procedure name and arguments (if available) from it.

5. The RPC server invokes the named procedure on the server and obtains a return value from it.

6. The return value is encoded into a response packet.

7. The response packet is transmitted back to the RPC client.

8. The RPC client receives the response packet, decodes it, and extracts the procedure's return value from it. This result value can then be used by the client within a script or program.

Obviously, this is a simplified version of the RPC programming model—it does not address issues such as procedure registration, state maintenance, error handling, or security. However, it should be sufficient to explain the fundamental principles of the programming model, and lay the foundation for the material in subsequent sections.

If you want to learn more about RPC, drop by this book's companion web site, which contains links to web sites with more information on the topic.

XML-RPC

XML-RPC, as defined on its official web site, is " . . . a spec and a set of implementa- tions that allow software running on disparate operating systems, running in different environments to make procedure calls over the Internet . . . "[1] It was created in 1998 to provide a simple portable framework for transmitting procedure calls and receiving responses over the Internet.

As the preceding definition states, XML-RPC actually consists of two parts: the XML-RPC specification itself, which defines the structure and format of XML-RPC procedure calls and responses; and a set of implementations for different platforms. Because XML-RPC was designed from the get-go to be easily portable, it won't sur- prise you to hear that it has spawned a diverse array of implementations. As of this writing, the official web site lists more than 50 different implementations in languages such as Lisp, AppleScript, JavaScript, C, Perl, Python, and PHP.

> **Déja Vu**
>
> If some of this sounds familiar, give yourself 10 points for attentiveness—because it should. Though the two specifications address different problems, XML-RPC shares a number of important traits with Web Distributed Data eXchange (WDDX) that was last seen in Chapter 5, "PHP and Web Distributed Data eXchange(WDDX)." Here's a brief list:
>
> - Neither WDDX nor XML-RPC is an official standard per se; they're both open specifications created by one company and popularized via the developer community.
>
> - Both specifications provide an open, extensible architecture for information exchange.
>
> - Both specifications use XML as their encoding toolkit. XML-RPC requires HTTP exclusively as its transmission layer, whereas WDDX can be transmitted over any protocol that supports text (HTTP, POP, FTP, SMTP, and so on).
>
> - Both specifications use similar data structures to represent native data types.
>
> - Both specifications' implementations are available for a wide variety of different languages and platforms.

1. UserLand Software, Inc. "XML-RPC Home Page." Available from the Internet: http://www.xmlrpc.org/. Last updated: November 5, 2001.

An XML-RPC procedure call is encoded as a well-formed XML document, with both procedure name and arguments enclosed within a `<methodCall>` document element. This procedure call is transmitted to the XML-RPC server as a standard HTTP POST request.

Listing 6.1 demonstrates an XML-RPC request to the server `some.quote.server`; the request itself is equivalent to calling the function `getRandomQuote("Shakespeare")`.

Listing 6.1 An XML-RPC Request

```
POST /RPC2 HTTP/1.0
User-Agent: Mozilla/4.0 (compatible; MSIE 5.0; Windows 95)
Host: some.quote.server
Content-Type: text/xml
Content-Length: 287

<?xml version="1.0" ?>
    <methodCall>
        <methodName>getRandomQuote</methodName>
        <params>
            <param>
                <value>
                    <string>Shakespeare</string>
                </value>
            </param>
        </params>
</methodCall>
```

As you can see, the XML-RPC request body is clearly demarcated into two sections. The `<methodName>` element contains the name of the procedure to be invoked on the remote server, whereas the `<params>` element encloses a list of arguments to be passed to the remote procedure. Individual arguments are represented by individual `<param>` elements, which in turn enclose a data-typed value (take a look at the following sidebar entitled "Atypically Yours" for a list of the various data types supported by XML-RPC).

The server decodes and interprets the request, processes it, and returns the result to the requesting client, again as an XML-encoded HTTP POST response. Listing 6.2 demonstrates what it might look like.

Listing 6.2 An XML-RPC Response to a Successful RPC Request

```
HTTP/1.0 200 OK
Server: QuoteServer/RPC
Connection: close
Content-Type: text/xml
Content-Length: 270

<?xml version="1.0"?>
<methodResponse>
```

continues

Listing 6.2 **Continued**

```
<params>
    <param>
        <value>
            <string>Good night, sweet prince, and flights of angels sing thee
            ➡to thy rest.</string>
        </value>
    </param>
</params>
</methodResponse>
```

Atypically Yours

The XML-RPC specification currently defines the following data types:

- Boolean values, represented by the `<boolean>` element

- Signed 32-bit integers, represented by the `<int>` or `<i4>` element

- Signed floating-point numbers, represented by the `<double>` element

- ASCII strings, represented by the `<string>` element (this is the default type)

- Date/time values, represented by the `<dateTime.iso8601>` element (these values must be encoded in ISO8601 format, but the XML-RPC specification does not make any assumption about the time zone offset used)

- Binary data encoded with BASE64, represented by the `<base64>` element

- Integer-indexed arrays, represented by the `<array>` element

- Structures, or string-indexed arrays, represented by the `<struct>` element

Every XML-RPC response must return an HTTP status code of 200 OK; however, the content of the response differs, depending on whether or not an error occurred while processing the XML-RPC request. The response to a successful RPC invocation looks like Listing 6.2: a document element named `<methodResponse>` that contains one `<params>` element enclosing the value returned by the procedure.

An unsuccessful RPC invocation generates an error, which looks like Listing 6.3.

Listing 6.3 **An XML-RPC Response to an Unsuccessful RPC Request**

```
HTTP/1.0 200 OK
Server: QuoteServer/RPC
Connection: close
Content-Type: text/xml
Content-Length: 585

<?xml version="1.0"?>
<methodResponse>
    <fault>
```

```
        <value>
            <struct>
                <member>
                    <name>faultCode</name>
                    <value>
                        <int>2</int>
                    </value>
                </member>
                <member>
                    <name>faultString</name>
                    <value>
                        <string>No quotes by that author</string>
                    </value>
                </member>
            </struct>
        </value>
    </fault>
</methodResponse>
```

In this case, though the document element remains the same, the `<params>` element is replaced by a `<fault>` element, which is itself a `<struct>` containing an error code and a human-friendly error string.

That pretty much covers the basics of XML-RPC. For more information and examples, you should refer to the official web site at `http://www.xmlrpc.org/`, which contains the complete XML-RPC specification (with examples and code samples), a list of implementations for different platforms, tutorials, FAQs, and a discussion forum.

SOAP

Similar in concept, yet far broader in scope and implication, is the Simple Object Access Protocol (SOAP), an emerging W3C standard for decentralized information exchange between peers in a networked environment. Designed specifically for information transfer between distributed applications and objects built on different platforms, and layered (like XML-RPC) on XML and HTTP, SOAP has the support of industry heavyweights such as Microsoft, IBM, HP, Ariba, Lotus, and SAP, and is expected to shortly reach W3C Recommendation status.

SOAP is, fundamentally, a framework for stateless data exchange between systems. It is a specification for the creation of structured, typed data packets designed for easy transmission across a network. As of this writing, the SOAP specification addresses merely the structure of SOAP packets and the SOAP processing model, leaving items such as the mechanics of packet transmission and routing, packet integrity, and security to be handled at the application layer.

It is not necessary that the data encoded using SOAP be an RPC request or response. SOAP can be used to transfer data of any kind—RPC is just one example of its applications.

A SOAP packet is a well-formed XML document consisting of the following three primary parts:

- The envelope that contains information on the encoding used for the SOAP packet.

- An optional header that can be used to transmit authentication information, transaction parameters, or trace data.

- The body that contains the actual data to be transmitted. In the context of this chapter, this data is either an RPC request or response (although SOAP can be used to transmit other kinds of data too).

Take a look at Listing 6.4, which demonstrates the SOAP equivalent of the RPC request you saw in Listing 6.1.

Listing 6.4 **A SOAP Request**

```
POST /SOAPServer HTTP/1.0
User-Agent: Mozilla/4.0 (compatible; MSIE 5.0; Windows 95)
Host: some.quote.server
Content-Type: text/xml
Content-Length: 360

<?xml version="1.0" ?>

<soap:Envelope xmlns:soap="http://schemas.xmlsoap.org/soap/envelope/"
⮑xmlns:xsd="http://www.w3.org/1999/XMLSchema" soap:encodingStyle=
⮑"http://schemas.xmlsoap.org/soap/encoding/">
    <soap:Body>
        <getRandomQuote>
            <xsd:string>Shakespeare</xsd:string>
        </getRandomQuote>
    </soap:Body>
</soap:Envelope>
```

As you can see, an RPC request is encoded within the body of the SOAP packet as a series of nested elements, with the name of the first element in the body corresponding to the name of the remote procedure. Arguments to the remote procedure are specified as elements within this outermost element.

Unlike XML-RPC, it is not necessary that a SOAP response return an HTTP status code of 200 OK; rather, the SOAP specification suggests the use of standard HTTP error codes to identify whether the request was successfully received and processed. The results of a successful RPC invocation would resemble Listing 6.5 (note the Response suffix added to the element containing the return value).

Listing 6.5 **A SOAP Response to a Successful SOAP Request**

```
HTTP/1.0 200 OK
Server: QuoteServer/SOAP
Connection: close
Content-Type: text/xml
Content-Length: 435

<?xml version="1.0" ?>

<soap:Envelope xmlns:soap="http://schemas.xmlsoap.org/soap/envelope/"
➥xmlns:xsd="http://www.w3.org/1999/XMLSchema"
soap:encodingStyle="http://schemas.xmlsoap.org/soap/encoding/">
    <soap:Body>
        <getRandomQuoteResponse>
            <xsd:string>Good night, sweet prince, and flights of angels sing thee
            ➥to thy rest.</xsd:string>
        </getRandomQuoteResponse>
    </soap:Body>
</soap:Envelope>
```

If an error occurs while processing the remote procedure, a fault is generated and returned to the client, with the fault information encoded within the body of the SOAP packet. Listing 6.6 demonstrates this with an example.

Listing 6.6 **A SOAP Response to an Unsuccessful SOAP Request**

```
HTTP/1.0 500 Internal Server Error
Server: QuoteServer/SOAP
Connection: close
Content-Type: text/xml
Content-Length: 545

<?xml version="1.0" ?>

<soap:Envelope xmlns:soap="http://schemas.xmlsoap.org/soap/envelope/"
➥xmlns:xsi="http://www.w3.org/1999/XMLSchema-instance"
➥xmlns:xsd="http://www.w3.org/1999/XMLSchema"
➥soap:encodingStyle="http://schemas.xmlsoap.org/soap/encoding/">
    <soap:Body>
        <soap:Fault>
            <faultstring xsi:type="xsd:string">Server error. Method not
            ➥found.&#10;&#10;getRandomQuote</faultstring>
            <faultcode xsi:type="xsd:string">soap:Client</faultcode>
        </soap:Fault>
    </soap:Body>
</soap:Envelope>
```

For more information and examples, you should refer to the W3C's SOAP primer at
`http://www.w3.org/TR/soap12-part0/`, which contains the official SOAP specification. (See the book's companion web site at `http://www.xmlphp.com` or
`http://www.newriders.com` for more specific links.) You might also want to visit
`http://www.soapware.org/`, a directory of SOAP implementations for numerous
different languages and platforms.

Simple Simon

When it comes to data types, SOAP offers far greater flexibility than XML-RPC. This is because SOAP
builds on the work done by the W3C's XML Schema Working Group, allowing developers to create and
use their own named data types in their SOAP packets.

The XML Schema specification defines two data types: simple and complex. Simple data types include
`string`, `int`, `boolean`, `decimal`, `float`, `double`, `duration`, `datetime`, `hexBinary`, and
`base64Binary`. These simple data types can be combined with each other to create new, complex data
types that are customized to the specific requirements of the application.

Consider Listing 6.7, which might make this clearer.

Listing 6.7   **Simple and Complex Data Types in an XML Schema**

```
<xsd:schema xmlns:xsd="http://www.w3.org/2001/XMLSchema">

<!-- a simple data type -->
<xsd:element name="movie" type="xsd:string"/>


<!-- a complex data type -->
<xsd:element name="movie">
    <xsd:complexType>
        <xsd:sequence>
            <xsd:element name="title" type="xsd:string"/>
            <xsd:element name="director" type="xsd:string"/>
        </xsd:sequence>
    </xsd:complexType>
</xsd:element>

</xsd:schema>
```

Listing 6.7 contains two alternative definitions for the element `movie`. The first uses a simple data type
(`string`) to define the type of data expected for the `movie` element; the second uses a combination of
two string data types to create a new more complex type definition for the same element.

For more information on how XML Schema data types work, you should refer to the XML Schema specification, available on the web at `http://www.w3.org/TR/xmlschema-0/`.

So Many Choices . . .

With so many similarities between WDDX, XML-RPC, and SOAP, you might be wondering which one to use, and when. Making the choice between these competing technologies becomes easier when you consider the problems they were originally designed to solve.

WDDX was developed in order to provide a simple structured framework for typed data exchange over the web. If your application needs to exchange typed information in a client-server environment, and WDDX components are available for your platform, WDDX is usually a good bet.

XML-RPC, on the other hand, is a specification focused solely on remote procedure invocation and response. As such, it is less versatile than WDDX when it comes to exchanging typed information between peers. This is not necessarily a bad thing—if all you're interested in is RPC, XML-RPC provides you with everything you need to do your job efficiently, without bogging you down in unnecessary features or convoluted structures.

SOAP, which includes ideas from both WDDX and XML-RPC, offers a more powerful and complete solution to the problem of data interchange between platforms and systems. As Eric Kidd succinctly puts it in his XML-RPC HOWTO, "If you like XML-RPC, but wish the protocol had more features, check out SOAP."[2]

For a more detailed comparison of these and other XML-based protocols, take a look at the W3C's XML Protocol Matrix at http://www.w3.org/2000/03/29-XML-protocol-matrix.

PHP and RPC

A PHP module for RPC has been available since version 4.1.0 of the language (released in December 2001). Created by Dan Libby of Epinions.com, this RPC extension (which goes by the distressingly unpronounceable name of XMLRPC-EPI-PHP) provides standard encoding, decoding, and server administration functions for XML-RPC and SOAP requests and responses. This extension is also available as a standalone C library at the project's official web site: http://xmlrpc-epi.sourceforge.net/.

If you're using a stock PHP binary, it's quite likely that you'll need to recompile PHP to add support for this library to your PHP build (detailed instructions for accomplishing this are available in this book's Appendix A, "Recompiling PHP to Add XML Support").

This chapter will focus exclusively on the XMLRPC-EPI-PHP extension. However, it should be noted that this RPC library is not the only game in town— both the XML-RPC web site (http://www.xmlrpc.org/) and SOAPWare (http://www.soapware.org/) list other PHP implementations of these protocols. Links to these alternative implementations are also available on this book's web site, and some of them are discussed in Chapter 8, "Open Source XML/PHP Alternatives."

2. Kidd, Eric. "The XML-RPC HOWTO." *SourceForge.Net* (2001). Available from the Internet: http://xmlrpc-c.sourceforge.net/xmlrpc-howto/

Teething Trouble

It's important to note, at the outset itself, that some of the examples in this chapter (those related to PHP and SOAP) will not work with the released versions of PHP 4.1.0 and 4.1.1. This is because those versions of the language come with version 0.41 of the XMLRPC-EPI-PHP extension, which does not include support for SOAP (de)serialization.

The affected listings in this chapter are:

- Listing 6.12 and its output, Listing 6.13

- Listing 6.19

- Listing 6.30 and Listing 6.31

In order to get these examples to work as advertised, you will need to upgrade to PHP 4.2.0 or better, which includes a newer version of the XMLRPC extension.

You might also like to take a look at SOAPx4, an alternative PHP-based SOAP implementation that's been discussed in Chapter 8, "Open Source XML/PHP Alternatives."

Note also that, as of this writing, the Windows version of PHP does not include an RPC extension, and therefore the examples in this chapter cannot be viewed in Windows. You will need a *NIX-based PHP build in order to try out the examples in this chapter.

Encoding and Decoding RPC Requests

PHP's RPC extension offers two functions designed specifically to encode RPC requests into XML. The first (and most commonly used) is the `xmlrpc_encode_request()` function that accepts, as function arguments, the name of the procedure to be called on the remote server and the parameters to be passed to it. Listing 6.8 demonstrates how it works.

Listing 6.8   **Encoding a Remote Procedure Call with PHP**

```php
<?php
// $numbers is an array of arguments to be passed to the remote procedure
$numbers = array(34, 78, 2, 674);

// encode procedure call
echo xmlrpc_encode_request("getRange", $numbers);
?>
```

The output of this code snippet is displayed in Listing 6.9.

Listing 6.9 **An XML-RPC Request**

```
<?xml version='1.0' encoding="iso-8859-1" ?>
<methodCall>
    <methodName>getRange</methodName>
    <params>
        <param>
            <value>
                <int>34</int>
            </value>
        </param>
        <param>
            <value>
                <int>78</int>
            </value>
        </param>
        <param>
            <value>
                <int>2</int>
            </value>
        </param>
        <param>
            <value>
                <int>674</int>
            </value>
        </param>
    </params>
</methodCall>
```

The second argument passed to `xmlrpc_encode_request()`—a variable containing arguments for the remote procedure—may be of any type supported by PHP, and it will automatically be encoded into a corresponding XML-RPC data type. Listing 6.10 demonstrates by encoding a PHP array of mixed type with `xmlrpc_encode_request`.

Listing 6.10 **Encoding Different Data Types with PHP**

```php
<?php
echo xmlrpc_encode_request("some_remote_method", array("name" => "John Doe",
➥34, "abracadabra"));
?>
```

Listing 6.11 has the output.

Listing 6.11 **An XML-RPC Request Containing Different Data Types**

```xml
<?xml version='1.0' encoding="iso-8859-1" ?>
<methodCall>
    <methodName>some_remote_method</methodName>
    <params>
        <param>
            <value>
                <struct>
                    <member>
                        <name>name</name>
                        <value>
                            <string>John Doe</string>
                        </value>
                    </member>
                    <member>
                        <name/>
                        <value>
                            <int>34</int>
                        </value>
                    </member>
                    <member>
                        <name/>
                        <value>
                            <string>abracadabra</string>
                        </value>
                    </member>
                </struct>
            </value>
        </param>
    </params>
</methodCall>
```

It's also possible to encode an RPC request as SOAP (rather than XML-RPC) data; this is accomplished by adding a third optional argument to the call to xmlrpc_encode_request() (see the sidebar entitled "What's in a Name?" for more output options). Listing 6.12 demonstrates how to encode a SOAP request.

Listing 6.12 **Encoding a SOAP Request**

```php
<?php
// $numbers is an array of arguments to be passed to the remote procedure
$numbers = array(34, 78, 2, 674);

// encode procedure call
echo xmlrpc_encode_request("getRange", $numbers, array("version" => "soap 1.1"));
?>
```

The output of this command is a SOAP envelope containing the remote procedure call and its arguments, as Listing 6.13 demonstrates.

Listing 6.13 **A SOAP Request**

```
<?xml version="1.0" encoding="iso-8859-1" ?>
<SOAP-ENV:Envelope xmlns:SOAP-ENV="http://schemas.xmlsoap.org/soap/envelope/"
➥xmlns:xsi="http://www.w3.org/1999/XMLSchema-instance"
➥xmlns:xsd="http://www.w3.org/1999/XMLSchema" xmlns:SOAP-
➥ENC="http://schemas.xmlsoap.org/soap/encoding/"
➥xmlns:si="http://soapinterop.org/xsd" xmlns:ns6="http://testuri.org" SOAP-
➥ENV:encodingStyle="http://schemas.xmlsoap.org/soap/encoding/">
    <SOAP-ENV:Body>
        <getRange>
            <xsd:int>34</xsd:int>
            <xsd:int>78</xsd:int>
            <xsd:int>2</xsd:int>
            <xsd:int>674</xsd:int>
        </getRange>
    </SOAP-ENV:Body>
</SOAP-ENV:Envelope>
```

Finding Fault

Wondering how to generate RPC faults on the server? Take a look at Listing 6.29.

It's also conceivable that you might need to generate XML for just a single procedure argument, rather than a complete RPC request—if, for example, you're incrementally building an RPC packet from a database or flat file. In this case, you can use the `xmlrpc_encode()` function, which returns an XML string containing the data-typed representation of the structure passed to `xmlrpc_encode()`. Listing 6.14 demonstrates encoding a single parameter.

Listing 6.14 **Encoding a Single Parameter**

```php
<?php
echo xmlrpc_encode(98.6);
?>
```

Listing 6.15 shows the output.

Listing 6.15 **The XML–RPC Result of Encoding a Single Parameter**

```
<?xml version="1.0" encoding="utf-8" ?>
<params>
  <param>
    <value>
      <double>98.600000</double>
    </value>
  </param>
</params>
```

Buyer Beware!

As of this writing, PHP's RPC extension does not allow you to build an RPC packet incrementally, as is possible with the WDDX extension's wddx_add_vars() function.

This works with arrays, too—as Listings 6.16 and 6.17 demonstrate.

Listing 6.16 **Encoding an Array**

```
<?php
$params = array("temperature" => "98.6", "convert_to" => "celsius");

// encode parameter
echo xmlrpc_encode($params);
?>
```

Listing 6.17 **The XML–RPC Result of Encoding an Array**

```
<?xml version="1.0" encoding="utf-8" ?>
<params>
  <param>
    <value>
      <struct>
        <member>
          <name>temperature</name>
          <value>
            <string>98.6</string>
          </value>
        </member>
        <member>
          <name>convert_to</name>
          <value>
            <string>celsius</string>
          </value>
        </member>
      </struct>
```

```
      </value>
    </param>
  </params>
```

Once encoded, the RPC request needs merely to be transmitted to the RPC server. This transmission may take place using any supported protocol; in the case of the web, this is usually HTTP. For a full-fledged example, take a look at Listing 6.26.

Making the Connection

It's important to note that the RPC extension that ships with PHP merely provides encoding and decoding functions, and a server and introspection API. It does not address the very important issue of how the request will be transmitted across the network, and how the response will be retrieved.

As it is right now, developers need to manually implement a network transmission layer. Listing 6.26 demonstrates an example of how this might work over HTTP, and the extension's official web site also provides an additional set of PHP-based utilities that implement this function (these utilities are also demonstrated in this chapter—take a look at Listing 6.29).

When the server receives the encoded RPC request, it needs to decode it, execute the procedure, obtain a return value, encode it as an RPC response, and transmit it back to the requesting client. At the server end of the connection, PHP's RPC extension automatically handles request decoding and response encoding via the `xmlrpc_server_call_method()` function (discussed in the next section); at the client end, however, the decoding of the server response needs to be implemented manually.

This is primarily accomplished by the `xmlrpc_decode()` function, a mirror of the `xmlrpc_encode()` function discussed in the preceding section. This function accepts an XML-RPC encoded response and decodes it into native PHP data types for subsequent use. Listing 6.18 demonstrates this.

Listing 6.18 **Decoding an XML-RPC Response**

```php
<?php

// sample response from server (XML-RPC)
$response = <<< END
<?xml version="1.0"?>
<methodResponse>
   <params>
     <param>
        <value>
           <struct>
              <member>
                 <name>start</name>
                 <value>
                 <int>2</int>
                 </value>
```

continues

Listing 6.18   **Continued**

```
                </member>
                <member>
                        <name>end</name>
                        <value>
                        <int>674</int>
                        </value>
                </member>
                    </struct>
                </value>
            </param>
        </params>
</methodResponse>
END;

// decode into native type and print
$output = xmlrpc_decode($response);

echo "Numbers provided fall in the range " . $output["start"] ." to " .
➥$output["end"];
?>
```

This works just as well with a SOAP-encoded response, too (see Listing 6.19).

Listing 6.19   **Decoding a SOAP Response**

```
<?php

// sample response from server (SOAP)
$response = <<< END
<?xml version="1.0"?>
<SOAP-ENV:Envelope xmlns:SOAP-ENV="http://schemas.xmlsoap.org/soap/envelope/"
➥xmlns:xsi="http://www.w3.org/1999/XMLSchema-instance"
➥xmlns:xsd="http://www.w3.org/1999/XMLSchema" xmlns:SOAP-
➥ENC="http://schemas.xmlsoap.org/soap/encoding/"
➥xmlns:si="http://soapinterop.org/xsd" xmlns:ns6="http://testuri.org" SOAP-
➥ENV:encodingStyle="http://schemas.xmlsoap.org/soap/encoding/">
    <SOAP-ENV:Body>
        <getRangeResponse>
          <item>
              <start xsi:type="xsd:int">2</start>
              <end xsi:type="xsd:int">674</end>
          </item>
        </getRangeResponse>
    </SOAP-ENV:Body>
</SOAP-ENV:Envelope>
```

```
END;

// decode into native type and print
$output = xmlrpc_decode($response);

echo "Numbers provided fall in the range " . $output["start"] ." to " .
➥$output["end"];
?>
```

The RPC extension also includes an `xmlrpc_decode_request()` function, which decodes an XML-encoded request string and returns the embedded remote procedure name and its arguments. It's unlikely that you'll ever need to use this function because (as you'll shortly see) the server can handle XML-encoded RPC requests without needing to decode them first, and the client will typically never need to decode a request (merely encode it). It's included with the library for the sake of completeness, and an example is included here for the same reason (see Listing 6.20).

Listing 6.20   **Decoding an XML-RPC Request**

```
<?php
// encode a request
$request = xmlrpc_encode_request("someMethod", array("red", "green", "blue"));

// decode it with xmlrpc_decode()
// $params will contain the name of the called procedure
// $output is an array containing passed parameters
$params = xmlrpc_decode_request($request, &$method);

// prints "Called method was: someMethod(red, green, blue)"
echo "Called method was: $method(" . join(", ", $params) . ")";
?>
```

Note that the variable containing the original remote procedure name must be passed to `xmlrpc_decode_request()` by reference.

Creating and Using an RPC Server

By itself, an RPC client is fairly useless; to be really valuable, it needs a server at the other end of the connection to process its requests and transmit information back to it. And so, PHP's RPC extension also provides a server API to support server instantiation and procedure registration and invocation.

There are a number of different steps involved here. So, let's look at a simple example to understand how the process works (see Listing 6.21).

Listing 6.21 **A Simple PHP-based RPC Server**

```php
<?php
// $request contains an XML-encoded request
$request = <<< END
<?xml version='1.0' encoding="iso-8859-1" ?>
<methodCall>
    <methodName>getRange</methodName>
    <params>
        <param>
            <value>
                <int>34</int>
            </value>
        </param>
        <param>
            <value>
                <int>78</int>
            </value>
        </param>
        <param>
            <value>
                <int>2</int>
            </value>
        </param>
        <param>
            <value>
                <int>674</int>
            </value>
        </param>
    </params>
</methodCall>
END;

// create server
$rpc_server = xmlrpc_server_create() or die("Could not create RPC server");

// register methods
xmlrpc_server_register_method($rpc_server, "getRange", "phpGetRange") or
➥die("Could not register method");

// call method
$response = xmlrpc_server_call_method($rpc_server, $request, NULL);

// print response
echo $response;

// clean up
xmlrpc_server_destroy($rpc_server);
```

```
// function to calculate highest
// and lowest in a number series
function phpGetRange ($method, $args, $add_args)
{
    sort ($args);
    return array ('start' => $args[0], 'end' => end ($args));
}


?>
```

Let's go through the process step-by-step:

1. Instantiating an RPC server is fairly simple: All it needs is a call to
   `xmlrpc_server_create()`.

   ```
   $rpc_server = xmlrpc_server_create() or die("Could not create RPC server");
   ```

   This function returns a handle to the server, stored in the variable `$rpc_server`, which is required for all subsequent server operations.

2. After the server has been instantiated, the next step is to register methods or pro-cedures with it—these are the same procedures that will be invoked by connect-ing clients. For this purpose, PHP offers the `xmlrpc_server_register_method()` function, which is used to register a PHP function to handle an exposed RPC procedure.

   The `xmlrpc_server_register_method()` accepts three arguments: a handle to the RPC server, the name of the procedure (as exposed to connecting clients), and the name of the PHP function to call when that procedure is invoked.

   ```
   xmlrpc_server_register_method($rpc_server, "getRange", "phpGetRange") or
   ➥die("Could not register method");
   ```

   In Listing 6.21, the `phpGetRange()` function is called when a connecting client executes an RPC call to the `getRange()` procedure.

   The `xmlrpc_server_register_method()` function can be used to register as many procedures as you like with the RPC server. The PHP functions regis-tered via the `xmlrpc_server_register_method()` function must be capable of accepting three arguments: the name of the called procedure, the arguments passed to it, and any additional user-defined arguments.

   ```
   function phpGetRange($method, $args, $add_args)
   {
   ...
   }
   ```

3. With the remote procedure(s) registered with the XML-RPC server, the `xmlrpc_server_call_method()` function is used to parse and process the XML-encoded RPC request from the client. As Listing 6.21 demonstrates, this function requires three arguments: a handle to the RPC server, the XML-encoded request string, and any additional data that may be required by the procedure.

```
$response = xmlrpc_server_call_method($rpc_server, $request, NULL);

echo $response;
```

In Listing 6.21, after the request is decoded by `xmlrpc_server_call_method()`, the `phpGetRange()` function is invoked. This function iterates through the number array passed to it to determine the highest and lowest in the series, and then returns an array containing these two values.

The `xmlrpc_server_call_method()` then encodes this return value as an XML document, for display or further processing. The return value may be encoded as either an XML-RPC response or a SOAP response (refer to the sidebar entitled "What's in a Name?" for more on how to do this).

4. After the remote procedure has been executed and a return value encoded into XML, the final step is to destroy the server and free up the memory it was occupying. This is accomplished via the aptly named `xmlrpc_server_destroy()` method.

```
xmlrpc_server_destroy($rpc_server);
```

The previous steps make up a fairly standard process, and you'll see them being used over and over again in the examples that follow.

What's in a Name?

Both the `xmlrpc_encode_request()` and the `xmlrpc_server_call_method()` functions can accept one optional argument: an array containing information on the format of the resulting XML.

This array is an associative array containing any or all of the following key-value pairs. The default value for each key is marked in bold.

- `"output_type"` => (`"php"`|`"xml"`): specifies whether the function should return an XML document or a PHP data structure.

- `"verbosity"` => (`"white_space"`|`"newlines_only"`|`"pretty"`): specifies whether the XML should be returned as indented, multiline data, or a single-line string.

- `"escaping"` => (`"cdata"`|`"non-ascii"`|`"non-print"`|`"markup"`): specifies if and how to escape special characters.

- `"version"` => (`"xmlrpc"`|`"soap 1.1"`|`"simple"`|`"auto"`): specifies the protocol to be used. Supported protocols include XML-RPC, SOAP 1.1, and a non-standard variant named simpleRPC. The `"auto"` value indicates that output should be sent in the same form as input.

- `"encoding"` => (`"iso-8859-1"`|`"utf-8"`|`...`): encoding to use for the output.

For example, the following code snippet generates an XML-RPC request as a single string:

```php
<?php
xmlrpc_encode_request($method, $params, array("version" => "xmlrpc", "verbosity"
=> "no_white_space"));
?>
```

Whereas, the following code snippet generates an indented, multiline SOAP response using UTF-8 encoding:

```php
<?php
xmlrpc_server_call_method($server, $request, $args, array("version" => "soap
1.1", "verbosity" => "pretty", "encoding" => "utf-8"));
?>
```

Note that SOAP support is not available in older versions of PHP's RPC extension. Refer to the earlier sidebar entitled "Teething Trouble" for more information on this.

Introspection

PHP's RPC extension also supports *introspection*, a fairly cool concept that allows your RPC server to display a certain degree of self-awareness about the procedures registered with it. A primitive introspection API makes it possible for developers to document the procedures they create, and provide this documentation to connecting clients using a simple XML vocabulary.

The Art of Self-Evaluation (Or, What the Heck Is Introspection?)

In a general sense, introspection refers to the capability of a piece of code to "discover" information about itself, and return this information when asked for it. So, for example, an object might be able to display a list of its exposed properties, together with information on what each one represents, or deliver a list of its public methods, together with the expected parameters and return values for each.

Obviously, this is not as magical or automatic as it sounds. The developer still needs to define these properties and describe them in a manner that can be used by an introspection API. However, by providing a simple description mechanism for an object's properties and methods, introspection makes it possible to analyze objects in a standard manner, automatically generate API documentation, and validate input parameters and output values.

In the long run, this reduces development times and makes code more maintainable—which is why introspection is generally considered a Good Thing, and one that should be used whenever possible.

An example might make this clearer. Consider Listing 6.22, which invokes, over RPC, the procedure system.listMethods().

Listing 6.22 **Listing Remote Procedures with** *system.listMethods()*

```php
<?php

// a sample request
$request = <<< END
<?xml version="1.0"?>
<methodCall>
    <methodName>system.listMethods</methodName>
    <params />
</methodCall>
END;

// create server
$rpc_server = xmlrpc_server_create() or die("Could not create RPC server");


// register methods

// execute request
$response = xmlrpc_server_call_method($rpc_server, $request, NULL, array("version"
 => "xml"));

// print response
echo $response;

// clean up
xmlrpc_server_destroy($rpc_server);


?>
```

Now, `system.listMethods()` is a built-in function that generates a list of methods currently registered with the RPC server and returns this list to the client. Listing 6.23 demonstrates the response to the procedure call.

Listing 6.23 **The Result of a Call to** *system.listMethods()*

```xml
<?xml version='1.0' encoding="iso-8859-1" ?>
<methodResponse>
  <params>
    <param>
      <value>
        <array>
          <data>
            <value><string>system.listMethods</string></value>
            <value><string>system.methodHelp</string></value>
            <value><string>system.methodSignature</string></value>
            <value><string>system.describeMethods</string></value>
            <value><string>system.multiCall</string></value>
```

```
      <value><string>system.getCapabilities</string></value>
      <value><string>getRandomQuote</string></value>
    </data>
   </array>
  </value>
 </param>
 </params>
</methodResponse>
```

This is a very basic example of introspection—the server is aware of all the methods currently registered with it and can provide this information to clients on demand. Of course, this information is not limited to a mere list of procedure names. The system.describeMethods() procedure provides more exhaustive information on registered procedures, including details such as expected arguments and argument types, expected return values, optional and required arguments, related methods, bugs, and version information; whereas the system.methodHelp() procedure provides information on the purpose of each registered procedure. There are a few other procedures as well (take a look at the next sidebar entitled "Talking Back" for a list).

As an illustration, consider Listing 6.24, which demonstrates what system.methodHelp() has to say about the getRandomQuote() function.

Listing 6.24   Obtaining an XML Description of the *getRandomQuote()* Procedure with *system.methodHelp()*

```
<?xml version='1.0' encoding="iso-8859-1" ?>
<methodResponse>
  <params>
    <param>
      <value><string>Retrieves a random quote by the specified
      author</string></value>
    </param>
  </params>
</methodResponse>
```

Talking Back

The system.listMethods() procedure is just one of a number of introspection functions provided by PHP's RPC extension. Here's a list of them all:

- system.listMethods()—Lists currently registered methods

- system.describeMethods()—Describes the available methods in detail

- system.methodHelp()—Returns documentation for a specified method

- system.methodSignature()—Returns signature for a specified method

- system.getCapabilities()—Lists server capabilities

Obviously, this information is not generated automatically; the developer needs to provide it to the RPC server while registering the corresponding procedure. For this purpose, PHP's RPC extension includes a function named `xmlrpc_server_register_introspection_callback()`, which names a callback function to handle introspection requests. Listing 6.25 has an example.

Listing 6.25 **Registering an Introspection Handler**

```php
<?php
xmlrpc_server_register_introspection_callback($rpc_server,
"generateIntrospectionData");
?>
```

In this case, the callback function `generateIntrospectionData()` is responsible for generating documentation in the approved XML vocabulary when it intercepts an introspection request. Listing 6.26 has a more detailed example.

Listing 6.26 **A more Complete Introspection Handler**

```php
<?php

// create server
$rpc_server = xmlrpc_server_create() or die("Could not create RPC server");

// register methods
xmlrpc_server_register_method($rpc_server, "getRandomQuote", "phpGetRandomQuote")
➥or die("Could not register method");

// function to run when introspection request comes through
xmlrpc_server_register_introspection_callback($rpc_server,
➥"generateIntrospectionData");

// generate an XML-RPC request for system.methodHelp
// this would normally come from an RPC client
$request = xmlrpc_encode_request("system.methodHelp", "getRandomQuote");

// call method
$response = xmlrpc_server_call_method($rpc_server, $request, NULL, array("version"
➥ => "xml"));

// print response
echo $response;

// clean up
xmlrpc_server_destroy($rpc_server);


// function to auto-generate documentation for procedures
// (introspection)
```

```
function generateIntrospectionData()
{
    $data = <<< END
<?xml version="1.0"?>
    <introspection version="1.0">
        <methodList>
            <methodDescription name="getRandomQuote">
                <author>Vikram Vaswani</author>
                <purpose>Retrieves a random quote by the specified author</purpose>
                <version>1.0</version>
                <signatures>
            <signature>
                    <params>
                        <value type="string" name="author">The name of the quote
                        ⇒author</value>
                    </params>
                    <returns>
                        <value type="string" name="quote">A quote by the specified
                        ⇒author</value>
                    </returns>
                </signature>
            </signatures>
            <errors>
            <item>Returns fault code 2 if no quotes by the specified author are
            ⇒available</item>
            </errors>
            <notes />
            <bugs/>
            <todo/>
        </methodDescription>
    </methodList>
</introspection>
END;

    return $data;

}

function phpGetRandomQuote($method, $args, $add_args)
{
    // code snipped out
}

?>
```

Note that the XML-encoded documentation generated by the callback function must conform to the rules laid down in the introspection specification, available from the extension's official web site at http://xmlrpc-epi.sourceforge.net/, and that the function must actually exist for the introspection data to be correctly returned.

By and large, introspection is a good idea. It provides application developers with an efficient, transparent mechanism of obtaining API documentation, thereby making remote services more accessible and easier to use—which, after all, is the holy grail of RPC. This book's web site includes links to a few web-based introspection clients that demonstrate this capability further.

A Few Examples

Over the preceding sections, you've seen quite a few examples of how the RPC library works and should now have a fairly clear understanding of the theory. This section puts it into practice with a few real-life demonstrations of how this technology can be used across the web.

Retrieving Meteorological Data with XML-RPC

I'll begin with something simple—a basic RPC client-server implementation for information delivery over HTTP. I'll be using a MySQL database as the data source, XML-RPC as the expression language for the procedure calls and responses, and PHP for the actual mechanics.

Requirements

Let's assume the existence of a fictional government department that is charged with the task of obtaining meteorological information and charting it for statistical purposes. In a rare fit of generosity, this department has decided to make some of its meteorological readings available to the general public, in the hope of encouraging amateur meteorologists (and interested science students) to take an interest in the subject. Consequently, this department needs some way to broadcast its raw data (at the moment, sets of temperature readings for different cities) over the web, to be available to any connecting client.

Here's a snippet of the MySQL database table that contains the temperature data (you may assume that this table is automatically updated on a regular basis by an independent process).

```
+------+-------+------+-------+
| city | t1    | t2   | t3    |
+------+-------+------+-------+
| BOM  | 27.6  | 26.9 | 26.1  |
| LON  | 10.5  | 11.9 | 10.8  |
| NYC  | 17.69 | 15.8 | 14.99 |
+------+-------+------+-------+
```

All that is required is an interface to this database so that users can connect to the system and obtain readings for any city (keyed against each city's unique three-letter city code).

RPC's client-server architecture provides a suitable framework for this kind of application. An RPC server can be used at one end of the connection to accept XML-encoded remote procedure calls (containing arguments such as the city code and the format in which data is required), and execute appropriate functions to retrieve the required data from the database. The results of invoking the procedure can then be sent back to the client for further processing or display.

Obviously, there are a number of different ways to implement this application (Perl, Java, WDDX, and even a plain-vanilla PHP script with MySQL hooks), so my usage of XML-RPC here is purely illustrative. In the long run, however, using XML-RPC might well turn out to be a good decision—because implementations of the protocol are available for different platforms, it would be possible for the fictional government organization to create other, non-web-based clients (for example, a Windows COM-based application) without any changes required to its RPC server.

The Server

The server is fairly easy to implement (and, in fact, hardly changes across subsequent examples), so I'll demonstrate that first. Listing 6.27 has the code.

Listing 6.27 **A Simple RPC Server**

```php
<?php
// get the request
$request = $HTTP_RAW_POST_DATA;

// create server
$rpc_server = xmlrpc_server_create() or die("Could not create RPC server");

// register methods
xmlrpc_server_register_method($rpc_server, "getWeatherData", "phpWeather") or
➥die("Could not register method");

// call method
$response = xmlrpc_server_call_method($rpc_server, $request, NULL,
➥array("verbosity" => "no_white_space"));

// print response
echo $response;

// clean up
xmlrpc_server_destroy($rpc_server);

// function to return weather data
// $args include a city code and a parameter indicating whether
// all three readings (raw) or a composite calculation (avg)
// are required
function phpWeather($method, $args, $add_args)
{
        // open connection to database
        $connection = mysql_connect("localhost", "rpc_agent", "secret") or die
➥("Unable to connect!");
```

continues

Listing 6.27 **Continued**

```php
mysql_select_db("weather_data") or die ("Unable to select database!");

// get data
$city = mysql_escape_string($args[0]["city"]);
$query = "SELECT t1, t2, t3 FROM weather WHERE city = '$city'";
$result = mysql_query($query) or die ("Error in query: $query. " .
➥mysql_error());

// if a result is returned
if (mysql_num_rows($result) > 0)
{
    // iterate through resultset
    list($t1, $t2, $t3) = mysql_fetch_row($result);

    // process data depending on requested output format
    if ($args[0]["format"] == "raw")
    {
        // return raw data
        return array("format" => "raw", "data" => array($t1, $t2, $t3));
    }
    else if ($args[0]["format"] == "avg")
    {
        // total and average readings
        // return average
        $total = $t1 + $t2 + $t3;

        // do this to avoid division by zero errors
        if ($total != 0)
        {
            $avg = $total/3;
        }
        else
        {
            $avg = 0;
        }

        return array("format" => "avg", "data" => $avg);
    }
}
else
{
    // return a fault
    return array("faultCode" => 33, "faultString" => "No data
    ➥available for that city");
}

// close database connection
mysql_close($connection);
}
?>
```

Most of this should be familiar to you from the previous sections of this chapter. The procedure getWeatherData(), which maps internally to the PHP function phpWeather(), is set up to accept two arguments: the three-letter city code and the data format (raw readings or arithmetic mean of raw readings) required by the client. This procedure is registered with the RPC server via the xmlrpc_server_register_method() function, and it is invoked when the server receives a POST request containing the XML-encoded RPC request.

> **Going POST-al**
>
> In case you're wondering, the special PHP variable $HTTP_RAW_POST_DATA returns the raw data sent to the server via the POST method (or, if you're using a command-line script, the data entered via the standard input). This data can then be parsed and processed by your script.

Internally, the phpWeather() function is pretty simple. It uses the arguments provided to it to connect to a MySQL database, retrieve the data from it, and then return it to the caller as an array containing either the average or the raw data. This returned array is then encoded into XML and sent back to the client as a POST response.

The Client

The RPC client needs to do a few important things:

- Accept user input as to the city and output format required.
- Encode this user input into an XML-RPC request, and POST it to the server.
- Receive the XML-encoded POST response and decode it.
- Display the received data as an HTML page.

Listing 6.28 has the complete code.

Listing 6.28   **A Simple XML–RPC Client**

```
<html>
<head>
<basefont face="Arial">
</head>

<body>


<?php
if(!$_POST['submit'])
{
?>
        <form action="<? echo $_SERVER['PHP_SELF']; ?>" method="POST">
        <b>City code:</b>
        <br>
        <input type="text" name="city" size="4" maxlength="3">
        <p>
```

continues

Listing 6.28   **Continued**

```
        <b>Data format:</b>
        <br>
        <input type="Radio" name="format" value="avg" checked>Average only
        <br>
        <input type="radio" name="format" value="raw">Raw data
        <p>
        <input type="submit" name="submit" value="Go!">
        </form>


<?php
}
else
{

        // where is the RPC server?
        $server = "weather.domain.com";
        $url = "/rpc/server.php";
        $port = 80;

        // RPC arguments
        $city = strtoupper($_POST['city']);
        $params = array("city" => $city, "format" => $_POST['format']);

        // encode XML-RPC request
        $request = xmlrpc_encode_request("getWeatherData", $params,
        ➥array("verbosity" => "no_white_space"));

        // open socket
        $fp = fsockopen($server, $port);

        if(!$fp)
        {
                echo "Could not open socket";
        }
        else
        {
                // create POST data string
                $post_data = "POST $url HTTP/1.0\r\nUser-Agent: PHP-RPC
                ➥Client\r\nContent-Type: text/xml\r\nContent-Length: " .
                ➥strlen($request) . "\r\n\r\n" . $request;

                // send POST data
                fwrite($fp, $post_data);

                // read the response
                $post_response = fread($fp, 14096);

                // close the socket
                fclose($fp);
```

```
        }

        // strip out HTTP headers in response
        // look for <?xml and get everything from there to the end of the response
        $response = substr($post_response, strpos($post_response, "<?xml"));

        // decode response
        $output = xmlrpc_decode($response);

        // more stringent error checks would be good here
        if(is_array($output))
        {
                // check to see if a fault was returned
                if (!isset($output[0]["faultCode"]))
                {
                        // no? this means valid data was returned
                        // format and display
                        if ($output["format"] == "avg")
                        {
                                echo "Average temperature reading for city $city is " .
                                ⇒$output["data"] . " (based on three readings)";
                        }
                        else if ($output["format"] == "raw")
                        {
                                echo "Last three temperature readings for city $city
                                ⇒(8-hour intervals) are:<br><ul>";
                                echo "<li>" . $output["data"][0];
                                echo "<li>" . $output["data"][1];
                                echo "<li>" . $output["data"][2];
                                echo "</ul>";
                        }
                }
                else
                {
                        // a fault occurred
                        // format and display fault information
                        echo "The following fault occurred:<br>";
                        echo $output[0]["faultString"] . " (fault code " .
                        ⇒$output[0]["faultCode"] . ")";
                }
        }
        else
        {
                // no array returned
                echo "Unrecognized response from server";
        }

}
?>
</body>
</html>
```

This entire script is split into two main sections. The first section merely displays an HTML form for user input; this form contains a text field for the city code and a pair of radio buttons to choose the data format required.

After the form is submitted, the script calls itself again; this time around, however, the $submit variable will exist, so the second half of the script will be executed. At this stage, the first order of business is to create an array to hold the remote procedure arguments, and create an XML-encoded RPC request with xmlrpc_encode_request().

Next, a socket is opened to the remote RPC server (actually a web server with PHP's RPC extension compiled in), and the XML data is sent to it as a POST request (note the various HTTP headers that must accompany the data packet). After the server has received the request, decoded it, and executed the remote procedure, the response is sent back (through the same socket connection) to the client as a POST response.

This POST response contains a bunch of HTTP headers, in addition to the XML-RPC response string. These need to be stripped out so that the remaining XML can be decoded into a native PHP data type with xmlrpc_decode(). Finally, depending on the data format requested (this format is included in the RPC response), the temperature reading(s) are displayed with an appropriate message.

Figure 6.3 and Figure 6.4 demonstrate what the client looks like, both before and after sending an RPC request.

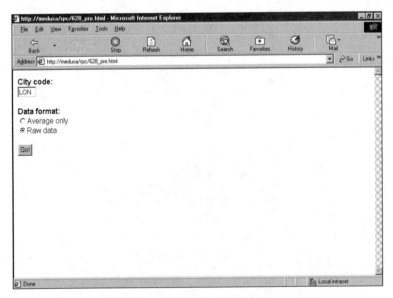

Figure 6.3   The XML-RPC client from Listing 6.28, prior to requesting weather data.

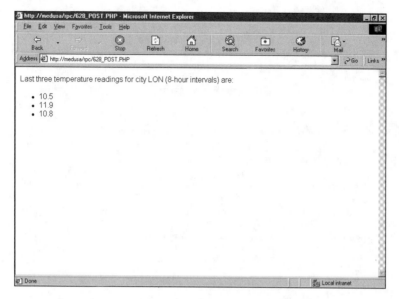

Figure 6.4   The XML-RPC client from Listing 6.28,
with the weather data requested.

The HTTP Files

If you want to learn more about the HTTP protocol and the POST method, you should take a look at the HTTP specification on the W3C's Protocols web page, at http://www.w3.org/Protocols/.

Now that was fairly complicated, especially the part involving sockets and HTTP headers—which is why it makes sense to package those bits of code into functions and then separate them from the main body of your script. And, if you look at the official web site for PHP's RPC extension, you'll see that the library author, Dan Libby, has done just this: He's packaged a number of network transmission functions as separate utilities that can be included and used in your RPC client.

Listing 6.29 demonstrates an alternative implementation of the script in Listing 6.28, using these packaged functions. As you will see, this listing is far simpler to read and understand.

Listing 6.29   **An Alternative XML-RPC Client**

```
<html>
<head>
<basefont face="Arial">
</head>

<body>
```

continues

Listing 6.29 **Continued**

```php
<?php
if($_POST['submit'])
{
?>
    <form action="<? echo $_SERVER['PHP_SELF']; ?>" method="POST">
    <b>City code:</b>
    <br>
    <input type="text" name="city" size="4" maxlength="3">
    <p>
    <b>Data format:</b>
    <br>
    <input type="Radio" name="format" value="avg" checked>Average only
    <br>
    <input type="radio" name="format" value="raw">Raw data
    <p>
    <input type="submit" name="submit" value="Go!">
    </form>

<?php
}
else
{
    include("utils.php");

    // where is the RPC server?
    $server = "weather.domain.com";
    $url = "/rpc/server.php";
    $port = 80;

    // RPC arguments
    $city = strtoupper($_POST['city']);
    $params = array("city" => $city, "format" => $_POST['format']);

    // encode, transmit request and receive, decode response
    $output = xu_rpc_http_concise(array("host" => $server, "uri" => $url,
    ➥"port" => $port, "method" => "getWeatherData", "args" => $params));

    if(is_array($output))
    {
        // check for faults
        if (!xu_is_fault($output))
        {
            // no fault!
            // data has been returned
            // format and display
            if ($output["format"] == "avg")
            {
                echo "Average temperature reading for city $city is " .
                ➥$output["data"] . " (based on three readings)";
```

```
        }
        else if ($output["format"] == "raw")
        {
                echo "Last three temperature readings for city $city
                ➥(8-hour intervals) are:<br><ul>";
                echo "<li>" . $output["data"][0];
                echo "<li>" . $output["data"][1];
                echo "<li>" . $output["data"][2];
                echo "</ul>";
        }
    }
    else
    {
            // fault! format and display
            echo "The following fault occurred:<br>";
            echo $output[0]["faultString"] . " (fault code " .
            ➥$output[0]["faultCode"] . ")";
    }
}
else
{
        // no array returned
        echo "Unrecognized response from server";
}

}
?>
</body>
</html>
```

In this case, everything related to HTTP header transmission and response translation has been extracted into the function xu_rpc_http_concise(), which accepts a number of arguments identifying the RPC server, remote procedure name and arguments, and response format. This function is defined in the file "utils.php", which you can download from the official site (http://xmlrpc-epi.sourceforge.net/). If you examine its internals, you'll see that it performs almost all the tasks so lovingly detailed in Listing 6.28, albeit with more stringent error checks.

The same holds true for the xu_is_fault() function, which merely checks the server response for a fault identifier, and returns true if it finds one.

Building an RPC-Based Mail Service

The previous example examined remote database access using the RPC framework. However, this is just one application of many; RPC makes it possible to expose and execute some very useful services over a network. The following example demonstrates one such service: an RPC-accessible mail service that checks a POP3 server for email and returns the number of messages in the specified mailbox.

Requirements

The requirements here are fairly simple: a server capable of accepting RPC requests and making POP3 (or IMAP) connections, and a client capable of encoding and decoding XML-encoded RPC data. Both client and server use SOAP as the encoding mechanism.

Note that it's not necessary that both client and server be implemented using PHP (although that's the way I've done it here); either client or server (or both) can be implemented in any SOAP-supported platform.

The Server

Listing 6.30 has the code for the server.

Listing 6.30 **A SOAP Server**

```php
<?php

include("utils.php");

$request = $HTTP_RAW_POST_DATA;

// create server
$rpc_server = xmlrpc_server_create() or die("Could not create RPC server");

// register methods
xmlrpc_server_register_method($rpc_server, "getTotalPOP3Messages",
➥"getTotalPOP3Messages") or die("Could not register method");

// call method
$response = xmlrpc_server_call_method($rpc_server, $request, NULL,
➥array("verbosity" => "no_white_space", "version" => "soap 1.1"));

// print response
echo $response;

// clean up
xmlrpc_server_destroy($rpc_server);

// function to return number of messages
function getTotalPOP3Messages($method, $args, $add_args)
{
        // check to see if the server supports POP3
        // you may need to recompile your PHP build
        // to enable this support
        if (function_exists('imap_open'))
        {
                // open connection to mail server
                $inbox = imap_open ("{". $args[0]["pop_host"] . "/pop3:110}",
                ➥$args[0]["pop_user"], $args[0]["pop_pass"]);
```

```
            if ($inbox)
            {
                    // get number of messages
                    $total = imap_num_msg($inbox);
                    imap_close($inbox);
                    return $total;
            }
            else
            {
                    return xu_fault_code(2, "Could not connect to POP3 server");
            }
        }
        else
        {
                return xu_fault_code(1, "POP3 support not available on RPC server");
        }
    }
?>
```

Again, the server code here is not very different from that seen in Listing 6.27. The primary difference here lies in the remote procedure—the getTotalPOP3Messages() function accepts a username, password, and mail host as procedure arguments, and attempts a connection to the specified mail host using PHP's POP3 functions. If the connection is successful, the function returns the number of messages found; if not, it generates an appropriate SOAP-Fault using one of the additional utility functions include()-d in "utils.php".

SOAP encoding is implemented by the simple expedient of specifying SOAP as the encoding mechanism to the xmlrpc_server_call_method() function. Because PHP's RPC extension supports both SOAP and XML-RPC (see the earlier sidebar entitled "Teething Trouble" for a few caveats related to this), switching between the two is a fairly simple matter, and one that is quickly accomplished.

The Client

In its internals, this client also resembles the previous ones. Take a look at Listing 6.31.

Listing 6.31 **A SOAP Client**

```
<html>
<head>
<basefont face="Arial">
</head>

<body>

<?php
if(!$_POST['submit'])
```

continues

Listing 6.31 **Continued**

```
{
        // display form
?>
        <table border="0" cellspacing="5" cellpadding="5">
        <form action="<? echo $_SERVER['PHP_SELF']; ?>" method="POST">
        <tr>
        <td><b>Username:</b></td>
        <td><input type="text" name="pop_user"></td>
        </tr>
        <tr>
        <td><b>Password:</b></td>
        <td><input type="password" name="pop_pass"></td>
        </tr>
        <tr>
        <td><b>POP Server:</b></td>
        <td><input type="text" name="pop_host"></td>
        </tr>
        <tr>
        <td colspan="2" align="center"><input type="submit" name="submit" value="Get
    ➥Total Messages!"></td>
        </tr>
        </form>
        </table>

<?php
}
else
{

        // include useful network connection functions
        include("utils.php");

        // where is the RPC server
        $server = "mail.service";
        $url = "/rpc/server.php";
        $port = 80;

        // RPC arguments
        $params = array("pop_user" => $_POST['pop_user'], "pop_pass" =>
    ➥$_POST['pop_pass'], "pop_host" => $_POST['pop_host']);

        // encode, transmit request and receive, decode response
        $result = xu_rpc_http_concise(array("host" => $server, "uri" => $url, "port"
    ➥=> $port, "method" => "getTotalPOP3Messages", "args" => $params, "output"
    ➥=> array("version" => "soap 1.1")));

        // check for faults
        if(is_array($result) && $result["faultcode"])
```

```
        {
              echo "The following error occurred: " . $result["faultstring"] . "
              ⇒(error code " . $result["faultcode"] . ")";
        }
        // if none present, display message count
        else
        {
              echo "$result messages in mailbox";
        }


}
?>
</body>
</html>
```

Again, the first half of the script sets up an HTML form for the user to enter mail account details; these details are then encoded into a SOAP envelope and sent to the SOAP server using the provided xu_rpc_http_concise() function. The decoded return value is then analyzed, and an appropriate message is displayed, depending on whether a fault was recorded or not.

Figure 6.5 and Figure 6.6 demonstrate what the client looks like, both before and after sending an RPC request.

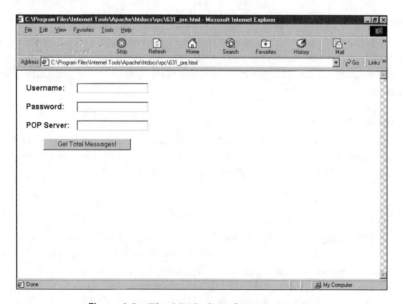

Figure 6.5 The SOAP client from Listing 6.31,
prior to retrieving mailbox information.

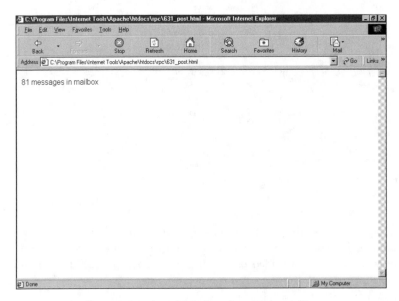

Figure 6.6   The SOAP client from Listing 6.31,
with the mailbox information requested.

Executing Shell Commands via RPC

Finally, an example that demonstrates the power inherent in RPC, and illustrates what a double-edged sword that power can be. The next (and final) example creates an RPC server that can accept any system or shell command from a client and execute this command on the server.

Requirements

Again, fairly simple: a client who accepts a command through user input, encodes it, and transmits it to a server that executes this command and returns the resulting output to the client. Both client and server communicate using XML-RPC, with HTTP as the network transport layer.

The Server

Listing 6.32 has the complete code for the server. This is probably one of the simplest servers created in this section: It merely exposes one procedure—execR()—that in turn simply uses PHP's backtick operator command (equivalent to the exec() command you read about in Chapter 2, "PHP and the Simple API for XML (SAX)") to execute the command received and return the output to the calling script.

Listing 6.32 **An XML–RPC Server**

```php
<?php

$request = $HTTP_RAW_POST_DATA;

// create server
$rpc_server = xmlrpc_server_create() or die("Could not create RPC server");

// register methods
xmlrpc_server_register_method($rpc_server, "execR", "execR") or die("Could not
➥register method");

// call method
$response = xmlrpc_server_call_method($rpc_server, $request, NULL);

// print response
echo $response;

// clean up
xmlrpc_server_destroy($rpc_server);



// execute command
function execR($method, $args, $add_args)
{
    $output = `$args[0]`;
    return $output;
}
?>
```

The Client

As you might guess, the client is equally simple—a form consisting of one text box, into which the user can enter the command to be executed on the remote server. This data is then encoded and sent to the server as an XML–RPC request with the command output coming back as an XML–RPC response.

Listing 6.33 has the complete code listing.

Listing 6.33 **An XML–RPC Client**

```html
<html>
<head>
<basefont face="Arial">
</head>
```

continues

Listing 6.33 **Continued**

```php
<body>


<?php
if(!$_POST['submit'])
{
?>

    <form action="<? echo $_SERVER['PHP_SELF']; ?>" method="POST">
    <b>Remote command:</b>
    <br>
    <input type="text" name="command">
    <input type="submit" name="submit" value="Go!">
    </form>

<?php
}
else
{
    include("utils.php");

    // where is the RPC server?
    $server = "remote.server";
    $url = "/rpc/server.php";
    $port = 80;

    // encode, transmit request and receive, decode response
    $output = xu_rpc_http_concise(array("host" => $server, "uri" => $url,
    ↪"port" => $port, "method" => "execR", "args" => $_POST['command']));

    echo $output;

}
?>
</body>
</html>
```

Figure 6.7 and Figure 6.8 demonstrate what the client looks like, both before and after sending an RPC request.

> **Red Alert**
>
> It cannot be stressed enough that an RPC server, such as the one discussed in Listing 6.32, should never, ever be implemented in a production environment. By allowing any client to execute any command on a remote system, you're immediately opening up a security hole of gaping proportions—one that can be used by malicious users to seriously damage your network or system.
>
> The example is included here only for illustrative purposes, to demonstrate the power that RPC provides; it's fitting to remember that this power can be easily turned against you if used improperly.

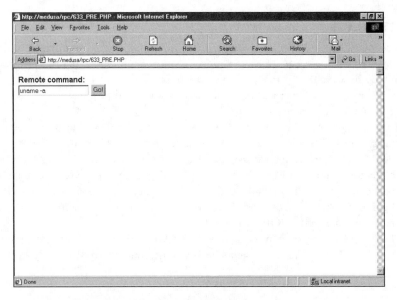

Figure 6.7 The XML–RPC client from Listing 6.33,
prior to executing a remote command.

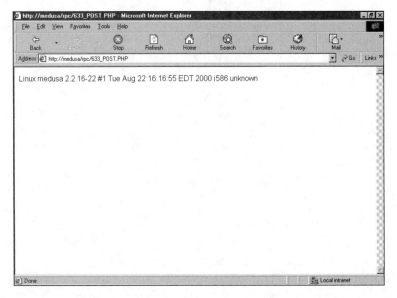

Figure 6.8 The XML–RPC client from Listing 6.33, after receiving the output
of the uname -a command from the XML–RPC server.

Summary

This chapter discussed RPC, explaining how they could be used to implement distributed, network-based applications. It then went on to apply RPC theory to the web, examining how XML and HTTP could be combined to encode and transport procedure calls over the Internet and discussing two XML-based protocols, XML-RPC and SOAP, which are designed to do just that.

With the broad overview out of the way, this chapter then proceeded to a detailed examination of PHP's RPC extension, examining how it could be used to encode and decode RPC data, create and manage an RPC server, and examine itself to automatically deliver documentation on its available procedures. Finally, two real-world examples (and one not-so-real-world illustration) put the theory to the test, demonstrating how PHP and XML can be used to build distributed web applications such as a meteorological data retrieval utility and a POP3 mail notification service.

The next chapter will focus on connecting XML with other data sources, using a MySQL database to dynamically generate XML data, and apply XSLT stylesheets to it.

"If we spoke a different language, we would perceive a somewhat different world."

~LUDWIG WITTGENSTEIN

7

PHP, XML, and Databases

XML WORKS BY MARKING UP DATA WITH descriptive tags. Databases work by tabulating information into rows and columns. Though the two approaches are fundamentally different, they share a common goal: to impose order on unstructured data in order to make it more useful.

Now, contrary to what you might have heard, XML is not the panacea for all the world's ills. The language does have limitations, which may render it unsuitable for use in particular situations—a fact amply attested to by the numerous web sites that continue to prefer databases for information storage and retrieval, even in this age of XML. Consequently, web application developers need a thorough understanding of the advantages and disadvantages of these two technologies, and must factor them into their calculations when making project-wide implementation decisions.

Often, however, merely understanding the issues involved is insufficient. When it comes to redeploying database-powered web applications to use XML, or exchanging information between sites or applications built on different back ends (some using XML, some using a database), a developer also needs a practical understanding of how to reconcile the two technologies in order to offer customers the most bang for their buck.

This chapter examines the relationship between XML and databases, demonstrating how technologies discussed previously in this book (SAX, DOM, and XSLT) can be mobilized to translate database records into well-formed XML documents, and vice-versa. It also includes a brief discussion of the pros and cons of these two technologies, with a view to helping you choose the right one for your particular requirements.

XML versus the Database

Nope, this isn't tonight's featured bout at the World Wresting Federation. It's a discussion stemming from one very basic question: What truly is the difference between storing information as XML and storing it in a database?

In the broad sense, there isn't much. After all, both are technologies designed to impose structure on raw data, thereby making it more useful to the applications that need it. XML accomplishes this with elements and attributes, a database with rows and columns. Both also come with some fairly powerful tools—databases with Structured Query Language (SQL) or some variant thereof, XML with the XML Path Language (XPath), and Extensible Stylesheet Language Transformations (XSLT)—that facilitate the manipulation of the data contained within them.

In a narrower, more technical sense, however, differences between the two technologies do exist. A database is designed for highly structured data; XML, on the other hand, favors data that is less structured and more hierarchical in nature. This is a fairly fundamental difference; although others do exist (and are discussed in greater length in the following sections), the consequences of ignoring this one can prove to be fairly serious.

In the web application arena, developers tend to prefer a traditional RDBMS over XML; too often, this choice is influenced less by technical reasons than by a better-the-devil-you-know psychosis. As you might imagine, this is not a good thing; in a production environment in which performance, portability, and ease of use are paramount, a developer needs to make implementation decisions based on sound technical reasons and a fundamental understanding of the issues and the technologies involved.

To that end, the following sections list the factors to be kept in mind when deciding between XML and a database.

Nature of the Data

If you have highly structured or volatile data—for example, stock symbols and their corresponding prices, or an address book with specific fields for contact information—a database is a far better choice than XML. This is because databases are designed to handle structured data (that's the whole point of those rigid rows and columns), and can offer a (much!) higher level of performance when manipulating this type of data.

When it comes to unstructured or irregularly structured information (recipes, poetry, lengthy dissertations, and so on), though, a traditional database tends to run into difficulties, because this type of data tends to resist easy classification into rows and columns. In such cases, XML is a much better choice; its self-describing approach offers document authors greater flexibility, allowing them to easily describe relationships between data fragments and thereby create data models that are efficient without necessarily conforming to the two-dimensional table paradigm.

That said, XML is not a good choice for volatile and frequently updated information simply because there exists no easy way to manipulate XML-encoded documents. It's far easier to put this type of information into a database and manipulate it with SQL than it is to store it in a text file and modify it with file read/write functions.

Data Retrieval Requirements

When deciding on whether to use XML or a database for your data, it's also important to take note of your data-retrieval requirements. If you're planning to work only with data organized in a clearly defined manner, you're fairly safe using a traditional database. An example of this is the retrieval of a name and telephone number from a table containing contact information. Because the required dataset is clearly defined and already maps into specific fields of a table, retrieving it via SQL is a snap.

If, however, the data you need to retrieve isn't so clearly defined, with the required dataset blurring or extending across the clearly defined boundaries of a table, the XML family of technologies is a far better choice. An example of this might be the retrieval of every alternate stanza in a poem—hard to do with SQL, yet fairly easy with XPath.

XPath, together with XSLT and XPointer, makes it extremely easy to create customized node collections from an XML document tree, and restructure this node collection into the format you require. Further, if your data contains complex recursive or nested structures, a traditional database will have difficulty organizing it in a format suitable for easy retrieval; XML, on the other hand, is well-suited to this task.

Performance

Data organized in a traditional database, which typically has built-in support for indexing and stored procedures, can usually be accessed faster than the corresponding XML-encoded version. Because XML documents are, at their core, ordinary text files, accessing individual data fragments involves parsing the text file line-by-line; this can degrade performance substantially, especially if there is a large amount of data involved.

A database also tends to handle simultaneous access better than an XML document, implementing a more secure and robust locking arrangement than is possible with a "regular" flat file.

Portability

There's a flip side to the performance argument, though. Because XML markup is stored as text, XML data is immediately portable across platforms; databases, on the other hand, may store data in proprietary formats that cannot be easily ported to other systems and platforms. If portability is a concern, or if you anticipate data manipulation by non-technical users, you can't get any more portable or simple than ASCII text; in these situations, it's worthwhile to consider whether XML might be a better solution than a database.

Standardization and Integration with Other Applications

Most databases support SQL, which provides a simple and efficient method of accessing records in a database. An upcoming W3C technology named XML Query is supposed to do for XML documents what SQL does for databases; at the moment, though, it's still under development. Consequently, most developers still need to write their own tools to access XML-encoded data, using either a SAX or DOM parser; this can add to development time and (because there isn't a common standard) possible integration difficulties with applications from other vendors.

Encoding your data into XML can also cause problems if it needs to be shared with applications or systems that don't understand the language. In such situations, too, a traditional database system (that exposes a standard API to developers) would be preferable.

It should be noted that there's no "one-size-fits-all" answer to the question of deciding which technology is most appropriate; the factors involved are fairly complex, and they vary from situation to situation. As technology evolves, the question may even become moot—many commercial databases now support XML as a data type; and a new database hybrid, the *native XML database*, offers the best of both worlds, combining the simplicity of XML with the feature set of traditional database systems.

Knowledge Is Power

Interested in learning more about XML, databases, and XML databases? Drop by the companion web site for this book for links to articles on the topic. Go to http://www.xmlphp.com or http://www.newriders.com.

Exporting Database Records To XML

As the web moves to an XML-based paradigm, one of the most common problems faced by developers involves converting legacy data, usually stored in a database, into corresponding XML data. With this in mind, let's look at some practical examples that demonstrate how data stored in an SQL-compliant database system can be converted into well-formed XML.

Note that the code listings in this section assume the existence of a MySQL database and a familiarity with PHP's database access functions (specifically, its MySQL functions). In case you don't already have MySQL, you can download it from http://www.mysql.com/, and SQL dump files for the database tables used in this section may be obtained from this book's companion web site.

Dynamically Generating XML from a Database

I'll begin with a simple example. Let's assume the existence of a table holding information on a personal CD collection. Here's a snippet from the table:

```
+----+-------------------------------+-----------------+
| id | title                         | artist          |
+----+-------------------------------+-----------------+
|  2 | Get A Grip                    | Aerosmith       |
|  3 | All That You Can't Leave Behind | U2            |
|  4 | Androgyny                     | Garbage         |
+----+-------------------------------+-----------------+
```

Now, the process of converting these rows and columns into XML would break down into the following steps:

1. Connect to the database.

2. Retrieve a result set.

3. Iterate through this result set, and create XML structures corresponding to the data retrieved.

4. Output the complete XML document.

XML does not possess any database manipulation capabilities. PHP, however, does, and because it also comes with a capable implementation of the DOM, it can be used to accomplish the preceding four steps with minimal difficulty. Listing 7.1 demonstrates the script that does all the work.

Listing 7.1 **A Dynamically Constructed XML DOM Tree from a Database**

```php
<?php

// query database for records
$connection = mysql_connect("cdserver", "joe", "cool") or die ("Unable to
➥connect!");
mysql_select_db("db712") or die ("Unable to select database!");
$query = "SELECT id, title, artist FROM cds";
$result = mysql_query($query) or die ("Error in query: $query. " . mysql_error());

if (mysql_num_rows($result) > 0)
{
        // create DomDocument object
        $doc = new_xmldoc("1.0");

        // add root node
        $root = $doc->add_root("cds");

        // iterate through result set
        while(list($id, $title, $artist) = mysql_fetch_row($result))
        {
                // create item node
                $record = $root->new_child("cd", "");
                $record->set_attribute("id", $id);

                // attach title and artist as children of item node
                $record->new_child("title", $title);
                $record->new_child("artist", $artist);
        }

// print the tree
echo $doc->dumpmem();
}
```

continues

Listing 7.1 **Continued**

```
// close connection
mysql_close($connection);
?>
```

Much of this should already be familiar to you, but let me take you through it anyway:

1. The first step is to connect to the database and execute a query to retrieve data from it; this is accomplished using PHP's standard MySQL functions.

   ```
   $connection = mysql_connect("cdserver", "joe", "cool") or die ("Unable to
   ➥connect!");
   mysql_select_db("db712") or die ("Unable to select database!");
   $query = "SELECT id, title, artist FROM cds";
   $result = mysql_query($query) or die ("Error in query: $query. " .
   ➥mysql_error());
   ```

2. Assuming that one or more records are returned, the next step is to create an XML document in memory. This is accomplished via the DOM extension's new_xmldoc() function, which returns an instance of the DOMDocument class.

   ```
   $doc = new_xmldoc("1.0");
   ```

3. Next, the document element, <cds>, is generated and added to the document, and a reference is returned to this newly minted node. This reference will be used in subsequent steps to construct the rest of the DOM tree.

   ```
   $root = $doc->add_root("cds");
   ```

4. With the preliminaries out of the way, all that's left is to iterate through the MySQL result set, and create XML representations of the data within it. In Listing 7.1, every record in the result set is represented as a <cd> element, with the fields within each record represented as attributes or children of this <cd> element.

   ```
   while(list($id, $title, $artist) = mysql_fetch_row($result))
   {
           $record = $root->new_child("cd", "");
           $record->set_attribute("id", $id);
           $record->new_child("title", $title);
           $record->new_child("artist", $artist);
   }
   ```

5. After the document has been completely generated, the dumpmem() object method is used to dump the XML tree as a string.

   ```
   echo $doc->dumpmem();
   ```

Cheat Sheet

This chapter makes extensive use of the following MySQL functions:

- `mysql_connect()` — Opens a connection to a MySQL database

- `mysql_select_db()` — Selects a particular MySQL database for use

- `mysql_query()` — Executes a query on the selected MySQL database

- `mysql_fetch_row()` — Fetches a single row of the MySQL result set

- `mysql_close()` — Closes a connection to a MySQL database

- `mysql_error()` — If an error occurs during query execution, returns the error string

More information on these functions, together with usage examples, can be obtained from your copy of the PHP manual or from the New Riders book *PHP Functions Essential Reference*, by Zak Greant, Graeme Merrall, Torben Wilson, and Brett Michlitsch (New Riders, 2001, ISBN: 0-7357-0970-X).

Listing 7.2 demonstrates what the output of Listing 7.1 looks like (note that the output has been manually indented for greater readability):

Listing 7.2 **A Dynamically Generated XML Document**

```xml
<?xml version="1.0"?>
<cds>
    <cd id="2">
        <title>Get A Grip</title>
        <artist>Aerosmith</artist>
    </cd>
    <cd id="3">
        <title>All That You Can't Leave Behind</title>
        <artist>U2</artist>
    </cd>
    <cd id="4">
        <title>Androgyny</title>
        <artist>Garbage</artist>
    </cd>
</cds>
```

Backtrack

Still not too clear about how Listing 7.1 works? Flip back to Chapter 3, "PHP and the Document Object Model (DOM)" (in particular, refer to Listing 3.15, which bears more than a passing resemblance to Listing 7.1), refresh your memory about how PHP's DOM extension works, and things should start making more sense.

X Marks the Spot

You might be interested to hear that version 4.x of the MySQL client application includes the ability to format an SQL result set as well-formed XML. For example, the command

```
$ echo 'USE db127; SELECT * FROM cds' | mysql -X
```

would return:

```
<?xml version="1.0"?>
<resultset statement="SELECT * FROM cds">
  <row>
        <id>1</id>
        <title>Get A Grip</title>
        <artist>Aerosmith</artist>
  </row>
  <row>
        <id>2</id>
        <title>Androgyny</title>
        <artist>Garbage</artist>
  </row>
</resultset>
```

This XML output may then be saved to a file, or sent to another application for further processing.

The MySQL client application may be downloaded from the official MySQL Web site, http://www.mysql.com/.

You don't have to restrict your activities to a single table, either; it's just as easy to build an XML document from multiple tables, either by joining them or by performing multiple queries at a time. Consider the following revised database schema, which links each CD to a track list stored in a separate table:

```
+----+------------------------------+---------------+
| id | title                        | artist        |
+----+------------------------------+---------------+
|  2 | Get A Grip                   | Aerosmith     |
|  3 | All That You Can't Leave Behind | U2         |
|  4 | Androgyny                    | Garbage       |
+----+------------------------------+---------------+
```

```
+----+-------------------------------------+------+
| cd | track                               | indx |
+----+-------------------------------------+------+
|  3 | Beautiful Day                       |   1  |
|  3 | Stuck In A Moment You Can't Get Out Of |  2  |
|  3 | Elevation                           |   3  |
|  2 | Eat The Rich                        |   1  |
|  2 | Livin' On The Edge                  |   2  |
+----+-------------------------------------+------+
```

Listing 7.3 demonstrates how this information can be represented in XML, extending Listing 7.1 to include a list of tracks for each CD.

Listing 7.3   **A Dynamically Constructed XML DOM Tree from Two Tables**

```php
<?php

// query database for records
$connection = mysql_connect("cdserver", "joe", "cool") or die ("Unable to
➥connect!");
mysql_select_db("db712") or die ("Unable to select database!");
$query = "SELECT id, title, artist FROM cds";
$result = mysql_query($query) or die ("Error in query: $query. " . mysql_error());

if(mysql_num_rows($result) > 0)
{
    // create DomDocument object
    $doc = new_xmldoc("1.0");

    // add root node
    $root = $doc->add_root("cds");

    // iterate through result set
    while(list($id, $title, $artist) = mysql_fetch_row($result))
    {
        $record = $root->new_child("cd", "");
        $record->set_attribute("id", $id);

        $record->new_child("title", $title);
        $record->new_child("artist", $artist);

        // add <tracks> node
        $tracks = $record->new_child("tracks", "");

        // query database for track listing for this CD
        $query2 = "SELECT track FROM tracks WHERE cd = '$id' ORDER BY indx";
        $result2 = mysql_query($query2) or die ("Error in query: $query2. " .
        ➥mysql_error());

        // print each track as a child of <tracks>
        while($row = mysql_fetch_row($result2))
        {
            $tracks->new_child("track", $row[0]);
        }
    }

// dump XML document to a string
$xml_string = $doc->dumpmem();
}
```

continues

Listing 7.3   **Continued**

```
// close connection
mysql_close($connection);

// print XML
echo $xml_string;
?>
```

In this case, an additional query has been inserted into the script. This one retrieves a list of tracks for each CD in the collection and appends this track list to each item in the collection. Listing 7.4 demonstrates the output.

Listing 7.4   **A Dynamically Generated XML Document**

```
<?xml version="1.0"?>
<cds>
      <cd id="2">
            <title>Get A Grip</title>
            <artist>Aerosmith</artist>
            <tracks>
                  <track>Eat The Rich</track>
                  <track>Livin' On The Edge</track>
            </tracks>
      </cd>
      <cd id="3">
            <title>All That You Can't Leave Behind</title>
            <artist>U2</artist>
            <tracks>
                  <track>Beautiful Day</track>
                  <track>Stuck In A Moment You Can't Get Out Of</track>
                  <track>Elevation</track>
            </tracks>
      </cd>
      <cd id="4">
            <title>Androgyny</title>
            <artist>Garbage</artist>
            <tracks/>
      </cd>
</cds>
```

Most of the time, this is a good place to stop. After all, the primary goal—to convert database records into XML—has been achieved. This XML can now be saved to a file for later use, parsed or transformed by an XML or XSLT engine, or transmitted over any text-capable communication system. However, it's instructive to see what happens next, if only to gain a deeper understanding of the complete process flow.

Emerging from a Cocoon

After the XML document has been generated, it may be processed and transformed by any XSLT-capable engine. Although PHP does come with a very capable XSLT extension, you can just as easily pass the dynamically generated XML to any other engine for processing.

One example of such an engine is Cocoon, a Java-based application that simplifies the process of publishing XML documents to the web. Fast and scalable, Cocoon is built around the JVM (for portability and performance), SAX (for fast document parsing), and XSLT (for document transformation). It supports content creation in (among others) HTML, WML, and PDF formats.

Cocoon has been developed by The Apache Group, and can be downloaded from
http://xml.apache.org/cocoon/.

Transforming Dynamically Generated XML with XSLT

The most common use of this dynamically generated XML usually involves transforming it into some other format via an XSL Transformation. I will do just that by using the very simple XSLT stylesheet illustrated in Listing 7.5.

Listing 7.5   **An XSLT Stylesheet Displays a Table of CDs and Tracks (*cds.xsl*)**

```
<?xml version="1.0"?>
<xsl:stylesheet version="1.0" xmlns:xsl="http://www.w3.org/1999/XSL/Transform">

<!-- set up page template -->
<xsl:template match="/">
      <html>
      <head>
      <basefont face="Arial" />
      </head>
      <body>
      <h3>My CD Collection</h3>
      <table border="1" cellspacing="0" cellpadding="5">
      <tr>
      <td align="center">Artist</td>
      <td align="center">Title</td>
      <td align="center">Track list</td>
      </tr>
      <xsl:apply-templates />
      </table>
      </body>
      </html>
</xsl:template>

<!-- look for CDs -->
<xsl:template match="//cd">
```

continues

Listing 7.5 **Continued**

```
    <tr>
    <td align="center" valign="top"><xsl:value-of select="artist" /></td>
    <td align="center" valign="top"><xsl:value-of select="title" /></td>
    <td align="left" valign="top">
        <ol>
        <!-- iterate through track list, print each <track> element as
        ⇒list item -->
        <xsl:for-each select="tracks/track">
        <li><xsl:value-of select="." /></li>
        </xsl:for-each>
        </ol>
     </td>
    </tr>
</xsl:template>
</xsl:stylesheet>
```

Listing 7.6 uses PHP's XSLT processing functions to combine this stylesheet with the dynamically generated XML output you saw in Listing 7.4.

Listing 7.6 **Dynamically Constructing and Transforming an XML DOM Tree**

```php
<?php

// query database for records
$connection = mysql_connect("cdserver", "joe", "cool") or die ("Unable to
⇒connect!");
mysql_select_db("db712") or die ("Unable to select database!");
$query = "SELECT id, title, artist FROM cds";
$result = mysql_query($query) or die ("Error in query: $query. " . mysql_error());


if(mysql_num_rows($result) > 0)
{
    // create DomDocument object
    $doc = new_xmldoc("1.0");

    // add root node
    $root = $doc->add_root("cds");

    // iterate through result set
    while(list($id, $title, $artist) = mysql_fetch_row($result))
    {
        $record = $root->new_child("cd", "");
        $record->set_attribute("id", $id);

        $record->new_child("title", $title);
        $record->new_child("artist", $artist);
```

```
            // add <tracks> node
            $tracks = $record->new_child("tracks", "");

            // query database for track listing for this CD
            $query2 = "SELECT track FROM tracks WHERE cd = '$id' ORDER BY indx";
            $result2 = mysql_query($query2) or die ("Error in query: $query2. " .
            ➥mysql_error());

            // print each track as a child of <tracks>
            while($row = mysql_fetch_row($result2))
            {
                $tracks->new_child("track", $row[0]);
            }

        }

// dump XML document to a string
$xml_string = $doc->dumpmem();
}

// close connection
mysql_close($connection);

// this time, don't print the XML
// instead, create an XSLT processor and transform it into HTML

if ($xml_string)
{
        // XSLT stylesheet
        $xslt_file = "cds.xsl";

        // create the XSLT processor
        $xp = xslt_create() or die("Could not create XSLT processor");

        // read in the XSLT data
        $xslt_string = join("", file($xslt_file));

        // set up buffers
        $arg_buffer = array("/xml" => $xml_string, "/xslt" => $xslt_string);

        // process the two files to get the desired output
        if($result = xslt_process($xp, "arg:/xml", "arg:/xslt", NULL, $arg_buffer))
        {
                // print output
                echo $result;
        }
        else
        {
                // else display error
```

continues

Listing 7.6 **Continued**

```
            echo "An error occurred: " . xslt_error($xp) . "(error code " .
            ➥xslt_errno($xp) . ")";
    }

    // free the resources occupied by the handler
    xslt_free($xp);
}
?>
```

The first part of Listing 7.6 is identical to Listing 7.3. It queries the database, retrieves track and title information, dynamically generates an XML document using PHP's DOM functions, and stores it in a string variable.

After the document has been generated, the focus shifts to PHP's XSLT processor, which is initialized with the `xslt_create()` function:

```
$xp = xslt_create() or die("Could not create XSLT processor");
```

Then, the XSLT stylesheet is read into a string variable, and both XML and XSLT strings are stored in the array `$arg_buffer` as named arguments:

```
$xslt_string = join("", file($xslt_file));

$arg_buffer = array("/xml" => $xml_string, "/xslt" => $xslt_string);
```

This argument buffer is then passed to the XSLT processor via `xslt_process()`, and the result of the transformation is then printed to the browser:

```
if($result = xslt_process($xp, "arg:/xml", "arg:/xslt", NULL, $arg_buffer))
{
    // print output
    echo $result;
}
```

Figure 7.1 shows what the output looks like.

Party Pooper

Wondering what XSLT is, and why it's decided to crash this particular party? Chapter 4, "PHP and Extensible Stylesheet Language Transformations (XSLT)," has the skinny.

Formatting Dynamically Generated XML With SAX

After you understand the basics, it's possible to apply the techniques demonstrated in the preceding examples to do some fairly complex things. Consider Listing 7.7, which uses PHP's MySQL functions to retrieve a complete list of all the records in a user-specified table, convert this result set to XML, and format it into a HTML representation using PHP's SAX parser.

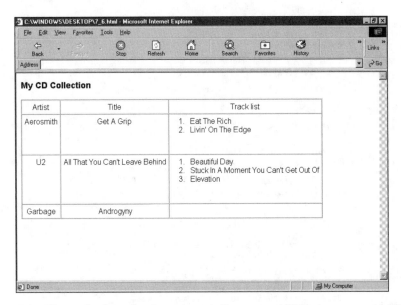

Figure 7.1   The result of transforming a dynamically generated XML document with XSLT.

Listing 7.7   **Reading a Database Table Using the DOM, and Formatting It into HTML with SAX**

```php
<?php
// database parameters
// get these via user input
$host = "localhost";
$user = "joe";
$pass = "cool";
$db = "web";
$table = "bookmarks";

// segment 1 begins

// query database for records
$connection = mysql_connect($host, $user, $pass) or die ("Unable to connect!");
mysql_select_db($db) or die ("Unable to select database!");
$query = "SELECT * FROM $table";
$result = mysql_query($query) or die ("Error in query: $query. " . mysql_error());

if(mysql_num_rows($result) > 0)
{
    // create DomDocument object
    $doc = new_xmldoc("1.0");
```

continues

Listing 7.7   **Continued**

```php
            // add root node
            $root = $doc->add_root("table");
            $root->set_attribute("name", $table);

            // create nodes for structure and data
            $structure = $root->new_child("structure", "");
            $data = $root->new_child("data", "");

            // let's get the table structure first
            // create elements for each field name, type and length
            $fields = mysql_list_fields($db, $table, $connection);
            for ($x=0; $x<mysql_num_fields($fields); $x++)
            {
                    $field = $structure->new_child("field", "");

                    $name = mysql_field_name($fields, $x);
                    $length = mysql_field_len($fields, $x);
                    $type = mysql_field_type($fields, $x);

                    $field->new_child("name", $name);
                    $field->new_child("type", $type);
                    $field->new_child("length", $length);
            }

            // move on to getting the raw data (records)
            // iterate through result set
            while($row = mysql_fetch_row($result))
            {
                    $record = $data->new_child("record", "");
                    foreach ($row as $field)
                    {
                            $record->new_child("item", $field);
                    }
            }

            // dump the tree as a string
            $xml_string = $doc->dumpmem();
}

// close connection
mysql_close($connection);

// segment 1 ends

// at this point, a complete representation of the table is stored in $xml_string
// now proceed to format this into HTML with SAX

// segment 2 begins
```

```
// array to hold HTML markup for starting tags
$startTagsArray = array(
'TABLE' => '<html><head></head><body><table border="1" cellspacing="0"
↪cellpadding="5">',
'STRUCTURE' => '<tr>',
'FIELD' => '<td bgcolor="silver"><font face="Arial" size="-1">',
'RECORD' => '<tr>',
'ITEM' => '<td><font face="Arial" size="-1">',
'NAME' => '<b>',
'TYPE' => '  <i>(',
'LENGTH' => ', '
);

// array to hold HTML markup for ending tags
$endTagsArray = array(
'TABLE' => '</body></html></table>',
'STRUCTURE' => '</tr>',
'FIELD' => '</font></td>',
'RECORD' => '</tr>',
'ITEM' => ' </font></td>',
'NAME' => '</b>',
'TYPE' => '',
'LENGTH' => ')</i>'
);

// call this when a start tag is found
function startElementHandler($parser, $name, $attributes)
{
     global $startTagsArray;
     if($startTagsArray[$name])
     {
          // look up array for this tag and print corresponding markup
          echo $startTagsArray[$name];
     }

}

// call this when an end tag is found
function endElementHandler($parser, $name)
{
     global $endTagsArray;
     if($endTagsArray[$name])
     {
          // look up array for this tag and print corresponding markup
          echo $endTagsArray[$name];
     }
}

// call this when character data is found
```

continues

Listing 7.7 **Continued**

```
function characterDataHandler($parser, $data)
{
     echo $data;
}

// initialize parser
$xml_parser = xml_parser_create();

// turn off whitespace processing
xml_parser_set_option($xml_parser,XML_OPTION_SKIP_WHITE, TRUE);
// turn on case folding
xml_parser_set_option($xml_parser, XML_OPTION_CASE_FOLDING, TRUE);

// set callback functions
xml_set_element_handler($xml_parser, "startElementHandler", "endElementHandler");
xml_set_character_data_handler($xml_parser, "characterDataHandler");

// parse XML
if (!xml_parse($xml_parser, $xml_string, 4096))
{
     $ec = xml_get_error_code($xml_parser);
     die("XML parser error (error code " . $ec . "): " . xml_error_string($ec) .
     ➥"<br>Error occurred at line " . xml_get_current_line_number($xml_parser) .
     ➥", column " . xml_get_current_column_number($xml_parser) . ", byte offset
     ➥" . xml_get_current_byte_index($xml_parser));
}

// all done, clean up!
xml_parser_free($xml_parser);

// segment 2 ends

?>
```

Listing 7.7 can be divided into two main segments:

- Retrieving database records and constructing an XML document from them
- Converting the XML document into an HTML page

The first segment is concerned with the retrieval of the records from the table (using a catch-all SELECT * FROM table query), and with the dynamic generation of a DOM tree in memory using the DOM functions discussed previously. Once generated, this tree would be stored in the PHP variable $xml_string, and would look a lot like Listing 7.8.

Listing 7.8   **An XML Representation of a MySQL Table**

```xml
<?xml version="1.0"?>
<table name="bookmarks">
      <structure>
            <field>
                  <name>category</name>
                  <type>string</type>
                  <length>255</length>
            </field>
            <field>
                  <name>name</name>
                  <type>string</type>
                  <length>255</length>
            </field>
            <field>
                  <name>url</name>
                  <type>string</type>
                  <length>255</length>
            </field>
      </structure>
      <data>
            <record>
                  <item>News</item>
                  <item>CNN.com</item>
                  <item>http://www.cnn.com/</item>
            </record>
            <record>
                  <item>News</item>
                  <item>Slashdot</item>
                  <item>http://www.slashdot.org/</item>
            </record>
            <record>
                  <item>Shopping</item>
                  <item>http://www.amazon.com/</item>
            </record>
            <record>
                  <item>Technical Articles</item>
                  <item>Melonfire</item>
                  <item>http://www.melonfire.com/</item>
            </record>
            <record>
                  <item>Shopping</item>
                  <item>CDNow</item>
                  <item>http://www.cdnow.com/</item>
            </record>
      </data>
</table>
```

Taking the Scenic Route

You may be wondering whether the long, convoluted process outlined in Listing 7.7 was even necessary. Strictly speaking, it wasn't—I could have achieved the same effect with PHP's MySQL functions alone, completely bypassing the DOM and SAX parsers (and obtaining a substantial performance benefit as a result). XML was added to the equation primarily for illustrative purposes, to demonstrate yet another of the myriad uses to which PHP's DOM and SAX extensions can be put when working with XML-based applications.

Note that the approach outlined in Listing 7.7 is not recommended for a production environment, simply because of the performance degradation likely to result from using it. When working with tables containing thousands of records, the process of retrieving data, converting it to XML, parsing the XML, and formatting it into HTML would inevitably be slower than the shorter, simpler process of directly converting the result set into HTML using PHP's native functions and data structures.

After the MySQL result set has been converted into XML, it's fairly simple to parse it using SAX, and to replace the XML elements with corresponding HTML markup. This HTML markup is then sent to the browser, which displays it as a neatly formatted table (see Figure 7.2).

Revisiting SAX

SAX, the Simple API for XML, provides an efficient, event-driven approach to parsing an XML document. If you're not familiar with how it works, or with the SAX functions used in Listings 7.7 and 7.11, drop by Chapter 2, "PHP and the Simple API for XML (SAX)," which should bring you up to speed.

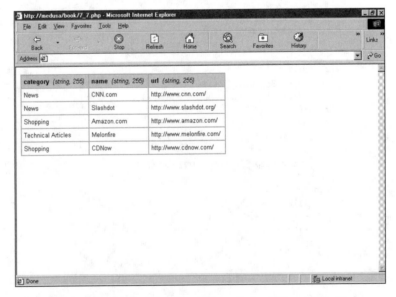

Figure 7.2   The result of formatting a dynamically generated, XML-encoded database schema into an HTML table with SAX.

It's interesting to note that I could just as easily have accomplished this using XSLT instead of SAX. The process is fairly simple (much like Listing 7.6), and you should attempt to work it out for yourself. In case you get hung up on some of the more arcane aspects of XSLT syntax, Listing 7.9 has a stylesheet you can use to perform the transformation.

Listing 7.9 **An XSLT Stylesheet to Format an XML Table Representation into HTML**

```
<?xml version="1.0"?>
<xsl:stylesheet version="1.0" xmlns:xsl="http://www.w3.org/1999/XSL/Transform">

<!-- set up page template -->
<xsl:template match="/">
      <html>
      <head>
      <basefont face="Arial" />
      </head>
      <body>
      <table border="1" cellspacing="0" cellpadding="5">
      <xsl:apply-templates select="//structure" />
      <xsl:apply-templates select="//data" />
      </table>
      </body>
      </html>
</xsl:template>

<!-- read structure data, set up first row of table -->
<xsl:template match="//structure">
      <tr>
      <!-- iterate through field list, print field information -->
      <xsl:for-each select="field">
      <td bgcolor="silver"><font face="Arial" size="-1"><b><xsl:value-of
      ↩select="name" /></b>  <i>(<xsl:value-of select="type" />, <xsl:value-of
      ↩select="length" />)</i></font></td>
      </xsl:for-each>
      </tr>
</xsl:template>

<!-- read records -->
<xsl:template match="//data">
      <!-- iterate through records -->
      <xsl:for-each select="record">
      <tr>
                <!-- iterate through fields of each record -->
                <xsl:for-each select="item">
                <td><font face="Arial" size="-1"><xsl:value-of select="."
                ↩/></font> </td>
```

continues

Listing 7.9 **Continued**

```
                        </xsl:for-each>
        </tr>
        </xsl:for-each>
</xsl:template>

</xsl:stylesheet>
```

Importing XML Data into a Database

Now that you know how to convert database records into well-formed XML documents, let's turn things around to look at how the process works in reverse. This section examines how data marked up with XML can be converted into SQL statements and inserted into a database.

Dynamically Constructing SQL Queries from an XML Document with SAX

Again, we'll begin with a simple example—consider the XML document in Listing 7.10.

Listing 7.10 **An XML Book List (*books.xml*)**

```
<?xml version="1.0"?>

<list>
        <item>
                <title>Waking Up With The Red-Eyed Bed Monster</title>
                <author>J. I. M. Somniac</author>
                <blurb>The blood-chillingly true story of one man's fight against
                ➥the monsters under his bed.</blurb>
        </item>

        <item>
                <title>The Case Of The Hungry Hippopotamus</title>
                <author>P. I. Hardhat</author>
                <blurb>A tough private eye is hired to solve the most challenging
                ➥case of his career.</blurb>
        </item>

        <item>
                <title>Making Money, Losing Friends</title>
                <author>T. Backstabber</author>
                <blurb>The bestselling self-help book for corporate executives on
                ➥the fast track.</blurb>
        </item>
```

```
        <item>
                <title>The Idiot's Guide to Sandwiches</title>
                <author>B. L. Tuhmatto</author>
                <blurb>Making tasty sandwiches has never been so easy!</blurb>
        </item>

</list>
```

The process of putting this XML-encoded data into a database involves the following four steps:

1. Parse the XML data.

2. Build a list of field-value pairs.

3. Dynamically generate a query to insert these field-value pairs into the database.

4. Execute the query.

It's possible to accomplish these tasks using SAX, XSLT, or the DOM. Most of the time, the process is fairly simple; the level of complexity varies depending on how generic you need your script to be. Listing 7.11 demonstrates the process, using SAX in a script designed specifically to handle the XML document described in Listing 7.10.

Listing 7.11 **Generating and Executing SQL Statements with SAX**

```php
<?php
// initialize some variables
$currentTag = "";

// this array will hold the values for the SQL statement
$values = array();

// this array will hold allowed fields/elements
$allowedFields = array("title", "author", "blurb");

// XML file to parse
$xml_file="books.xml";

// database parameters
$host = "localhost";
$user = "john";
$pass = "doe";
$db = "library";
$table = "books";

// called when parser finds start tag
function startElementHandler($parser, $name, $attributes)
{
        global $currentTag;
```

continues

Listing 7.11   **Continued**

```php
        $currentTag = $name;
}

// called when parser finds end tag
function endElementHandler($parser, $name)
{
        global $values, $currentTag;
        // import database link and table name
        global $connection, $table;

        // if ending <item> tag
        // implies end of record
        if (strtolower($name) == "item")
        {
                // generate the query string
                $query = "INSERT INTO books";
                $query .= "(title, author, blurb) ";
                $query .= "VALUES(\"" . join("\", \"", $values) . "\");";

                // uncomment for debug
                // print $query;

                // execute query
                $result = mysql_query($query) or die ("Error in query: $query. " .
                ⇒mysql_error());

                // reset all internal counters and arrays
                $values = array();
                $currentTag = "";
        }

}

// called when parser finds cdata
function characterDataHandler($parser, $data)
{

        global $currentTag, $values, $allowedFields;
        // lowercase tag name
        $currentTag = strtolower($currentTag);

        // look for tag in $allowedFields[] array
        // to see if it is to be included in query
        if (in_array($currentTag, $allowedFields) && trim($data) != "")
        {
                // add field=>value pairs to $values array
                $values[$currentTag] = mysql_escape_string($data);
        }
}

// initialize parser
```

```
$xml_parser = xml_parser_create();

// turn off whitespace processing
xml_parser_set_option($xml_parser,XML_OPTION_SKIP_WHITE, TRUE);
// turn on case folding
xml_parser_set_option($xml_parser, XML_OPTION_CASE_FOLDING, FALSE);

// set callback functions
xml_set_element_handler($xml_parser, "startElementHandler", "endElementHandler");
xml_set_character_data_handler($xml_parser, "characterDataHandler");

// open connection to database
$connection = mysql_connect($host, $user, $pass) or die ("Unable to connect!");
mysql_select_db($db) or die ("Unable to select database!");

// read XML file
if (!($fp = fopen($xml_file, "r")))
{
    die("File I/O error: $xml_file");
}

// parse XML
while ($data = fread($fp, 4096))
{
    // error handler
    if (!xml_parse($xml_parser, $data, feof($fp)))
    {
        $error_code = xml_get_error_code($xml_parser);
        die("XML parser error (error code " . $error_code . "): " .
        ⇥xml_error_string($error_code) . "<br>Error occurred at line " .
        ⇥xml_get_current_line_number($xml_parser));
    }
}

// all done, clean up!
xml_parser_free($xml_parser);
mysql_close($connection);

?>
```

Again, most of this should already be familiar to you from Chapter 2, but I'll run through the highlights quickly anyway.

1. An instance of the SAX parser is initialized and configured to invoke the callback functions startElementHandler(), endElementHandler(), and cdataHandler() when it encounters starting elements, ending elements, and character data respectively:

   ```
   $xml_parser = xml_parser_create();
   xml_set_element_handler($xml_parser, "startElementHandler",
   "endElementHandler");
   xml_set_character_data_handler($xml_parser, "characterDataHandler");
   ```

2. Because we already decided that this script is to be customized to the XML document presented in Listing 7.10, it's possible to clearly identify which XML elements contain the data we're interested in at the outset, and write code to handle these elements appropriately. A study of the XML data in Listing 7.10 reveals that the elements `<title>`, `<author>`, and `<book>` hold the information that is to be inserted into the database; consequently, every time the parser finds character data, it must first check the corresponding element name. If it matches any of the three names listed previously, it adds the element-value pair to the associative array `$values`.

```
if (in_array($currentTag, $allowedFields) && trim($data) != "")
{
    // add field=>value pairs to $values array
    $values[$currentTag] = mysql_escape_string($data);
}
```

3. When the parser encounters a closing item element—indicating the end of a particular record—the elements of the `$values` array are manipulated to create a single query string, which is then applied to the database via PHP's `mysql_query()` function:

```
if (strtolower($name) == "item")
{
    $query = "INSERT INTO books";
    $query .= "(title, author, blurb) ";
    $query .= "VALUES(\"" . join("\", \"", $values) . "\");";

    $result = mysql_query($query) or die ("Error in query: $query. " .
    ➥mysql_error());
}
```

4. After all the elements within the document have been processed, the parser is terminated, and the database connection is closed.

```
xml_parser_free($xml_parser);
mysql_close($connection);
```

Listing 7.12 demonstrates the output of this script.

Listing 7.12 **A Series of SQL Statements Dynamically Generated from an XML File**

```
INSERT INTO books(title, author, blurb) VALUES("Waking Up With The Red-Eyed Bed
➥Monster", "J. I. M. Somniac", "The blood-chillingly true story of one man\'s
➥fight against the monsters under his bed.");

INSERT INTO books(title, author, blurb) VALUES("The Case Of The Hungry
➥Hippopotamus", "P. I. Hardhat", "A tough private eye is hired to solve the most
➥challenging case of his career.");
```

```
INSERT INTO books(title, author, blurb) VALUES("Making Money, Losing Friends",
➥"T. Backstabber", "The bestselling self-help book for corporate executives on
➥the fast track.");

INSERT INTO books(title, author, blurb) VALUES("The Idiot\'s Guide to Sandwiches",
➥"B. L. Tuhmatto", "Making tasty sandwiches has never been so easy!");
```

Now, Listing 7.11 makes certain assumptions about the field names and the number of values in each SQL statement. These assumptions may not always be true, so let's see if we can develop something a little more generic by using the XML document in Listing 7.13 as the base.

Listing 7.13 **A More Generic XML Table Representation** (*data.xml*)

```
<?xml version="1.0"?>
<table name="readings">
        <record>
                <a>56</a>
                <b>1222</b>
                <c>78.5</c>
        </record>
        <record>
                <x>45</x>
                <y>-10</y>
        </record>
        <record>
                <x>12</x>
                <b>10459</b>
                <a>756</a>
                <y>9</y>
        </record>
</table>
```

This XML document is a little more generic than the one demonstrated in Listing 7.10. The table name is specified as an attribute of the document element `<table>`, whereas individual table records are enclosed within `<record>` elements. Every record contains a series of field names (elements) and field values (character data). The field names within each `<record>` may be variable, as may be the total number of fields per record.

Listing 7.14 builds on the basic concepts demonstrated in Listing 7.11 and the generic XML document described in Listing 7.13 to create a more generic parser—one that makes no assumptions about the number of values in each record, and retrieves the field names from the XML data itself (rather than having them hard-coded into the script).

Listing 7.14   **A More Generic XML-to-SQL Converter**

```php
<?php
// initialize some variables
$currentTag = "";

// these two arrays will hold the fields and values for the SQL statement
$fields = array();
$values = array();

// XML file to parse
$xml_file="data.xml";

// database parameters
// get these via user input
$host = "localhost";
$user = "john";
$pass = "doe";
$db = "db423";

// called when parser finds start tag
function startElementHandler($parser, $name, $attributes)
{
    global $currentTag, $table;
    $currentTag = $name;

    // get table name
    if (strtolower($currentTag) == "table")
    {
        $table = $attributes["name"];
    }

}

// called when parser finds end tag
function endElementHandler($parser, $name)
{
    global $fields, $values, $count, $currentTag;

    // import database link and table name
    global $connection, $table;

    // if </record> tag
    // implies end of record
    if (strtolower($name) == "record")
    {
        // generate the query string
        $query = "INSERT INTO $table";
        $query .= "(" . join(", ", $fields) . ")";
        $query .= " VALUES(\"" . join("\", \"", $values) . "\");";
```

```
                // uncomment for debug
                // print $query;

                // execute query
                mysql_query($query) or die ("Error in query: $query. " .
                ➥mysql_error());

                // reset all internal counters and arrays
                $fields = array();
                $values = array();
                $count = 0;
                $currentTag = "";
        }

}

// called when parser finds cdata
function characterDataHandler($parser, $data)
{
        global $fields, $values, $currentTag, $count;
        if (trim($data) != "")
        {
                // add field-value pairs to $fields and $values array
                // the index of each array is used to correlate the field-value pairs
                $fields[$count] = $currentTag;

                // escape quotes with slashes
                $values[$count] = mysql_escape_string($data);
                $count++;
        }
}


// initialize parser
$xml_parser = xml_parser_create();

// turn off whitespace processing
xml_parser_set_option($xml_parser,XML_OPTION_SKIP_WHITE, TRUE);
// turn on case folding
xml_parser_set_option($xml_parser, XML_OPTION_CASE_FOLDING, FALSE);

// set callback functions
xml_set_element_handler($xml_parser, "startElementHandler", "endElementHandler");
xml_set_character_data_handler($xml_parser, "characterDataHandler");

// open connection to database
$connection = mysql_connect($host, $user, $pass) or die ("Unable to connect!");
mysql_select_db($db) or die ("Unable to select database!");
```

continues

Listing 7.14 **Continued**

```
// read XML file
if (!($fp = fopen($xml_file, "r")))
{
     die("File I/O error: $xml_file");
}

// parse XML
while ($data = fread($fp, 4096))
{
     // error handler
     if (!xml_parse($xml_parser, $data, feof($fp)))
     {
          $ec = xml_get_error_code($xml_parser);
          die("XML parser error (error code " . $ec . "): " .
          ➥xml_error_string($ec) . "<br>Error occurred at line " .
          ➥xml_get_current_line_number($xml_parser));
     }
}

// all done, clean up!
xml_parser_free($xml_parser);
mysql_close($connection);

?>
```

This is fairly involved, so an explanation is in order:

1. The first step is to set up a bunch of required variables: the name of the XML
    file to be parsed, database access parameters, and so on. Note that, unlike Listing
    7.11, there's no need to specify a table name here—that information will be
    sourced directly from the XML document.

    ```
    $currentTag = "";
    $fields = array();
    $values = array();
    $host = "localhost";
    $user = "john";
    $pass = "doe";
    $db = "db423";
    ```

2. Next, the SAX parser is initialized, parsing options are set, and callback functions
    are defined:

    ```
    $xml_parser = xml_parser_create();
    xml_parser_set_option($xml_parser,XML_OPTION_SKIP_WHITE, TRUE);
    xml_parser_set_option($xml_parser, XML_OPTION_CASE_FOLDING, FALSE);
    xml_set_element_handler($xml_parser, "startElementHandler",
    ➥"endElementHandler");
    xml_set_character_data_handler($xml_parser, "characterDataHandler");
    ```

A connection is also opened to the database in preparation for the queries that will follow:

```
$connection = mysql_connect($host, $user, $pass) or die ("Unable to
↩connect!");
mysql_select_db($db) or die ("Unable to select database!");
```

3. With everything in place, we're ready to roll. The xml_parse() function is used to parse the XML data, invoking the specified callback functions as it finds elements and character data in the document.

    ```
    xml_parse($xml_parser, $data, feof($fp));
    ```

4. Every time the parser encounters a start tag, it invokes the startTagHandler() function, which assigns the element name to the $currentTag variable and makes it globally available to other functions in the script (specifically, to the characterDataHandler() function, which is the only one that actually uses it). It also checks the element name to see whether it is the document element <table>; if so, it retrieves the table name.

    ```
    $currentTag = $name;
    // get table name
    if (strtolower($currentTag) == "table")
    {
          $table = $attributes["name"];
    }
    ```

5. Whenever the parser encounters character data, it creates a field-value pair, placing the element (field) name—available from the $currentTag variable—in the $fields array, and the character data (value) in the corresponding slot in the $values array.

    ```
    $fields[$count] = $currentTag;
    $values[$count] = mysql_escape_string($data);
    ```

6. After the parser hits the end of an individual record—a closing <record> element—the end tag handler uses the collected field-value pairs to build an INSERT statement, and executes this statement via a call to the mysql_query() function. It then resets all the variables used—$currentTag and the field and value arrays—in preparation for parsing the next record.

    ```
    if (strtolower($name) == "record")
    {
          $query = "INSERT INTO $table";
          $query .= "(" . join(", ", $fields) . ")";
          $query .= "VALUES(\"" . join("\", \"", $values) . "\");";
          mysql_query($query) or die ("Error in query: $query. " .
          ↩mysql_error());
    }
    ```

7. After parsing has concluded, both the parser and the database connection are
    gracefully terminated.

```
xml_parser_free($xml_parser);
mysql_close($connection);
```

Looking Ahead

If you found Listing 7.14 interesting, you'll probably also enjoy the section on Metabase in Chapter 9,
"Case Studies."

Listing 7.15 demonstrates the output.

Listing 7.15   **A Series of SQL Statements Generated from an XML File**

```
INSERT INTO readings(a, b, c) VALUES("56", "1222", "78.5");

INSERT INTO readings(x, y) VALUES("45", "-10");

INSERT INTO readings(x, b, a, y) VALUES("12", "10459", "756", "9");
```

Now, although this is fairly complicated, it works quite well. But don't be fooled
into thinking it's the only way—if there's anything this chapter demonstrates, it's
that the XML/PHP combination offers more than one way to skin a cat. In this
case, cat-skinning technique number two involves using an XSLT stylesheet to
generate the query string, with PHP standing by to actually execute the query.

Dynamically Constructing SQL Queries from an XML Document with XSLT

As you may already know, XSLT provides an efficient, powerful mechanism to transform
an XML document into a new result document—here, a series of SQL statements. A
number of basic XSLT constructs—including loops, conditional statements, and XPath
node tests—are available to accomplish this. They are used with great success in Listing
7.16, which lists the complete stylesheet code to perform this transformation.

Listing 7.16   **An XSLT Stylesheet to Construct *SQL INSERT* Statements (*sql.xsl*)**

```
<?xml version="1.0"?>
<xsl:stylesheet version="1.0" xmlns:xsl="http://www.w3.org/1999/XSL/Transform">

<!-- output as text, strip whitespace -->
<xsl:output method="text" indent="no" />
<xsl:strip-space elements="*"/>

<!-- look for the table node  -->
<xsl:template match="/table" >
        <!-- iterate through each record -->
        <xsl:for-each select="record">
```

```
<!-- get the table name -->
<xsl:text>INSERT INTO </xsl:text>
<xsl:value-of select="/table/@name" />
<xsl:text>(</xsl:text>

<!-- iterate through child elements and get field names -->
<xsl:for-each select="child::*">
      <xsl:value-of select="name()" />
      <xsl:if test="position() != last()">, </xsl:if>
</xsl:for-each>

<xsl:text>) VALUES(</xsl:text>

<!-- iterate through child elements and get values -->
<xsl:for-each select="child::*">
      <xsl:text>"</xsl:text>
      <xsl:value-of select="." />
      <xsl:text>"</xsl:text>
      <xsl:if test="position() != last()">
            <xsl:text>,</xsl:text>
      </xsl:if>
</xsl:for-each>

   <xsl:text>);</xsl:text>

   </xsl:for-each>
</xsl:template>

</xsl:stylesheet>
```

Listing 7.17 processes this stylesheet using PHP's XSLT API.

Listing 7.17 **An XSLT-Based XML-to-SQL Converter**

```
<?php

// XML file
$xml_file = "data.xml";

// XSLT stylesheet
$xslt_file = "sql.xsl";

// database parameters
$host = "localhost";
$user = "john";
$pass = "doe";
$db = "db423";
```

continues

Listing 7.17 **Continued**

```php
// create the XSLT processor
$xp = xslt_create() or die("Could not create XSLT processor");

// process the two files to get the desired output
if($result = xslt_process($xp, $xml_file, $xslt_file))
{
    // uncomment for debug
    // echo $result;

    // open connection to database
    $connection = mysql_connect($host, $user, $pass) or die ("Unable to
    ➥connect!");
    mysql_select_db($db) or die ("Unable to select database!");

    // split XSLT output into individual queries
    $queries = explode(";", $result);

    // execute each query
    foreach($queries as $query)
    {
        if(!empty($query))
        {
            mysql_query($query) or die ("Error in query: $query. " .
            ➥mysql_error());
        }
    }

    // close database connection
    mysql_close($connection);
}
else
{
    // else display error
    echo "An error occurred: " . xslt_error($xp) . "(error code " .
    ➥xslt_errno($xp) . ")";
}

// clean up
xslt_free($xp);
?>
```

In this case, the output from the XSL Transformation is equivalent to that in Listing 7.15—a series of SQL statements, returned as a single string. These SQL statements are separated from each other and individually executed via PHP's `mysql_query()` function.

Things to Do on a Rainy Day

Obviously, INSERT statements aren't the only types of SQL statements you can build—it's just as easy to dynamically construct UPDATE and DELETE statements from XML data. And you don't have to do it using just SAX or XSLT either—this type of conversion lends itself very well to DOM-type tree traversal and node manipulation. PHP's DOM extension represents every node on the DOM tree as an object, exposing properties such as the element name and value; consequently, it's not too hard to manipulate these properties to build an INSERT or UPDATE statement.

In order to gain a better understanding of the XML-to-SQL conversion process, you should attempt to duplicate the preceding examples using the DOM; for variety, try constructing a series of UPDATE instead of INSERT statements.

Summary

This chapter took an in-depth look at the relationship between PHP, XML, and databases, and demonstrated how to encode database records as XML, and vice-versa. In an attempt to assist developers in choosing the appropriate technology for their specific requirements, it first evaluated the pros and cons of each approach, examining the two technologies vis-à-vis each other. Then, forsaking theory for in-depth, practical examples, it built on your knowledge of SAX, XSLT, and the DOM to illustrate how painless the conversion process is, and how many different ways there are to accomplish it.

And speaking of choice, you'll be interested to hear that the next chapter offers you even more of it, exploring some of the alternatives available to simplify XML-based application development with PHP. Most of these alternatives are open-source projects, and some of them give PHP's native XML functions a serious run for their money.

*"The absence of alternatives clears
the mind marvelously"*

~HENRY KISSINGER

8

Open Source PHP/XML Alternatives

THE NICE THING ABOUT THE OPEN SOURCE community is that you're never short of choices. This is particularly true in the case of a language such as PHP, which allows developers tremendous freedom in extending and contributing to the core API. This open source approach has been the driving force behind PHP's popularity, and has also led to the creation of a huge pool of robust, free PHP widgets by independent developers all over the planet.

That's where this chapter comes in—it discusses alternative implementations of the PHP functions described in earlier chapters. Created by PHP developers from around the world and released to the community at large, these implementations make it possible to perform advanced XML processing with PHP—even in environments in which PHP's native XML extensions are not supported!

This chapter examines four popular open source XML/PHP implementations, each designed to meet a specific requirement. In addition to a brief description of the way each works, this chapter also re-creates examples from previous chapters using these non-native implementations, in order to demonstrate their viability in the real world.

Alternatives to PHP's Native Functions: What You Should Know

Before getting into the details of different PHP-XML implementations, I'd like to take a few minutes to answer a very basic question, one which may already have occurred to you: Why, really, do you need to know about alternatives to PHP's built-in XML functions?

The short answer? Most of the time, you don't. As demonstrated in previous chapters of this book, PHP comes with a remarkably full-featured library of functions designed to streamline the process of creating, parsing, and processing XML documents. These functions address most of the tasks XML developers have to grapple with—everything from parsing and formatting XML documents to using XML to represent and pass data between systems—in a simple and efficient manner, and are frequently updated to keep pace with emerging XML technologies and new developments in the field.

As you've seen, though, many of PHP's XML extensions aren't enabled by default, and activating them typically requires you to recompile your PHP build. As long as you're working in a development environment that's controlled by you, this isn't a big deal—you can just reconfigure PHP and compile a new build that supports the functions you need (instructions for doing this are available in Appendix A, "Recompiling PHP to Add XML Support"). But when you're working in an environment that isn't under your control (for example, your web hosting provider's Internet server), then the situation gets a little more complicated.

There are a couple of very important differences between developing software on a system you control, and developing software on a system controlled by someone else. In the former case, you typically have superuser privileges, which allow you to compile and install anything you like, whenever and wherever you like, on the system. Superuser privileges also allow you to customize the development environment to your needs, altering system configuration files and environment variables with abandon, and to update system libraries with newer versions as they become available.

Web hosting services, especially those that host multiple domains on a single server, are far less accommodating to developers. Such services typically decide on a standard development environment for each server, and offer this standard package to all customer web sites hosted on that server. This development environment may not have all the features you need; in fact, it may not even contain all the software you need! But as one customer among many, there's not much you can do about it.

Sensitive to both security and performance issues, most hosting services are also loathe to install "bleeding-edge" software on their systems (or let you do it for them). This can seriously hamper your ability to develop software that takes advantage of new features in vibrant, rapidly evolving open source projects. And, because your activities on these shared servers are restricted, you're again dependent on your service provider for software updates and upgrades. Some providers make it a point to update their software every few months, whereas others are far less attentive to the problem (and their customers).

Of course, this problem can easily be solved by throwing money at it: Buy (or rent) a server of your own, hook it up to the Internet, and download-compile-install to your heart's content. Most professional software development companies adopt this approach; however, smaller companies and independent developers may not find it economically viable.

When it comes to PHP, the problem is exacerbated by the diverse range of extensions and libraries available for the language. The standard PHP build offered by your hosting service may not be tuned to your specific needs or contain support for all the extensions you require—and, most of the time, your only option is to grin and bear it.

Or is it?

In the best traditions of open source software, the PHP developer community is constantly creating and releasing new and innovative PHP libraries to the Web. Some of these libraries are specifically targeted at developers working with XML and PHP and are produced as alternatives to PHP's native XML functions. All of them are available free of charge and can be integrated into a PHP application with minimal difficulty (you don't need to recompile your PHP build to use them, which makes them very useful in restricted development environments). If you're faced with the kind of situation described previously, and if your pleas for a software upgrade are falling on deaf ears, you might find them handy. Take a look.

Buyer Beware!

It should be noted at the outset that this chapter is neither an exhaustive list of XML/PHP alternatives available on the Web, nor a definitive API reference or programming guide to the software implementations showcased within it. Given the speed at which new software appears (and disappears) online, such an attempt would invariably be both incomplete and inaccurate. Rather, the goal of this chapter is merely to demonstrate some of the alternatives available to XML/PHP developers, and to briefly discuss (via examples and code listings) how they may be used in application development.

Note also that all the implementations discussed in this chapter require a PHP build that has been compiled with basic XML support. This support is included by default in PHP 4.x.

An Alternative PHP/DOM Implementation: eZXML

A DOM parser written in PHP, the eZXML class provides a primitive, though effective, alternative to PHP's native DOM extension. Developed as part of a larger publishing system by eZ Systems, it is freely available under the GPL from http://developer.ez.no/.

Version Control

All the examples in this section use version 1.0.3 of the eZXML class.

The eZXML class works in much the same way as PHP's native DOM library, creating a series of nested objects to represent the structure of an XML document. Each of these objects exposes standard properties, which can be used to traverse the object tree; and access specific elements, attributes, or data. In order to illustrate how this works, consider the simple XML document in Listing 8.1.

Listing 8.1   **A Simple XML Document (*list.xml*)**

```
<?xml version="1.0"?>
<shoppinglist>
     <item quantity="1">cauldron</item>
     <item quantity="5">eye of newt</item>
     <item quantity="1">tail of lizard</item>
     <item quantity="24">bat wings</item>
</shoppinglist>
```

The eZXML class can be used to read this XML document and convert it into a PHP structure, as Listing 8.2 demonstrates.

Listing 8.2   **Creating an Object Representation of an XML Document with eZXML**

```
<?php

// include class definition
include("ezxml.php");

// XML file
$xml_file = "list.xml";

// parse XML file into single string
$xml_string = join("", file($xml_file));

// create Document object
$doc = eZXML::domTree($xml_string, array("TrimWhiteSpace" => "true"));

// print structure
// uncomment the next line to view the object created
// print_r($doc);

?>
```

The domTree() method of the eZXML class accepts an XML string as input and returns an object representing the XML document. This returned object is itself a collection of node objects, each one containing information about the corresponding XML node. (You can examine the structure of the returned object by uncommenting the last line of Listing 8.2.) This information, accessible as object properties, can be used to process the XML document, either to modify its structure or to format the data contained within it. For example, every node object comes with `name`, `content`, `type`, and `children` properties, which can be used to obtain information on the corresponding XML node name, value, type (whether element, attribute or text), and children respectively.

In order to demonstrate this, let's try something a little more complicated: converting an XML document into HTML. Consider Listing 8.3, which contains an invoice marked up in XML.

Listing 8.3 **An XML Invoice (*invoice.xml*)**

```
<?xml version="1.0"?>

<invoice>

    <customer>
        <name>Joe Wannabe</name>
        <address>
            <line>23, Great Bridge Road</line>
            <line>Bombay, MH</line>
            <line>India</line>
        </address>
    </customer>

    <date>2001-09-15</date>

    <reference>75-848478-98</reference>

    <items>
        <item cid="AS633225">
            <desc>Oversize tennis racquet</desc>
            <price>235.00</price>
            <quantity>1</quantity>
            <subtotal>235.00</subtotal>
        </item>

        <item cid="GT645">
            <desc>Championship tennis balls (can)</desc>
            <price>9.99</price>
            <quantity>4</quantity>
            <subtotal>39.96</subtotal>
        </item>
```

continues

Listing 8.3   **Continued**

```
                <item cid="U73472">
                        <desc>Designer gym bag</desc>
                        <price>139.99</price>
                        <quantity>1</quantity>
                        <subtotal>139.99</subtotal>
                </item>

                <item cid="AD848383">
                        <desc>Custom-fitted sneakers</desc>
                        <price>349.99</price>
                        <quantity>1</quantity>
                        <subtotal>349.99</subtotal>
                </item>
        </items>

        <delivery>Next-day air</delivery>

</invoice>
```

Listing 8.4 parses this XML document, replacing XML elements with corresponding
HTML markup to create an HTML document suitable for display in a web browser.
(Note that as of this writing, the eZXML class cannot handle processing instructions,
and so simply ignores them.)

Listing 8.4   **Converting an XML Document into HTML with eZXML**

```
<html>
<head>
<basefont face="Arial">
</head>
<body bgcolor="white">

<font size="+3">Sammy's Sports Store</font>
<br>
<font size="-2">14, Ocean View, CA 12345, USA http://www.sammysportstore.com/</font>
<p>
<hr>
<center>INVOICE</center>
<hr>
<?php

// include class definition
include("ezxml.php");

// arrays to associate XML elements with HTML output
$startTagsArray = array(
'CUSTOMER' => '<p> <b>Customer: </b>',
'ADDRESS' => '<p> <b>Billing address: </b>',
'DATE' => '<p> <b>Invoice date: </b>',
```

```
'REFERENCE' => '<p> <b>Invoice number: </b>',
'ITEMS' => '<p> <b>Details: </b> <table width="100%" border="1" cellspacing="0"
➥cellpadding="3"><tr><td><b>Item description</b></td><td><b>Price</b></td>
➥<td><b>Quantity</b></td><td><b>Sub-total</b></td></tr>',
'ITEM' => '<tr>',
'DESC' => '<td>',
'PRICE' => '<td>',
'QUANTITY' => '<td>',
'SUBTOTAL' => '<td>',
'DELIVERY' => '<p> <b>Shipping option:</b> ',
'TERMS' => '<p> <b>Terms and conditions: </b> <ul>',
'TERM' => '<li>'
);

$endTagsArray = array(
'LINE' => ', ',
'ITEMS' => '</table>',
'ITEM' => '</tr>',
'DESC' => '</td>',
'PRICE' => '</td>',
'QUANTITY' => '</td>',
'SUBTOTAL' => '</td>',
'TERMS' => '</ul>',
'TERM' => '</li>'
);

// XML file
$xml_file = "invoice.xml";

// read file into string
$xml_string = join("", file($xml_file));

// parse XML string and create object
$doc = eZXML::domTree($xml_string, array("TrimWhiteSpace" => "true"));

// start printing
print_tree($doc->children);

// this recursive function accepts an array of nodes as argument,
// iterates through it and:
//        - marks up elements with HTML
//        - prints text as is
function print_tree($nodeCollection)
{
    global $startTagsArray, $endTagsArray, $subTotals;

    for ($x=0; $x<sizeof($nodeCollection); $x++)
    {
```

continues

Listing 8.4   **Continued**

```
              // how to handle elements
              if ($nodeCollection[$x]->type == 1)
              {
                    // print HTML opening tags
                    echo $startTagsArray[strtoupper($nodeCollection[$x]->name)];

                    // recurse
                    print_tree($nodeCollection[$x]->children);

                    // once done, print closing tags
                    echo $endTagsArray[strtoupper($nodeCollection[$x]->name)];
              }


              // how to handle text nodes
              if ($nodeCollection[$x]->type == 3)
              {
                    // print text as is
                    echo($nodeCollection[$x]->content);
              }

      // PIs are ignored by the class


        }
    }

?>
</body>
</html>
```

Wondering why this looks familiar? That's because it's a rewrite of an example from Chapter 3, "PHP and the Document Object Model (DOM)." That example (Listing 3.10) used PHP's native DOM library to perform the conversion from XML to HTML; this one uses the eZXML class to achieve the same result.

Very simply, the XML invoice in Listing 8.3 is converted into a structured object representation by eZXML, and the print_tree() function is used to recursively iterate through this object and display the content within it, with appropriate markup. The information needed to map a specific XML element into corresponding HTML markup is stored in the PHP associative arrays $startTagsArray and $endTagsArray.

If you have a few minutes to spare, you might want to compare Listing 8.4 with the original version in Listing 3.10 in order to better understand the differences between the two approaches.

Although the eZXML class does not have all the bells and whistles of PHP's native DOM extension, it can (as Listing 8.4 demonstrated) nevertheless be used to perform some fairly complex XML processing. If you're looking for a functional DOM implementation for your PHP project, this one is worth a look.

An Alternative PHP/XPath Implementation: PHP.XPath

In the words of its developers, PHP.XPath is " . . . a PHP class for searching an XML document using XPath, and making modifications using a DOM style API . . . [it] does not require the DOM XML PHP library"[1]. The class, which is maintained as an open source project on the SourceForge network (http://www.sourceforge.net) by Nigel Swinson, Sam Blum, and Daniel Allen, is released under the Mozilla Public License, and is freely downloadable from http://www.sourceforge.net/projects/phpxpath.

As the previous description suggests, there isn't anything very complicated about the PHP.XPath class. It accepts XML data (either a file or a string) as argument, parses the data, and creates an object representing the XML document. The methods exposed by this object allow developers to create XML nodesets based on XPath expressions; add, edit, and delete nodes from the document tree; and extract character data embedded within specific XML elements. In order to demonstrate how the class works, let's consider a simple example (see Listing 8.5).

Listing 8.5   **A simple XML Document (*market.xml*)**

```
<?xml version="1.0"?>
<sentence>
Today in the market, I spy
<vegetable color='green'>cabbages</vegetable>,
<fruit color='red'>apples</fruit>,
<fruit color='green'>pears</fruit>,
<vegetable color='purple'>aubergines</vegetable>, and
<fruit color='orange'>oranges</fruit>
</sentence>
```

The Number Game

All the examples in this section use version 2.1 of the PHP.XPath class.

1. SourceForge.net. "Project: PHP.XPath Summary." Available from the Internet: http://www.sourceforge.net/projects/phpxpath.

Listing 8.6 demonstrates using the PHP.XPath class to obtain a collection of all the <fruit> elements within the document (via an XPath expression), and print the contents of each of these elements in an HTML list.

Listing 8.6 **Extracting a Node Collection from an XML Document with PHP.XPath**

```
<html>
<head></head>
<body>

The following fruits were encountered in this document:
<ul>
<?php

// include class
require("XPath.class.php");


/*
the first step is to instantiate an object of the class

the constructor accepts the name of an XML file as argument;
it then parses this XML file and creates a context for subsequent XPath queries
*/

$xpath = new XPath("market.xml");


/*
next, retrieve a collection of <fruit> nodes

the match() method accepts an XPath expression as argument,
and returns a node collection matching that expression, as an array
*/

$nodeCollection = $xpath->match("//fruit");


// want to see what it looks like?
// uncomment the following line
// print_r($nodeCollection);


/*
finally, iterate through the returned node collection
and print the content of each node

the getData() method returns the content (character data)
of a particular node
*/
```

```
foreach($nodeCollection as $node)
{
     echo  "<li>" . $xpath->getData($node);
}
?>
</ul>
</body>
</html>
```

The PHP.XPath class exposes a number of different methods; however, the two you're likely to use most often are the match() and getData() methods. The match() method evaluates a specific XPath expression within the context of the selected XML document and returns an array of nodes matching the expression; whereas the getData() method extracts the content, or character data, of a specified node.

With this fundamental understanding in place, it's possible to use the PHP.XPath class for even more complex operations. In order to illustrate this, I will rewrite the data tabulation program first seen in Listing 3.12, using the PHP.XPath class instead of PHP's native DOM and XPath functions. Listing 8.7 contains the XML source, which needs to be collated, averaged, and presented in a 2x2 table.

Listing 8.7   **A Compilation of Experiment Readings (*data.xml*)**

```
<?xml version="1.0"?>
<project id="49">

     <!-- data for 3 cultures: Alpha, Beta and Gamma, tested at temperatures
     ➥ranging from 10C to 50C -->
     <!-- readings indicate cell counts 4 hours after start of experiment -->

     <record>
          <culture>Alpha</culture>
          <temperature>10</temperature>
          <reading>25000</reading>
     </record>

     <record>
          <culture>Beta</culture>
          <temperature>10</temperature>
          <reading>4000</reading>
     </record>

     <record>
          <culture>Alpha</culture>
          <temperature>10</temperature>
```

continues

Listing 8.7 **Continued**

```
        <reading>23494</reading>
    </record>

    <record>
        <culture>Alpha</culture>
        <temperature>20</temperature>
        <reading>21099</reading>
    </record>

    <record>
        <culture>Gamma</culture>
        <temperature>40</temperature>
        <reading>768</reading>
    </record>

    <record>
        <culture>Gamma</culture>
        <temperature>10</temperature>
        <reading>900</reading>
    </record>

    <!-- snip -->
</project>
```

Listing 8.8 has the code that actually does all the work.

Listing 8.8 **Averaging and Tabulating Experiment Readings with PHP.XPath**

```
<html>
<head>
<basefont face="Arial">
</head>
<body bgcolor="white">
<?php

// include class definition
require("XPath.class.php");

// XML file
$xml_file = "data.xml";

// create arrays to hold culture/temperature list
$cultures = array();
$temperatures = array();

// create XPath object
$xpath = new XPath($xml_file);
```

```php
// get a list of "culture" nodes
$nodeset = $xpath->match("//culture");

// ...and create an array containing
// the names of all available cultures
for ($x=0; $x<sizeof($nodeset); $x++)
{
    $cultures[] = $xpath->getData($nodeset[$x]);
}

// strip out duplicates
$cultures = array_unique($cultures);

// do the same thing for temperature points
$nodeset = $xpath->match("//temperature");

for ($x=0; $x<sizeof($nodeset); $x++)
{
    $temperatures[] = $xpath->getData($nodeset[$x]);
}

$temperatures = array_unique($temperatures);

// sort both arrays
natsort($temperatures);
natsort($cultures);
?>
<table border="1" cellspacing="5" cellpadding="5">

<tr>
<td> </td>
<?php
// first row of table, print culture names
foreach($cultures as $c)
{
    echo "<td>$c</td>";
}
?>
</tr>

<?php
foreach($temperatures as $t)
{
    // create as many rows as there are temperature points
    echo "<tr>";
    echo "<td>$t</td>";

    // for each intersection (culture, temperature)
    // print average of available readings
    foreach($cultures as $c)
    {
```

continues

Listing 8.8 **Continued**

```php
        echo "<td>" . intersection($t, $c) . "</td>";
    }

    echo "</tr>";
}
?>

</table>

<?php
// this function collects all readings for
// a particular culture/temperature
// totals them and averages them
function intersection($temperature, $culture)
{
    // get a reference to the XPath object
    global $xpath;

    // set up variables to hold total and frequency
    $total = 0;
    $count = 0;

    // get a list of "reading" nodes
    // for records with culture c and temperature t
    $nodeset = $xpath->match("//record[culture='" . $culture . "' and
➥temperature='" . $temperature . "']/reading");

    // iterate through nodeset
    // add the readings
    foreach ($nodeset as $reading)
    {
        $total += $xpath->getData($reading);
        $count++;
    }

    // and then average them
    if ($count > 0)
    {
        return $total/$count;
    }

    return 0;
}

?>
</body>
</html>
```

Listing 8.8 uses three different XPath expressions. The first two are used to create a list of available cultures and temperature points (they are required for the row and column headings of the table), whereas the third XPath returns a list of nodes matching a specific culture and temperature. With all this in place, all that's left is to add the readings associated with each of these nodes to reach a total number, and divide that total number by the number of nodes (readings) to obtain an average cell count.

Again, most of the work here is done by the match() and getData() methods, which make it possible to easily create subsets of XML elements matching a specific criteria, and retrieve the data contained within them.

This is just one example of many. The PHP.XPath class comes with a remarkably full-featured API, which opens up numerous possibilities to the creative developer. Examples and documentation are available at the official web site for the project (http://www.sourceforge.net/projects/phpxpath), together with introductory material to get you started.

Plug In, Click Through

Drop by this book's companion web site for links to other open source XML/PHP alternatives.

An Alternative PHP/XML-RPC Implementation: XML-RPC for PHP

Before XML-RPC support appeared in PHP, Edd Dumbill's XML-RPC implementation was the only real choice for PHP developers working with the protocol. Powerful, flexible, and easy to use, this XML-RPC implementation provides developers with a full-featured alternative to the XML-RPC-EPI extension that first shipped with PHP 4.1.0. Released under the BSD license, it can be downloaded from http://phpxmlrpc.sourceforge.net/.

Completely object-oriented in nature, Edd Dumbill's implementation begins with the construction of a fundamental unit: an XML-RPC value, or xmlrpcval, object. This object is then used as the basis for other more complex objects: an XML-RPC request, or xmlrpcmsg, object; and an XML-RPC response, or xmlrpcresp, object. Finally, client and server objects are available to handle data transmission between the two ends of the XML-RPC connection.

In order to better understand this, consider Listing 8.9, which demonstrates the construction of an XML-RPC request using these objects.

Pre-Flight Check

All the examples in this section use version 1.02 of XML-RPC for PHP.

Listing 8.9   **Constructing an XML-RPC Request**

```php
<?php

// include the class definitions
include("xmlrpc.inc");

/*
create an instance of the xmlrpcmsg object

the xmlrpcmsg object constructor requires two parameters:
xmlrpcmsg(procedure, array of xmlrpcval objects)

the xmlrpcval object constructor also requires two parameters:
xmlrpcval(value, type)

allowed xmlrpcval types are "i4", "int", "boolean", "double", "string",
➡"dateTime.iso8601", "base64", "array", "struct";
*/

$rpc = new xmlrpcmsg("getRandomQuote", array(new xmlrpcval("Churchill", "string")));

/*
the serialize() method serializes the xmlrpcmsg object into an
XML representation, suitable for transmission to an XML-RPC server
*/

echo $rpc->serialize();
?>
```

Listing 8.9 uses two objects: the fundamental `xmlrpcval` object for argument values; and the `xmlrpcmsg` object, which uses the `xmlrpcval` object in the construction of a complete XML-RPC request. Listing 8.10 demonstrates the output.

Listing 8.10   **An XML-RPC Request**

```xml
<?xml version="1.0"?>
<methodCall>
     <methodName>getRandomQuote</methodName>
     <params>
          <param>
               <value>
                    <string>Churchill</string>
               </value>
          </param>
     </params>
</methodCall>
```

Construction of an XML-RPC response is accomplished in a similar manner, except that this time an xmlrpcresp object is used. Listing 8.11 demonstrates how such a response might be constructed.

Listing 8.11   **Constructing an XML-RPC Response**

```php
<?php
// include class definitions
include("xmlrpc.inc");

/*
create an instance of the xmlrpcresp object

the xmlrpcresp object constructor requires three parameters:
xmlrpcresp(return value as xmlrpcval object, fault code, fault string)
*/

$rpc = new xmlrpcresp(new xmlrpcval("A fanatic is one who won't change his mind
⇒and won't change the subject", "string"));


/*
the serialize() method serializes the xmlrpcresp object into an
XML representation, suitable for transmission to an XML-RPC client
*/

echo $rpc->serialize();
?>
```

Listing 8.12 demonstrates the output of Listing 8.11.

Listing 8.12   **An XML-RPC Response**

```xml
<methodResponse>
     <params>
          <param>
               <value>
                    <string>A fanatic is one who won't change his mind and
                    ⇒won't change the subject</string>
               </value>
          </param>
     </params>
</methodResponse>
```

With message construction out of the way, all that remains is the transmission layer for messages between the client and server. In this implementation, transmission is handled by two additional objects: xmlrpc_server and xmlrpc_client. They provide methods to send XML-RPC requests, receive XML-RPC responses, decode XML-RPC <value>s into native PHP data types, and log debug messages.

In order to illustrate how this works, consider Listing 8.13 and Listing 8.14, which re-create the meteorological server and client from Listing 6.26 and Listing 6.27, again bypassing PHP's native XML-RPC extension in favor of this object-based implementation. Listing 8.13 demonstrates the code for the server.

Listing 8.13 **A Simple XML-RPC Server**

```php
<?php
// include class definitions
include("xmlrpc.inc");
include("xmlrpcs.inc");

// create server object
// the object constructor is used to map public procedure names to internal
➥function names
$server = new xmlrpc_server(array("getWeatherData" => array("function" =>
➥"phpWeather")));

// function to retrieve weather data
// and return it in requested format (raw or average)
function phpWeather($params)
{
    // get reference to associative array passed to server by client
    $struct = $params->getParam(0);

    // get value of "city" key
    // the structmem() method returns a reference to a particular key of the array
    // the scalarval() method extracts the corresponding value
    $member = $struct->structmem("city");
    $city = $member->scalarval();

    // get value of "format" key
    $member = $struct->structmem("format");
    $format = $member->scalarval();

    // initialize error variables
    $error_msg = "";
    $error_code = 0;

    if (!$city)
    {
        // no city code available
        // set error flag
        $error_msg = "Missing city code";
        $error_code = 998;
    }
```

```
else
{
      // open connection to database
      $connection = mysql_connect("localhost", "rpc_agent", "secret") or
      ➥$error = "Unable to connect to database";
      mysql_select_db("weather_db") or $error = "Unable to select database";

      // get data
      $query = "SELECT t1, t2, t3 FROM weather WHERE city = '" . $city . "'";
      $result = mysql_query($query) or $error = "Error in query: $query. " .
      ➥mysql_error();

      // if a result is returned
      if (mysql_num_rows($result) > 0)
      {
      // get column values
            list($t1, $t2, $t3) = mysql_fetch_row($result);

            // close database connection
            mysql_close($connection);
      }
      else
      {
            // set error flag
            $error_msg = "No data available for that city";
            $error_code = 999;
      }
}

// if error flag set
if ($error_msg)
{
      // return an XML-RPC fault as an xmlrpcresp object
      return new xmlrpcresp(0, $error_code, $error_msg);
}
else
{
      // process data depending on requested output format
      if ($format == "raw")
      {
            // return raw data  as associative
            // array ("format" => $format, "data" = array($t1, $t2, $t3))

            // note that the xmlrpcresp object is constructed
            // from a collection of xmlrpcval objects
            $data = array(new xmlrpcval($t1, "int"), new xmlrpcval($t2,
            ➥"int"), new xmlrpcval($t3, "int"));
            $result = new xmlrpcval(array("format" => new xmlrpcval($format,
            ➥"string"), "data" => new xmlrpcval($data, "array")), "struct");
            return new xmlrpcresp($result);
```

continues

Listing 8.13 **Continued**

```
            }
            else if ($format == "avg")
            {
                    // total and average readings
                    $total = $t1 + $t2 + $t3;

                    // do this to avoid division by zero errors
                    if ($total != 0)
                    {
                            $avg = $total/3;
                    }
                    else
                    {
                            $avg = 0;
                    }

                    // return average as associative array ("format" => $format,
                    ➥"data" = $avg)
                    $result = new xmlrpcval(array("format" => new xmlrpcval($format,
                    ➥"string"), "data" => new xmlrpcval($avg, "int")), "struct");
                    return new xmlrpcresp($result);

            }
        }
    }

?>
```

And Listing 8.14 demonstrates the code for the client.

Listing 8.14 **A Simple XML–RPC Client**

```
<html>
<head>
<basefont face="Arial">
</head>

<body>


<?php
// form not yet submitted
// display form
if(!$_POST['submit'])
{
?>
```

```
        <form action="<? echo $_SERVER['PHP_SELF']; ?>" method="POST">
        <b>City code:</b>
        <br>
        <input type="text" name="city" size="4" maxlength="3">
        <p>
        <b>Data format:</b>
        <br>
        <input type="Radio" name="format" value="avg" checked>Average only
        <br>
        <input type="radio" name="format" value="raw">Raw data
        <p>
        <input type="submit" name="submit" value="Go!">
        </form>

<?php
}
else
{

        // include class definitions
        include("xmlrpc.inc");

        // construct array of parameters
        // this is an associative array of the form ("city" => $city, "format" =>
        ➥$format)
        $params = new xmlrpcval(array("city" => new xmlrpcval($_POST['city'],
        ➥"string"), "format" => new xmlrpcval($_POST['format'], "string")),
        ➥"struct");

        // create an XML-RPC request object
        $msg = new xmlrpcmsg("getWeatherData", array($params));

        // uncomment next line to see serialized request
        // echo $msg->serialize();

        // create an XML-RPC client
        // the object constructor requires the XML-RPC server location as parameters
        $client = new xmlrpc_client("/rpc/server.php", "weather.domain.com", 80);

        // uncomment next line to see client debug messages
        // $client->setDebug(1);

        // send RPC request, read response
        // the send() method is a transparent method to send data to the server
        // it returns the server's response as an xmlrpcresp object
        $response = $client->send($msg);

        // create xmlrpcval object to hold value
        $result = $response->value();
```

continues

Listing 8.14 **Continued**

```
// assuming no fault took place...
if (!$response->faultCode())
{
    // this object is an associative array
    // of form("format" => $format, "data" = array|scalar)
    // get the format
    $member = $result->structmem("format");
    $format = $member->scalarval();

    // check data format requested
    // if raw readings requested
    if ($format == "raw")
    {
        echo "Last three temperature readings for city $city (8-hour
        ➥intervals) are:<br><ul>";

        $member = $result->structmem("data");

        // iterate through data array and display values
        for($x=0; $x<$member->arraysize(); $x++)
        {
            $obj = $member->arraymem($x);
            echo "<li>" . $obj->scalarval();
        }

    echo "</ul>";
    }
    // if average reading requested
    else if ($format == "avg")
    {

        // display single value
        $member = $result->structmem("data");
        echo "Average temperature reading for city $city is " .
        ➥$member->scalarval() . " (based on three readings)";
    }

}
// if fault generated
// display fault information
else
{
    // the faultString() and faultCode() methods return
    // the error string and error code respectively
    echo  "The following error occurred: <br>";
    echo $response->faultString() . " (error code " . $response->faultCode() . ")";
```

```
      }
   }

?>
</body>
</html>
```

As demonstrated previously, both client and server objects come with specific methods to ease the task of transmitting an RPC request and decoding the response. A simple `send()` method handles most of the work at the client end of the connection, whereas ancillary methods such as `scalarval()`, `arraymem()`, and `structmem()` (designed specifically to manipulate composite XML-RPC data types such as `<struct>`s and `<array>`s) make it possible to easily convert these data types to native PHP structures.

An interesting item here are the addition of the `faultString()` and `faultCode()` methods, which allow developers to check for the presence of an XML-RPC fault in the server-generated response and take appropriate measures to handle this fault.

This XML-RPC implementation is one of the more robust and full-featured ones available online. In addition to basic RPC functions, it also includes a very capable introspection API, support for HTTPS transactions, and a number of utility functions for converting between PHP and XML-RPC data types. Finally, because it's been under development for awhile, it's also fairly well-documented; if you plan to use it in one of your projects, you might want to visit this book's companion web site, which offers links to articles and reference material on the topic to help you get started.

An Alternative PHP/SOAP Implementation: SOAPx4

SOAPx4 is a PHP implementation of the Simple Object Access Protocol (SOAP) and Web Services Description Language (WSDL). Developed by Dietrich Ayala, these two standards are implemented as a pair of PHP classes (one for the server, and one for the client), and are freely available under the GNU LGPL at `http://dietrich.ganx4.com/soapx4/`.

SOAPx4 uses an approach similar to that demonstrated in Edd Dumbill's XML-RPC implementation (discussed in the preceding section). Here too, the fundamental unit is a `soapval` object, which represents a single SOAP value. Multiple `soapval` objects can be built into a SOAP message, complete with header and body sections. This `soapmsg` object, once serialized, is suitable for transmission to any SOAP-compliant server or client.

Crunching Numbers

All the examples in this section use version 0.5 of SOAPx4.

Consider Listing 8.15, which demonstrates the construction of a SOAP request using these objects.

Listing 8.15 **Constructing a SOAP Request**

```php
<?php
// include class definitions
include("class.soap_client.php");

/*
create an instance of the soapval object
the soapval object constructor requires three parameters
soapval(name, type, value)
*/

$val = new soapval("author", "string", "Oscar Wilde");

/*
the serializeval() method serializes the value into XML
*/
// uncomment the line below to see the serialized value
// print $val->serializeval();

/*
create an instance of the soapmsg object
the soapmsg object constructor requires two parameters:
soapmsg(procedure, array of soapval objects)
*/

$msg = new soapmsg("getRandomQuote", array($val));

/*
the serialize() method creates a complete SOAP packet
*/

print $msg->serialize();
?>
```

Listing 8.16 demonstrates the SOAP packet resulting from Listing 8.15.

Listing 8.16 **A SOAP Request**

```
<xml version="1.0"?>
<SOAP-ENV:Envelope xmlns:SOAP-ENV="http://schemas.xmlsoap.org/soap/envelope/"
➥xmlns:xsd="http://www.w3.org/2001/XMLSchema" xmlns:xsi="http://www.w3.org/
➥2001/XMLSchema-instance" xmlns:SOAP-ENC="http://schemas.xmlsoap.org/soap/
➥encoding/" xmlns:si="http://soapinterop.org/xsd" xmlns:ns6="http://testuri.org"
➥SOAP-ENV:encodingStyle="http://schemas.xmlsoap.org/soap/encoding/">
     <SOAP-ENV:Body>
          <ns6:getRandomQuote>
```

```
            <author xsi:type="xsd:string">Oscar Wilde</author>
        </ns6:getRandomQuote>
    </SOAP-ENV:Body>
</SOAP-ENV:Envelope>
```

In a similar manner, it's also possible to construct a SOAP response. Listing 8.17 demonstrates how.

Listing 8.17 **Constructing a SOAP Response**

```php
<?php
// include class definitions
include("class.soap_client.php");

// create an instance of the soapval object
$val = new soapval("quote", "string", "One man's poetry is another man's poison");

// create an instance of the soapmsg object
// note that, in this implementation, the same object is used
// to create both requests and responses
$msg = new soapmsg("getRandomQuoteResponse", array($val));

// the serialize() method creates a SOAP packet
print $msg->serialize();
?>
```

And Listing 8.18 demonstrates the generated SOAP response.

Listing 8.18 **A SOAP Response**

```xml
<?xml version="1.0"?>
<SOAP-ENV:Envelope xmlns:SOAP-ENV="http://schemas.xmlsoap.org/soap/envelope/"
➡xmlns:xsd="http://www.w3.org/2001/XMLSchema" xmlns:xsi="http://www.w3.org/2001/
➡XMLSchema-instance" xmlns:SOAP-ENC="http://schemas.xmlsoap.org/soap/encoding/"
➡xmlns:si="http://soapinterop.org/xsd" xmlns:ns6="http://testuri.org"
➡SOAP-ENV:encodingStyle="http://schemas.xmlsoap.org/soap/encoding/">
    <SOAP-ENV:Body>
        <ns6:getRandomQuoteResponse>
            <quote xsi:type="xsd:string">One man's poetry is another man's
            ➡poison</quote>
        </ns6:getRandomQuoteResponse>
    </SOAP-ENV:Body>
</SOAP-ENV:Envelope>
```

SOAPx4 also includes two high-level classes, one to instantiate a server and the other to instantiate a client. These high-level classes substantially simplify the work involved in creating and manipulating SOAP requests and responses. In order to better demonstrate how these work, I'll use SOAPx4 to reprise the RPC-based mail service from Chapter 6, "PHP and XML-Based Remote Procedure Calls (RPC)," (Listing 6.29 and Listing 6.30). Listing 8.19 demonstrates the code for the SOAP server.

Listing 8.19 **A SOAP Server**

```php
<?php

// include class definitions
include("class.soap_client.php");
include("class.soap_server.php");

// instantiate a server object
$server = new soap_server;

// uncomment next line to see server debug messages
// $server->debug_flag = true;

/*
the add_to_map() method adds a procedure to the server's list
of exposed public methods

the second and third argument specify the data type of the input (arguments) to,
and output (return values) from, the procedure respectively.
*/

$server->add_to_map("getTotalPOP3Messages", array("SOAPStruct"), array("int"));

/*
the service() function services the SOAP request
and sends a SOAP response back to the client
*/

$server->service($HTTP_RAW_POST_DATA);

// function to return number of messages
function getTotalPOP3Messages($struct)
{
    // make sure the server supports POP3
    // if you're using PHP, you may need to recompile your build
    // to enable this support
    $inbox = imap_open ("{". $struct["pop_host"] . "/pop3:110}",
    ➥$struct["pop_user"], $struct["pop_pass"]);

    // if connection successfully opened
    if ($inbox)
    {
        // get number of messages
        $total = imap_num_msg($inbox);
        imap_close($inbox);
        return $total;
```

```
        }
        else
        {
                // else generate a SOAP fault
                $params = array("faultcode" => "75", "faultstring" => "No connection
            ➥available", "detail" => "Could not connect to POP3 server");
                $faultmsg  = new soapmsg("Fault", $params,
            ➥"http://schemas.xmlsoap.org/soap/envelope/");
                return $faultmsg;
        }


}

?>
```

There are two important methods to be aware of when using a SOAP server created
with the SOAPx4 class. After an instance of the server class has been created, the
add_to_map() method is used to register procedures with the server, together with
information on the expected data types of input arguments and return values. Then,
the service() method is used to service the incoming SOAP request and return a
SOAP packet containing the response.

The SOAP client at the other end of the connection needs to generate a SOAP
request and decode the response packet containing the results of the procedure call.
In SOAPx4, this can be accomplished with just a few lines of code, as Listing 8.20
demonstrates.

Listing 8.20   **A SOAP Client**

```
<html>
<head>
<basefont face="Arial">
</head>

<body>

<?php
if(!$_POST['submit'])
{
// display form
?>
<table border="0" cellspacing="5" cellpadding="5">
<form action="<? echo $_SERVER['PHP_SELF']; ?>" method="POST">
<tr>
<td><b>Username:</b></td>
<td><input type="text" name="pop_user"></td>
</tr>
<tr>
<td><b>Password:</b></td>
<td><input type="password" name="pop_pass"></td>
```

continues

Listing 8.20 **Continued**

```
</tr>
<tr>
<td><b>POP Server:</b></td>
<td><input type="text" name="pop_host"></td>
</tr>
<tr>
<td colspan="2" align="center"><input type="submit" name="submit" value="Get Total
➥Messages!"></td>
</tr>
</form>
</table>

<?php
}
else
{

    // include class definitions
    include("class.soap_client.php");

    // where is the SOAP server
    $server = "http://mail.service/rpc/server.php";

    // arguments
    $params = array("pop_user" => $_POST['pop_user'], "pop_pass" =>
➥$_POST['pop_pass'], "pop_host" => $POST['pop_host']);

    // instantiate a new client class
    $client = new soapclient($server);

    // uncomment next line to see client debug messages
    // $client->debug_flag = true;

    /*
    the call() function packages and transmits a SOAP request
    to the server, and reads and decodes the response packet

    it requires four parameters:
    - the procedure name
    - an array of arguments, as soapval objects
    - a namespace
    - a SOAPAction
    */

    echo $client->call("getTotalPOP3Messages", array(new soapval("pop_params",
➥"SOAPStruct", $params)), "urn:soapserver", "urn:soapserver");
}
?>
</body>
</html>
```

Creating a SOAP client with SOAPx4 is also fairly easy: Instantiate an object of the class `soapclient`, pass it to the location of the SOAP server, and use the object's `call()` method to transmit a remote procedure call to the server and retrieve the response. This response can then be used within your script, in whatever manner you desire. In Listing 8.20, the SOAP response will contain either an integer indicating the number of messages in the user's mailbox, or (if an error occurred) a fault string and code.

More information, together with usage examples and a series of interoperability tests (for both SOAP and WSDL), is available on the project's official web site. Note that, as of this writing, there isn't much documentation available for this class or the methods it exposes. Thus, expect to spend some quality time with the online examples in order to get up and running with your application.

Summary

PHP's XML extensions, especially those that ship with newer versions of the language, are more than sufficient for most development tasks. However, if your PHP build doesn't support a particular XML extension, and you're not in a position to recompile a new build, your development efforts can get rapidly derailed. Further, many of PHP's built-in extensions are still experimental and in a state of flux. In such a situation, an external class that is more stable (and perhaps also easier to use) is often a viable option.

A number of open source XML/PHP projects are available to work around the problem. Implemented as PHP classes that can easily be included in your application, they allow you, the developer, to reproduce the functionality of PHP's native XML functions in environments in which these native functions are not supported.

This chapter provided a quick-and-dirty crash course in the basics of each implementation, demonstrating its viability in real-world application development with simple examples and re-creations of applications from previous chapters. Each of these implementations is freely available on the Internet, together with supporting examples and (in most cases) good documentation.

If the implementations discussed in this chapter don't meet your requirements, don't despair. The PHP developer community is fairly restless, and it's quite likely that someone, somewhere, has decided to create and release a piece of code that does exactly what you need. Drop by this book's companion web site for a more comprehensive, frequently updated list of available XML/PHP alternatives, and take a look for yourself.

The next (and final) chapter of this book takes things a step further, demonstrating how all the theory you've learned thus far can be applied in the real world. Case studies, coming up next.

"In theory there is no difference between theory and practice.

In practice there is."

~YOGI BERRA (AND JAN L.A. VAN DE SNEPSCHEUT)

9

Case Studies

O UT WHERE THE RUBBER MEETS THE ROAD, it doesn't matter how many programming books you have stacked on your coffee table, or how many buzzwords you know. What matters is your ability to understand a problem, analyze the requirements of the solution, and deploy different technologies to achieve the best (most efficient and cost-effective) result.

Needless to say, this is harder than it sounds.

Developing the skills—technical and otherwise—to do this can take years of hard work, exposure to a wide variety of technologies, and a great deal of patience. Making a decision on which technology or combination of technologies to deploy in a particular situation requires a thorough understanding of what each one can (and cannot) do . . . and practical knowledge is key to gaining that understanding.

That's precisely why almost every chapter in this book includes practical examples of what you can do with PHP and XML, and why this chapter comes as a fitting endnote. It examines two real-world applications built on the XML/PHP combination in an attempt to demonstrate the practical usage of all the theory you've imbibed over the preceding pages.

In this chapter, you'll read about Metabase, a database-independent API that uses XML to store and manage database schema definitions; and patTemplate, a template-driven rendering engine that allows for the easy transformation of XML data into

HTML documents. Both are open-source software projects that address real problems; both are available free of charge on the web; and both highlight the potential of the XML/PHP combination to build scalable, robust, and real-world software solutions.

Metabase

Metabase is a database abstraction layer for SQL-compliant databases. Developed by Manuel Lemos as an open-source software project, Metabase is available under the BSD license, and can be downloaded from `http://www.phpclasses.org/browse.html/package/20.html`.

Design Goals

Metabase was designed to accomplish two main goals:

- Provide a database-independent API for PHP applications
- Provide a database-independent mechanism for maintaining and updating database schema

Metabase accomplishes the first goal using just PHP, and the second using a combination of PHP and XML.

Application Components

Metabase consists of the following components, implemented as PHP classes:

- A database-independent public interface, or API, that developers can use in their application
- Database-specific "drivers" that implement public interface methods for each database type
- A manager to handle database schema comparison, installation, and upgrade
- A Metabase-specific parser, which verifies the syntax and structure of an XML-encoded database schema
- A generic XML parser, which is used to convert any XML document into a native PHP structure

Abstract Thinking

If you've worked with databases before, you already know that PHP comes with a different set of database-manipulation functions for each database type. For example, opening a connection to a MySQL database is accomplished via the `mysql_connect()` function, whereas opening an equivalent connection to an Oracle database is accomplished via the `OCILogon()` function.

With this in mind, it follows that any change to the database server used in a PHP application immediately implies a change to the application code—specifically, to the native PHP functions used to manipulate the database. This is both tedious (a developer needs to manually inspect the code and alter it to use the functions specific to the new database) and time-consuming (the entire application needs to be retested in order to verify that things still work as advertised).

That's where a database abstraction layer comes in. A *database abstraction layer* provides an interface that can be used with any database type, thereby providing the developer with a uniform API to develop applications that are portable across databases. This interface (which may be represented as public functions or object methods) is internally mapped to the corresponding native PHP functions for each database type, with the abstraction layer possessing the intelligence necessary to decide which native function to call when the corresponding public function or object method is invoked. For example, an abstraction layer might expose a generic connect() function, which internally invokes either mysql_connect(), OCILogon(), or odbc_connect(), depending on the database type it has been configured for.

Thus, by providing a public interface that is independent of the database being used, a database abstraction layer provides a simple solution to the problem of developing portable database-independent PHP applications.

So that's the good news. Now, here's the bad news: In the real world, database abstraction layers are usually slower than native functions, take advantage of fewer database features, and are slower to catch up with the native API.

Usage Examples

Before getting into an analysis of the code, it's instructive to look at a couple of usage examples in order to see how Metabase fulfills the design goals stated previously. Consider Listing 9.1, which shows the abstraction layer in action:

Listing 9.1 **Retrieving Data from a MySQL Database with the Metabase API**

```php
<?php
// require Metabase public interface files
require("metabase_interface.php");
require("metabase_database.php");

// configure Metabase with database type and connection parameters
$error = MetabaseSetupDatabase(array("Type" => "mysql", "User" => "john",
 ↪"Password" => "doe"), $db);

// select a database
MetabaseSetDatabase($db, "db127");

// check for errors
if($error != "")
{
    die("Database setup error: $error\n");
```

continues

Listing 9.1 **Continued**

```php
}

// generate and execute query
$query = "SELECT * FROM addressbook";
$result = MetabaseQuery($db, $query);

// if an error occurred while executing the query
// report the error and exit
if(!$result != 0)
{
    echo "The following error occurred: " . MetabaseError($db);
    MetabaseFreeResult($db, $result);
    exit;
}

// get number of rows in result set
$rows = MetabaseNumberOfRows($db, $result);

// if no rows available
if(!$rows)
{
    echo "No data available.";
}
// print data in each row
else
{
    echo "<table><tr><td>name</td><td>email</td></tr>";
    for($row=0; $row<$rows; $row++)
    {
        echo "<tr><td>", MetabaseFetchResult($db, $result, $row,
        ➥"name"),"</td>";
        echo "<td>",MetabaseFetchResult($db, $result, $row,
        ➥"email"),"</td></tr>";
    }
echo "</table>";
}

?>
```

In this case, although I'm using a MySQL database, I'm not accessing the data within it using PHP's native MySQL functions. Rather, I'm using the Metabase API, which provides equivalent functionality with the additional benefit of portability across databases. If, for example, I decided to move to a PostgreSQL database, I would only need to alter one line in the preceding script above—the call to `MetabaseSetupDatabase()`—and everything else would continue to work as before.

> **OOPs!**
>
> Fans of object-oriented programming will be glad to hear that Metabase supports an alternative object-based interface to database manipulation. So, although you can certainly do this:
>
> ```
> MetabaseSetDatabase($db, "db127");
> ```
>
> Metabase also allows you to do this:
>
> ```
> $result=$db->SetDatabase("db127");
> ```
>
> In this case, $db is an object created via a call to the `MetabaseSetupDatabaseObject()` function.
>
> Take a look at the Metabase manual for more information on this feature.

In addition to the database-independent API demonstrated in Listing 9.1, Metabase also comes with a fairly powerful module for working with database schema. This module uses a combination of PHP and XML to simplify the task of schema creation and maintenance, and is the primary focus of the case study. In order to illustrate how it works, consider the following simple table definition:

```
Table : addressbook
+----------+------------+------+-----+---------+-------+
| Field    | Type       | Null | Key | Default | Extra |
+----------+------------+------+-----+---------+-------+
| id       | int(11)    |      |     | 1       |       |
| name     | char(255)  | YES  |     | NULL    |       |
| address  | char(150)  | YES  |     | NULL    |       |
| tel      | int(11)    | YES  |     | NULL    |       |
| fax      | int(11)    | YES  |     | NULL    |       |
+----------+------------+------+-----+---------+-------+
```

Now, consider Listing 9.2, which creates a Metabase-compliant representation of this table definition in well-formed XML.

Listing 9.2 **A Database Table Definition in XML (*addressbook.xml*)**

```xml
<?xml version="1.0"?>
<database>
      <!-- database name -->
      <name>db1097</name>

      <!-- table definition -->
      <table>
            <name>addressbook</name>
            <!-- field declarations -->
            <declaration>
                  <field>
                        <name>id</name>
                        <type>integer</type>
                        <notnull>1</notnull>
```

continues

Listing 9.2 **Continued**

```
                        <default>1</default>
                </field>
                <field>
                        <name>name</name>
                        <type>text</type>
                        <length>255</length>
                </field>
                <field>
                        <name>address</name>
                        <type>text</type>
                        <length>150</length>
                </field>
                <field>
                        <name>tel</name>
                        <type>integer</type>
                </field>
                <field>
                        <name>fax</name>
                        <type>integer</type>
                </field>
        </declaration>
    </table>
</database>
```

By using simple XML structures to express database schema semantics, Metabase allows developers—even those who are not familiar with the intricacies of database creation—to easily create and maintain database schema definitions, and to use these definitions in their development efforts.

Metabase can accept an XML document in this format, parse it, and create a corresponding database table. Listing 9.3 contains a PHP script that uses the Metabase public interface to do just this.

Listing 9.3 **Creating a Table Using a Metabase-Compliant XML Table Definition**

```php
<?php
// include all required files
require("xml_parser.php");
require("metabase_parser.php");
require("metabase_interface.php");
require("metabase_database.php");
require("metabase_manager.php");

// where is the schema
$schema = "addressbook.xml";
```

```
// set up variable interpolation array
$variables = array();

// set up Metabase configuration
$arguments = array("Type" => "mysql", "User" => "john", "Password" => "doe");

// instantiate the Metabase manager
$manager = new metabase_manager_class;

// set up database
$result = $manager->UpdateDatabase($schema, $schema . ".old", $arguments,
⇒$variables);
?>
```

Not My Type

It's sad but true: Different database management systems are not always consistent in their support for basic data types. And this lack of consistency can cause serious difficulties when porting data over from one database system to another.

As a database abstraction layer, Metabase has an interesting solution to this problem. It defines a set of "base data types"[1] that are independent of the database system, and which may be used transparently by developers within their applications. These base data types include date, time, numeric (integer, float, and decimal), string, and Boolean types.

When it comes to actually inserting the data into the database, the Metabase API internally does the hard work of translating the base data type into a native data type supported by the underlying database system. For applications that must support multiple database backends, this feature is extremely useful because it allows developers to work with a uniform set of data types without worrying about compatibility issues between different database systems.

In the event of any change to the database schema, Metabase also allows you to update the XML document with the new schema; it then takes care of altering the database to conform to the new schema, and of porting existing records to this altered database. As demonstrated in Listing 9.1 and Listing 9.3, all these tasks are accomplished via the database-independent Metabase API, which currently supports a number of different databases (including Oracle, MySQL, PostgreSQL, mSQL, and ODBC), and is therefore a viable real-world alternative for developers looking to create portable database-driven web applications.

1. Lemos, Manuel. *Class: Metabase—Database Independent Access and Management.* PHP Classes Repository. Available from the Internet: http://www.phpclasses.org/browse.html/package/20.html or http://phpclasses.org/goto/browse.html/file/60.html

Implementation Overview

Now that you've seen how Metabase works, let's briefly focus on what happens behind the scenes (you might find it helpful to refer to the source code of the application while reading this section).

Metabase is implemented as a collection of different PHP classes, each one performing a clearly defined set of functions. These classes are the following:

- `metabase_database_class`: A class that provides base functionality to driver classes, and that may be reused or overridden in the actual driver classes

- `metabase_`*dbtype*`_class`: A database-specific class that implements Metabase public interface functions for a particular database type

- `metabase_manager_class`: A class that processes database schema documents, compares different schema documents to build a list of differences, and makes the database changes necessary to install or upgrade to the new schema

- `metabase_parser_class`: A class that validates the XML-encoded database schema

- `xml_parser_class`: A generic XML parser for parsing any XML document

Putting the Pieces Together

It should be noted that the generic XML parser used by Metabase, the `xml_parser_class` class, is not included in the standard Metabase distribution. You can download it separately from `http://phpclasses.upperdesign.com/browse.html/package/4`.

As Listing 9.1 demonstrated, the first order of business is to configure Metabase by providing it with information on the database type, username, and password:

```
MetabaseSetupDatabase(array("Type" => "mysql", "User" => "john", "Password" =>
➥"doe"), $db);
```

This allows the Metabase public interface (defined in the file `metabase_interface.php`) to select the appropriate database driver for subsequent queries. Listing 9.4 demonstrates this with a snippet of the function code.

Listing 9.4 **The Functions for Configuration of the Metabase Public Interface** (from *metabase_interface.php*)

```php
<?php
// some parts of these functions
// have been deleted for greater readability
Function MetabaseSetupDatabase($arguments,&$database)
{
    global $metabase_databases;

    $database=count($metabase_databases)+1;
    if(strcmp($error=MetabaseSetupInterface($arguments,$metabase_databases
➥[$database]),""))
    {
```

```
                Unset($metabase_databases[$database]);
                $database=0;
        }
        else
                $metabase_databases[$database]->database=$database;
        return($error);
}


Function MetabaseSetupInterface(&$arguments,&$db)
{
        switch(IsSet($arguments["Type"]) ? $arguments["Type"] : "")
        {
                case "msql";
                        $include="metabase_msql.php";
                        $class_name="metabase_msql_class";
                        $included="METABASE_MSQL_INCLUDED";
                        break;
                case "mssql";
                        $include="metabase_mssql.php";
                        $class_name="metabase_mssql_class";
                        $included="METABASE_MSSQL_INCLUDED";
                        break;
                case "mysql";
                        $include="metabase_mysql.php";
                        $class_name="metabase_mysql_class";
                        $included="METABASE_MYSQL_INCLUDED";
                        break;
                case "pgsql";
                        $include="metabase_pgsql.php";
                        $class_name="metabase_pgsql_class";
                        $included="METABASE_PGSQL_INCLUDED";
                        break;

                        // and so on...

                include($include_path.$include);
        }
        $db=new $class_name;
        if(IsSet($arguments["Host"]))
                $db->host=$arguments["Host"];
        if(IsSet($arguments["User"]))
                $db->user=$arguments["User"];
        if(IsSet($arguments["Password"]))
                $db->password=$arguments["Password"];
        return($db->Setup());
}
?>
```

As Listing 9.4 demonstrates, the Metabase API function MetabaseSetupDatabase()
internally invokes MetabaseSetupInterface(), which uses the database type to include
the appropriate database driver file.

Now, when a Metabase API function is called by the application, the Metabase interface layer diverts the request to the appropriate database driver, which uses PHP's native function(s) for that database to perform the selected action. The result of the function call(s) is then sent back to the application from the database driver via the Metabase interface layer.

This hierarchical flow can be better represented by Figure 9.1.

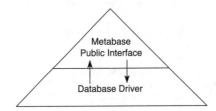

Figure 9.1 Interaction between the Metabase public API and the database-specific driver.

So, for example, a call to the Metabase function `MetabaseNumberOfRows()` in a MySQL environment would first get intercepted by the Metabase interface layer and then diverted to the MySQL database driver, which would execute the function using PHP's native MySQL functions.

This can be clearly seen from the following code snippets. Listing 9.5 contains the definition for the `MetabaseNumberOfRows()` function as it appears in the Metabase interface layer.

Listing 9.5 **The Definition for the *MetabaseNumberOfRows()* API Function (from *metabase_interface.php*)**

```php
<?php
Function MetabaseNumberOfRows($database,$result)
{
     global $metabase_databases;

     return($metabase_databases[$database]->NumberOfRows($result));
}
?>
```

As you can see, this function definition is merely a stub pointing to the `NumberOfRows()` function, which is individually defined for each database driver. Listing 9.6 demonstrates what the one for MySQL looks like.

Listing 9.6   **The Definition for the MySQL-Specific** *NumberOfRows()* **Function (from** *metabase_mysql.php*)

```php
<?php
Function NumberOfRows($result)
{
      return(mysql_num_rows($result));
}
?>
```

And Listing 9.7 demonstrates what the one for PostgreSQL looks like.

Listing 9.7   **The definition for the PostgreSQL-specific** *NumberOfRows()* **function (from** *metabase_pgsql.php*)

```php
<?php
Function NumberOfRows($result)
{
      return(pg_numrows($result));
}
?>
```

Thus, the two-tiered approach illustrated in Figure 9.1 makes it possible to create database-specific drivers while still exposing a uniform interface to developers.

In the event that the API function called involves the creation or alteration of a database (remember the second design goal?), the two-tier hierarchy illustrated in Figure 9.1 gets modified to include a couple of additional layers. Figure 9.2 illustrates the change.

In this case, Metabase first creates an instance of the XML parser class (defined in the file xml_parser.php) to parse the XML-compliant schema definition, and to convert this XML document into a native PHP object.

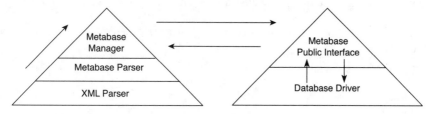

Figure 9.2   Interaction between the Metabase manager, XML parser, and public interface.

The XML parser used by Metabase converts the marked-up database schema definition into a single PHP associative array. The indices of this array are the path of the tag or data elements, and the corresponding values are the actual tag or data element values.

This can be better understood with an example. Consider Listing 9.8, which uses this XML parser to parse a simple XML document.

Listing 9.8   **Using Metabase's XML Parser to Convert an XML Document into a Structured PHP Object**

```php
<?php
// include XML parser
require("xml_parser.php");

// create a simple XML document
$xml_str = <<< END
<?xml version="1.0"?>
<scream>Mommy, Mommy, the <martians>little green men</martians> are back!</scream>
END;

// instantiate an XML parser object
$xml_parser=new xml_parser_class;

// uncomment the next line to store element positions
// as part of the structure
// $xml_parser->store_positions = 1;

// parse the XML document
$xml_parser->Parse($xml_str, 1);

// uncomment the next line to see the resulting structure
// print_r($xml_parser);
?>
```

When the resulting structure is dissected with print_r(), it looks like Listing 9.9.

Listing 9.9   **The Object Created after Parsing an XML Document with Metabase's XML Parser**

```
xml_parser_class Object
(
    [xml_parser] => 0
    [error] =>
    [error_number] => 0
    [error_line] => 0
    [error_column] => 0
    [error_byte_index] => 0
```

```
[error_code] => 0
[stream_buffer_size] => 4096
[structure] => Array
    (
        [0] => Array
            (
                [Tag] => scream
                [Elements] => 3
                [Attributes] => Array
                    (
                    )

            )

        [0,0] => Mommy, Mommy, the
        [0,1] => Array
            (
                [Tag] => martians
                [Elements] => 1
                [Attributes] => Array
                    (
                    )

            )

        [0,1,0] => little green men
        [0,2] =>  are back!
    )

[positions] => Array
    (
    )

[store_positions] => 0
[case_folding] => 0
[target_encoding] => ISO-8859-1
[simplified_xml] => 0
[fail_on_non_simplified_xml] => 0
)
```

This PHP structure is then passed on to the Metabase parser class (defined in the file metabase_parser.php), which performs Metabase-specific error checks, and tests on the schema—for example, verifying that every <database> element has a corresponding <name> element under it, or ensuring that <field> elements contain appropriate values.

Listing 9.10 demonstrates this by reproducing some snippets culled directly from the class code.

Listing 9.10 **Some of the Error Checks Performed by the Metabase Parser Class** (from *metabase_parser.php*)

```php
<?php
// some parts of this function
// have been deleted for greater readability
Function Parse($data,$end_of_data)
{
    // snip

    if(strcmp($this->xml_parser->structure["0"]["Tag"],"database"))
            return($this->SetParserError("0","it was not defined a valid database
            ⇒definition"));

    if(!IsSet($database_tags["name"]))
            return($this->SetParserError("0","it was not defined the database name
            ⇒property"));

    if(!strcmp($database_values["name"],""))
            return($this->SetParserError($database_tags["name"],"It was not
            ⇒defined a valid database name"));

        // and so on...
}
?>
```

These error checks, together with others in the script, perform the very important function of verifying that the schema is valid before using it to create one or more database tables.

Tying Up Loose Ends

If you actually peek into the internals of the Metabase parser class (defined in the file metabase_parser.php), you'll notice that a good portion of the code consists of error checks. In case you're wondering whether this is really necessary, you might want to keep in mind that PHP's SAX parser is a non-validating XML parser, and consequently does not support using a DTD to verify the integrity of the marked-up schema definition. Therefore, the only way to validate the XML data is to manually parse it and aggressively check the elements and data within it for structural or type errors.

After all the error checks have been completed successfully, the next step is to compare the current definition with the previous one (if it exists), and build a list of changes between the two versions. This list of changes (again structured as an array of arrays) is then passed on to the Metabase interface layer (specifically to the MetabaseAlterTable() function), and then to the driver for that specific database—which takes care of performing the actual table modification, dropping, renaming, and adding columns to the table.

Obviously, this is a broad overview of how Metabase works—a line-by-line explanation of the code is beyond the scope of this chapter, especially when you consider that the application consists of well over eight thousand lines of code. That said, if you have the time (and patience), it's instructive to read through the source code of the application, if only to increase your familiarity with code modularization, error handling, and object-oriented programming techniques.

Concluding Remarks

By providing developers with a uniform, database-independent mechanism for executing SQL queries, Metabase makes it possible to write web applications that can be ported across databases with minimal difficulty, time, and cost. It's also a good example of the type of applications that the XML/PHP combination makes possible, illustrating clearly how the simplicity of XML can be combined with the power of PHP's XML parser to create a robust and useful real-world solution.

patTemplate and patXMLRenderer

patTemplate is a rendering engine that attempts to simplify web application development by using a template-based framework to separate presentation information from data. It does this by using simple templates to hold presentation semantics—formatting, layout, alignment, and so on—and inserting placeholders in these templates to represent data elements. When these templates are rendered by the engine, the placeholders embedded within them are replaced by actual data, which may be dynamically retrieved from a database, a text file, or any other data source.

patXMLRenderer builds on the functionality offered by patTemplate, adding an XML parser to the mix. This allows data encoded in XML to be retrieved and used in a template, with the XML parser automatically creating appropriate variables and handing them off to the template engine for inclusion in the final output.

Together, patTemplate and patXMLRenderer provide a simple, efficient solution to the problem of generating HTML (or other ASCII) documents from XML-encoded data. Part of a larger suite of PHP-based application tools, they are developed and maintained by Stephan Schmidt, and can be downloaded free of charge from `http://www.php-tools.de/`.

Design Goals

The patXMLRenderer publishing system was designed around the following goals:

- Separate content from its presentation
- Allow for the easy transformation of raw data into any other format
- Provide an extensible framework for the development of new application modules

It accomplishes these goals using a combination of PHP and XML programming techniques.

Application Components

Assuming an XML data source, a patXMLRenderer publishing system consists of two primary components:

- A template engine (patTemplate) that handles the creation and management of document templates and performs variable interpolation
- An XML parser (patXMLRenderer) that parses one or more XML documents, retrieves data from them, and merges this raw data with the templates to produce a composite result.

Usage Examples

As before, let's look at a couple of simple examples before diving into the code that drives the application. Consider Listing 9.11, which contains a simple template.

Listing 9.11 **A Template for a Simple HTML Document** (*superhero.tmpl*)

```
<!-- this template sets up the main page -->
<patTemplate:tmpl name="superhero">
<html>
<head></head>
<body>
<font face="Arial" size="+1">My friends call me {NICKNAME}, although my real name
➥is {REALNAME}. Why don't we get together for dinner sometime?</font>
</body>
</html>
</patTemplate:tmpl>
```

Each template is enclosed within a pair of `<patTemplate:tmpl>`...`</patTemplate:tmpl>` elements and has a unique name (in this case, `"superhero"`). As you'll see in Listing 9.12, this name attribute is used when assigning values to different template variables.

The uppercase strings you see enclosed within curly braces within the template definition (`REALNAME`, `NICKNAME`) are template variables; they serve as placeholders for actual data and will be replaced during the rendering phase.

Listing 9.12 demonstrates the PHP script that initializes the template engine, assigns values to the template variables, and puts the two together to create a composite result.

Listing 9.12 **Assigning Data to Template Variables and Displaying the Composite Result**

```php
<?php
// include template engine
include("include/patTemplate.php");

// initialize template engine
$template = new patTemplate();

// set base path for templates
$template->SetBaseDir("templates");

// read template data
$template->ReadTemplatesFromFile("superhero.tmpl");

// define values for template variables
$template->AddVar("superhero", "NICKNAME", "The Incredible Hulk");
$template->AddVar("superhero", "REALNAME", "Bruce Banner");

// display output
$template->DisplayParsedTemplate();
?>
```

Listing 9.13 contains the resulting HTML document, with Figure 9.3 demonstrating what it looks like in a browser.

Listing 9.13 **The HTML Document Generated by Listing 9.12**

```html
<html>
<head></head>
<body>
<font face="Arial" size="+1">My friends call me The Incredible Hulk, although my
➥real name is Bruce Banner. Why don't we get together for dinner sometime?</font>
</body>
</html>
```

Checking Out the Competition

If you're interested in developing template-driven web sites, you might want to also look at the FastTemplate and Smarty template engines, which share some semantic similarities with the patTemplate class. Both are available on the web at http://www.thewebmasters.net/ and http://freshmeat.net/projects/smarty/, respectively.

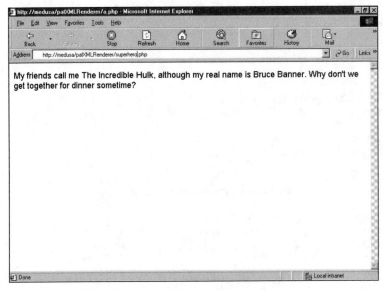

Figure 9.3 The HTML document generated by
Listing 9.12, as it appears in a Web browser.

Let's see what happens when XML is added to the mix. Consider Listing 9.14, an
XML shopping list.

Listing 9.14 **An XML Shopping List** (*shoppinglist.xml*)

```
<?xml version="1.0"?>
<shoppinglist>
    <item>
        <name>eye of newt</name>
        <quantity>3</quantity>
    </item>
    <item>
        <name>tongue of lizard</name>
        <quantity>2</quantity>
    </item>
    <item>
        <name>scouring powder</name>
        <quantity>7 boxes</quantity>
    </item>
    <item>
        <name>cauldron</name>
        <quantity>1</quantity>
    </item>
</shoppinglist>
```

Now, let's convert this XML-encoded list into a web page. The first step is to create a series of templates (compliant to the patTemplate format described earlier) to define the formatting and layout of this web page. Listing 9.15 contains the templates I'd like to use.

Listing 9.15 **A Series of Templates for an HTML Shopping List**

```
<!-- this template sets up the main container -->
<patTemplate:tmpl name="shoppinglist">
<html>
<head></head>
<body>
<h2>My Shopping List</h2>
<ul>
{CONTENT}
</ul>
</body>
</html>
</patTemplate:tmpl>

<!-- this sets up the list element for each <item> element -->
<patTemplate:tmpl name="item">
<li>{CONTENT}</li>
</patTemplate:tmpl>

<!-- this prints the content of each <name> element within an <item> element -->
<patTemplate:tmpl name="name">
{CONTENT}
</patTemplate:tmpl>

<!-- this prints the content of each <quantity> element within an <item> element,
➥in italics and parentheses -->
<patTemplate:tmpl name="quantity">
<i>({CONTENT})</i>
</patTemplate:tmpl>
```

As you can see, the desired output is fairly simple—an HTML document with the items in the shopping list displayed as elements of a bulleted list. In Listing 9.15, this simple HTML document is broken up into individual pieces, with each piece represented as a separate template.

The CONTENT marker that appears within each template is a special placeholder variable that is used by patXMLRenderer when it generates the final output. When a template is parsed by the rendering engine, the CONTENT placeholder is automatically replaced with the contents of the corresponding XML element (this may be either character data or other nested XML elements).

Those Amazing Acrobatic Attributes!

The CONTENT placeholder variable is not the only one recognized by patXMLRenderer. The class also allows you to import the values of XML attributes into the template, simply by using template variables corresponding to the attribute names.

Consider Listing 9.16, which has an XML document containing elements and element attributes.

Listing 9.16   **A Simple XML Document (*size.xml*)**

```
<?xml version="1.0"?>
<size units="inches">
     <height>20</height>
     <width>40</width>
</size>
```

When patXMLRenderer reads and combines this XML document with the template in Listing 9.17, the attribute values are automatically imported into the template as template variables and used to replace the template placeholders.

Listing 9.17   **A Template that Uses XML Attributes as Template Variables**

```
<!-- this template sets up the main container -->
<patTemplate:tmpl name="size">
<html>
<head></head>
<body>
Dimensions: {CONTENT} {UNITS}
</body>
</html>
</patTemplate:tmpl>

<!-- template for printing height -->
<patTemplate:tmpl name="height">
{CONTENT} x
</patTemplate:tmpl>

<!-- template for printing width -->
<patTemplate:tmpl name="width">
{CONTENT}
</patTemplate:tmpl>
<!-- output is "Dimensions: 20 x 40 inches" -->
```

This capability to automatically convert XML attributes into template variables is unique to patXMLRenderer, and is one of the class' most useful features.

Finally, Listing 9.18 has the PHP script that initializes both the template engine and the XML parser, and generates the required output.

Listing 9.18   **Merging Templates with XML Data and Displaying the Composite Result**

```php
<?php
// include config files
include("config/conf.php");

// include template and rendering engines
include("include/patTemplate.php");
include("include/patXMLRenderer.php");

// initialize template engine
$template = new patTemplate();

// set base path for templates
$template->SetBaseDir("templates");

// initialize rendering engine
$randy = new patXMLRenderer();

// set base path for XML data
$randy->setXMLDir("xml");

// set data file
$randy->setXMLFile("shoppinglist.xml");

// connect template to rendering engine
$randy->setTemplate($template);

// set template file
$randy->addTemplateFile("shoppinglist.tmpl");

// load templates, XML
$randy->initRenderer();

// parse XML file, merge data into template and display output
$randy->displayRenderedContent();
?>
```

In this case, because the data will be coming directly from an XML file, there's no real need to manually define values for template variables with the addVar() method. Instead, when the patXMLRenderer engine is initialized, it parses the XML document, matches XML elements to templates (on the basis of the name attribute in the template definition), and replaces the placeholders in the template with data from the

XML document. If you flip back to Listing 9.14, you'll see the correspondence between the XML elements used there and the `name` attributes used in Listing 9.15.

Listing 9.19 contains the resulting HTML code, and Figure 9.4 demonstrates what it looks like in a web browser.

Listing 9.19 **The HTML Document Generated by Listing 9.18**

```
<!-- output reindented for greater readability -->
<html>
<head></head>
<body>
<h2>My Shopping List</h2>
<ul>
<li>eye of newt<i>(3)</i></li>
<li>tongue of lizard<i>(2)</i></li>
<li>scouring powder<i>(7 boxes)</i></li>
<li>cauldron<i>(1)</i></li>
</ul>
</body>
</html>
```

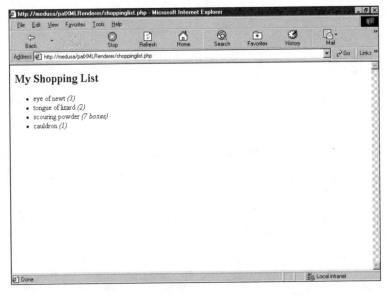

Figure 9.4 The HTML document generated by Listing 9.18, as it appears in a web browser.

Though these are simple examples, they clearly demonstrate the potential of this system on a content-heavy web site. By separating the presentation of the data from the data itself, this system makes it possible to decouple the graphical interface of a web site from the data that appears within that interface, so web designers and content editors can (finally) work independently of each other.

Extending Yourself

One of the nice things about patXMLRenderer is its capability to incorporate and use new extensions (remember the third design goal?), thereby allowing developers to add custom functionality to the class.

Each extension has its own namespace; the XML parser uses this unique namespace to store extension-specific variables and execute extension-specific methods.

As an example, consider Listing 9.20, which illustrates usage of a custom time extension. This extension provides a bunch of useful date and time formatting functions for use in a template.

Listing 9.20   **Using patXMLRenderer's Time Extension**

```
<?xml version="1.0"?>
<doc>
      <!-- include time extension -->
      <randy:addextension namespace="time"
file="time/patXMLRendererTimeExtension.php"
extension="patXMLRendererTimeExtension"/>
      <modified>This page was last modified on <time:format format=
      ➥"D d M Y">2002-06-04</time:format></modified>
</doc>
<!-- outputs "This page was last modified on Tue 04 Jun 2002" -->
```

This capability to add custom extensions to the class is unique to patXMLRenderer, and it is what makes the class different from (and more powerful than) your average XSLT processor. Extensibility makes it a snap to add new functionality to the class on an as-needed basis, while still retaining the feature set and scalability of the base application.

A number of extensions for patXMLRenderer are available on the official web site for the project. Check them out at http://www.php-tools.de/

Implementation Overview

As stated previously, the system consists of two components, which are implemented as PHP classes:

- The patTemplate class, which handles the creation and management of document templates and performs variable interpolation

- The patXMLRenderer class, which takes care of parsing XML documents, converting attribute values and character data into template variables, and displaying the rendered content

If you look at the source code for the patTemplate class, you'll see that it's fairly simple. It first reads and parses the available template(s), and then creates PHP arrays to hold the template name(s) and data. Listing 9.21 demonstrates a snippet from the readTempatesFromFile() method of this class.

Listing 9.21 **A Function to Read and Parse Templates (from** *patTemplate.php*)

```php
<?php
// some parts of this function
// have been deleted for greater readability
Function readTemplatesFromFile($file)
{
    // Tag depth
    $this->depth = -1;
    // Names, extracted from the Tags
    $this->template_names = array();
    // All HTML code, that is found between the tags
    $this->template_data = array();
    // Attributes, extracted from tags
    $this->template_types  = array();

    $this->last_opened = array();
    $this->last_keep = array();
    $this->whitespace  = array();

    $this->createParser($file);

    $open_tag = array_pop($this->last_opened);
    if($open_tag != NULL)
        die ("Error in template '".$file."': &lt;/".$open_tag."&gt; still open
        ↦at end of file.");
}
?>
```

In case you're wondering, the createParser() method of the class is used to actually parse the template file and obtain information on the templates within it.

After all the templates have been parsed, the next step is to obtain a list of template variables and values (remember that these variables must be manually defined by the application using the AddVar() method, as was done in Listing 9.12), and replace the variable placeholders in the template with their corresponding values. This is accomplished via the parseTemplate() method, which internally calls the parseStandardTemplate() method (see Listing 9.22).

Listing 9.22 **A Function to Replace Variables in a Template with Their Actual Values** (from *patTemplate.php*)

```php
<?php
// some parts of this function
// have been deleted for greater readability

function parseStandardTemplate($name, $mode="w")
{
     $name = strtoupper($name);

     // get a copy of the plain content

     $temp = $this->getTemplateContent($name);

     $vars = $this->getVars($name);
     $vars[$this->tag_start."PAT_ROW_VAR".$this->tag_end] = 1;
     while(list($tag, $value) = each($vars))
     {
          if(is_array($value))
          {
               $value = $value[0];
          }
          $temp = str_replace($tag, $value, $temp);
     }

// snip

}
?>
```

After variable interpolation has taken place (see the call to str_replace() in Listing 9.22), all that's left is to display the resulting output. This is taken care of by a little method called DisplayParsedTemplate(), which merely echoes the result to the output device.

So long as your activities are restricted only to patTemplate, the process described in the preceding paragraphs holds good. However, if you have a large amount of data, manually defining the values for a large number of template variables can get tedious. In such situations, it's easier to mark up your data in XML and let patXMLRenderer automatically import this data into your template(s).

A close look at the source code for the patXMLRenderer class reveals that most of the activity begins with the initRenderer() method, which sets the name of the XML file to parse, and also creates some global variables for use in the patTemplate class. Listing 9.23 has a snippet from this method.

Listing 9.23   **A Function to Initialize the XML Parser and Set Some Global Template Variables (from** *patXMLRenderer.php***)**

```php
<?php
// some parts of this function
// have been deleted for greater readability

function initRenderer()
{
    if(!$this->xmlFile)
        $this->setXMLFile($this->defaultFile);

    // add some global variables
    $file = ($this->xmlDir!="") ? $this->xmlDir."/".$this->xmlFile :
    ➥$this->xmlFile;

    // snip

    // add global variables
    $this->template->addGlobalVar("XMLFILE", $this->xmlFile);
    $this->template->addGlobalVar("XMLSOURCE", $file);
    $this->template->addGlobalVar("PAGE_LAST_UPDATED", date( "Y-m-d H:i:s",
    ➥filemtime($file)));

    // snip

    $this->xmlSource = $file;
}
?>
```

Next, the `getRenderedContent()` method starts the process of parsing the XML file via the `parseXMLFile()` method. The `parseXMLFile()` method creates a parser via the `createParser()` method and processes it in chunks (see Listing 9.24).

Listing 9.24   **The Functions to Create an XML Parser and Parse the XML Document (from** *patXMLRenderer.php***)**

```php
<?php
// some parts of this function
// have been deleted for greater readability

function parseXMLFile($file)
{
    $file = ($this->xmlDir!="") ? $this->xmlDir."/".$file : $file;

    // snip
```

```
     $parser = $this->createParser();

     if(!( $fp = fopen( $file, "r" )))
          die("patXMLRenderer could not open XML file :".$file );

     flock($fp, LOCK_SH );
     $counter = 0;
     while($data = fread($fp, filesize($file)))
     {
         if (!xml_parse($parser, $data, feof($fp)))
         {
             die(sprintf("XML error: %s at line %d in file %s",
               ▸xml_error_string(xml_get_error_code($parser)),
               ▸xml_get_current_line_number($parser), $file));
         }
     }
     xml_parser_free($parser);
     $data = $this->finalData[$this->parsers];
     flock($fp, LOCK_UN);

     // snip

     return $data;
}

function createParser()
{
     // snip

     // init XML Parser
     $parser = xml_parser_create();
     xml_set_object($parser, &$this);
     xml_set_element_handler($parser, "startElement", "endElement");
     xml_set_character_data_handler($parser, "characterData");
     xml_set_external_entity_ref_handler($parser, "externalEntity");
     xml_set_processing_instruction_handler($parser, "processingInstruction");
     xml_parser_set_option($parser, XML_OPTION_CASE_FOLDING, true);
     return $parser;
}
?>
```

As the parser steps through the document, callback functions are called to handle the different structures found—you may remember this from Chapter 2, "PHP and the Simple API for XML (SAX)." These callbacks—specifically the end element handler endElement()—take care of creating variable-value pairs from the character data in the XML document (see Listing 9.25 for a snippet from this function).

Listing 9.25   **A Function to Assign Attribute Values and Character Data from the XML Document to Template Variables (from *patXMLRenderer.php*)**

```php
<?php
function endElement($parser, $name)
{
     // snip
     if($this->getOption( "transform" ) == "on")
     {
          if( $this->getOption("replaceentities") == "on" &&
          ⮑is_array($attributes))
          {
               reset($attributes);
               while(list($key, $value) = each($attributes))
               $attributes[$key] = htmlspecialchars($value);
          }
          $this->template->addVars($tag, $attributes);
          $this->template->addVar($tag, "PAT_TAG_NAME", $tag);
          $this->template->addVar($tag, "PAT_TAG_REP", $tagcounter);
          $this->template->addVar($tag, "CONTENT", $data);
          unset( $this->tagCounter[$this->parsers][($tagDepth + 1)]);
          if($this->template->exists($tag))
          {
               $data = $this->template->getParsedTemplate($tag);
               $this->template->clearTemplate($tag);
          }
     }
}
?>
```

After all the template variables have been defined, the `patTemplate` class' `getParsedTemplate()` method is called to perform the variable interpolation, and the output is returned to the browser.

Isn't it simple when you know how?

Concluding Remarks

patTemplate and patXMLRenderer demonstrate how the combination of an XML parser (which parses an XML document and retrieves data from it) with a PHP-based template engine (which separates content from presentation by means of placeholder variables) can substantially streamline the development process of a web application. This separation of presentation semantics from raw data not only increases efficiency by allowing a software development team to work independently of an interface design team, it also makes application code easier to maintain, update, and test. And no matter which way you look at it, this adds up to a Good Thing.

Summary

You've now reached the end of this book. In a fitting conclusion, this chapter demonstrated the fundamental premise of this book—the synergy between PHP and XML—with case studies of two real-world development projects.

As clearly illustrated in this chapter, XML and PHP are both powerful technologies, and together offer the creative developer ample opportunity to create new and innovative software applications. Expect to see more and more of these applications as the technologies evolve and the developer community's awareness of their joint capabilities increases.

That's it for the moment. I hope you found this book interesting, informative, and enjoyable, and that it offered you some insight into the different things you can do with XML and PHP. Until next time . . . be good!

"A journey of a thousand leagues begins with a single step."

~LAO TZU

A

Recompiling PHP to Add XML Support

IN YOUR SOJOURN THROUGH THIS BOOK, you may have noticed that many of the examples require special extensions to be compiled into PHP in order to function correctly. In the event that your PHP build doesn't already include support for these XML-specific extensions, you will need to recompile PHP to activate support for these extensions.

Some of these extensions can be activated simply by adding an appropriate compile-time parameter during the build process; others require more complex configuration, including the installation of specific external libraries. This appendix documents the entire process, describing how the different pieces can be put together to create a PHP build that supports all the technologies discussed in this book.

It should be noted at the outset that this appendix is intended only as an overview of the process of recompiling PHP as a static Apache module with support for XML-specific extensions. It is *not* intended to replace the installation instructions that ship with each of the packages described as follows. In the event that you encounter difficulties in installing or compiling any of the packages discussed in this chapter, you should refer to the package's installation instructions or web site for detailed troubleshooting information.

With that caveat out of the way, let's get started!

Plug and Play

If your Apache build supports DSO modules, you should look at PHP's INSTALL file for more information on the process of compiling PHP as a DSO module, and check the section titled "Adding PHP" for a list of the compile-time options necessary to enable XML support.

If you have no idea what the previous sentence means, ignore it and keep reading.

Obtaining the Software

The first step is to make sure that you have all the software you need. Here is your shopping list:

- The most important item is, obviously, PHP itself. The PHP (version 4.1.0 or better) source code distribution is available from http://www.php.net/.

- If you intend to run PHP as an Apache module (recommended), you'll also need the Apache web server. Apache (version 1.3.20 or better) source code is available from http://www.apache.org/.

- In order to activate PHP's DOM and XSLT support, you also need a few external libraries:

  - The zlib library (version 1.1.3 or better) is available from http://www.gzip.org/zlib/.

  - The expat library (version 1.95.2 or better) is available from http://sourceforge.net/projects/expat/.

  - The GNOME XML library, a.k.a. libxml (version 2.4.2 or better), is available from http://www.xmlsoft.org/.

  - The Sablotron library (version 0.71 or better) is available from http://www.gingerall.com/.

- Many of the examples in this book assume that you have a MySQL database server up and running on your system. In case you don't, you will want to download and install it. MySQL (version 3.23.23 or better) is available from http://www.mysql.com/.

- Because you will be compiling all this software afresh, you also need a C++ compiler. Your development environment should already have one of these; however, in case it doesn't, you can try the GCC compiler. GCC is available at http://gcc.gnu.org/.

- Finally, you need the tar and gunzip utilities to decompress and extract files from their distribution archives. Binaries for both can be downloaded from the GNU web site at http://www.gnu.org/.

In case you were wondering, all this software is freely available on the Internet, and can be downloaded at no charge.

> ### Version Control
> Here are the software versions used when developing this book:
>
> - zlib 1.1.3
> - expat 1.95.2
> - libxml 2.4.9
> - Sablotron 0.71
> - PHP 4.1.1 and PHP 4.2.0
> - Apache 1.3.20
> - MySQL 3.23.23
> - GCC 2.96
> - tar 1.13.17
> - gunzip 1.3

Compiling and Installing the Software

After you've successfully downloaded all the sources, the next step is to configure, compile, and install the different packages. The next sections show you how.

Step 1—Unpacking the Sources

Unpack all the sources to a temporary area on your system (I'll be using /tmp/sources/).

```
$ cd /tmp/sources/
$ tar -xzvf libxml2-2.4.9.tar.gz
$ tar -xzvf expat-1.95.2.tar.gz
$ tar -xzvf Sablot-0.71.tar.gz
$ tar -xzvf zlib-1.1.3.tar.gz
$ tar -xzvf apache_1.3.20.tar.gz
$ tar -xzvf php-4.1.1.tar.gz
```

You should end up with a directory structure that looks something like this:

```
$ ls -l /tmp/sources/
drwxrwxrwx    5 root      root         4096 Feb  4 15:51 Sablot-0.71
drwxr-xr-x    8 root      root         4096 Feb  4 16:22 apache_1.3.20
drwxr-xr-x    7 root      root         4096 Feb  4 15:26 expat-1.95.2
drwxrwxrwx   11 root      root         4096 Feb  4 15:13 libxml2-2.4.9
drwxrwxr-x   16 root      root         4096 Feb  4 16:13 php-4.1.1
drwxr-xr-x    7 root      root         4096 Feb  4 15:15 zlib-1.1.3
```

Step 2—Adding the External Libraries

Next, configure, build, and install the external libraries required by PHP. Here's how:

1. Configure, build, and install expat.

```
$ cd expat-1.95.2
$ ./configure
$ make
$ make install
```

Unless you specified a different directory, the expat library should get installed to /usr/local/lib/. (You can specify a different directory by adding the --prefix to the configure script.)

Run the library linker ldconfig to tell the system about the newly installed library.

```
$ /sbin/ldconfig
```

The Root of All Errors . . .

You probably do not require superuser, or root, privileges while configuring and building these libraries. However, you do require superuser privileges when running the final make install and ldconfig commands because these commands access restricted areas of the system.

2. Configure, build, and install zlib.

```
$ cd ../zlib-1.1.3
$ ./configure
$ make
$ make install
```

Unless you specified a different directory, the zlib library should get installed to /usr/local/lib/. (You can specify a different directory by adding the --prefix to the configure script.)

Run the library linker ldconfig to tell the system about the newly installed library.

```
$ /sbin/ldconfig
```

3. Configure, build, and install libxml.

```
$ cd ../libxml2-2.4.9
$ ./configure
$ make
$ make install
```

Unless you specified a different directory, the libxml library should get installed to /usr/local/lib/. (You can specify a different directory by adding the --prefix to the configure script.)

Run the library linker `ldconfig` to tell the system about the newly installed library.

```
$ /sbin/ldconfig
```

4. Configure, build, and install Sablotron.

```
$ cd ../Sablot-0.71
$ ./configure
$ make
$ make install
```

Unless you specified a different directory, the Sablotron library should get installed to `/usr/local/lib`. (You can specify a different directory by adding the `--prefix` to the `configure` script.)

Run the library linker `ldconfig` to tell the system about the newly installed library.

```
$ /sbin/ldconfig
```

Looking in the Wrong Places

Make sure that the location these libraries get installed to (`/usr/local/lib/`, in this case) is specified in the system's library configuration file (usually `/etc/ld.so.conf`), or else the final call to `ldconfig` will have no effect whatsoever.

Step 3—Adding PHP

After all the external libraries have been built and installed, it's time to configure, build, and install PHP. Here's how (do one of the following):

- If you want to compile PHP as a module into the Apache web server, you need to first configure it appropriately. To do this, first change into the Apache directory and run Apache's configuration script.

```
$ cd ../apache_1.3.20
$ ./configure
```

This is a necessary precondition to compiling PHP as an Apache module because it tells PHP where to find Apache's header files.

Now, move back to the PHP directory, and configure PHP with support for all required XML extensions.

```
$ cd ../php-4.1.1
$ ./configure --with-apache=../apache_1.3.20 --enable-track-vars
➥--with-mysql --with-dom --enable-sockets --enable-wddx --with-xmlrpc
➥--enable-xslt --with-xslt-sablot --with-zlib-dir=/usr/local/lib/
$ make
$ make install
```

You should now have a PHP module suitable for use with the Apache web server. This module should have been copied automatically into the Apache source tree.

The MySQL Files

PHP 4.x comes with built-in support for MySQL (note the additional `--with-mysql` parameter to the PHP `configure` script). However, if you're compiling PHP as a module for a web server and plan to use other MySQL-based server modules with it, you should not rely on this built-in support, but should instead use your locally installed copy of the MySQL client libraries and header files.

Note that this appendix does not include any information on configuring or installing MySQL on your system. For more information on this, you should refer to the documentation available at `http://www.mysql.com/`

- If you want to compile a standalone PHP binary, you don't need to bring Apache into the picture at all. Simply change into your PHP directory and run the `configure` script with the following options:

```
$ cd ../php-4.1.1
$ ./configure --enable-track-vars --with-mysql --with-dom --enable-sockets
➥--enable-wddx --with-xmlrpc --enable-xslt --with-xslt-sablot
➥--with-zlib-dir=/usr/local/lib/
$ make
$ make install
```

You should now have a PHP binary installed to `/usr/local/bin/`, which can be used to execute any PHP script from the command line. Skip the following steps and proceed directly to the section titled "Testing the Software" to verify that your PHP build has support for all the required extensions.

Step 4—Adding Apache

If you decided to compile PHP as an Apache module, the next step is to compile and install Apache. Move back into the Apache directory, configure Apache to use the PHP module created in the first choice of "Step 3—Adding PHP," and build and install it.

```
$ cd ../apache_1.3.20
$ ./configure --prefix=/usr/local/apache
➥--activate-module=src/modules/php4/libphp4.a
$ make
$ make install
```

When All Else Fails, RTFM!

If you have trouble installing PHP as an Apache module, you should check the "Verbose Install" section of PHP's `INSTALL` file.

Step 5—Configuring Apache to Work with PHP

After Apache has been installed, open up Apache's configuration file, `httpd.conf`, in your favorite text editor, and add the following lines to it so that Apache knows how to handle files with the `.php` extension:

```
AddType application/x-httpd-php .php
AddType application/x-httpd-php-source .phps
DirectoryIndex index.php index.html
```

Step 6—Starting Apache

Start the Apache web server via the included `apachectl` script.

```
$ /usr/local/apache/bin/apachectl start
```

Time Flies When You're Having Fun

You should be aware that the process of recompiling PHP with XML support is fairly time-consuming. Expect to spend between 30 to 60 minutes compiling and installing the various packages to your system.

Table A.1 shows an estimate of how long it takes to compile each package on different systems.

Table A.1 **A Comparison of the Time Taken to Recompile PHP with XML Support on Different Systems**

Package	Estimated Time on a P-200 with 64MB RAM	Estimated Time on a Duron-800 with 128MB RAM
expat	3 minutes	1 minute
zlib	3 minutes	30 seconds
libxml	9 minutes	2 minutes
Sablotron	12 minutes	3 minutes
PHP	20 minutes	7 minutes
Apache	5 minutes	3 minutes
Total	52 minutes .	16 1/2 minutes

A Note for Windows Users

The preceding sections document the process of recompiling PHP with XML support on Linux and other UNIX variants. If you're using Windows, most of what you've just read is irrelevant to you. This is because Windows users get a pre-built PHP binary, which already includes support for most common extensions, and they need only to activate these extensions via the Windows `php.ini` configuration file.

The extensions that need to be activated in the `php.ini` configuration file (look in the section titled "Dynamic Extensions") are the following:

- `php_domxml.dll`
- `php_xslt.dll`
- `php_sockets.dll`

You can activate these extensions by removing the semicolon (;) at the beginning of the corresponding line in `php.ini`. Remember to restart the web server for your changes to take effect.

Note that the Windows versions of PHP 4.1.1 and 4.2.0 include built-in support for WDDX, but no support for the XML-RPC extension.

For detailed instructions on getting PHP and Apache to talk nicely to each other on the Windows platform, refer to the installation instructions that ship with the Windows version of PHP, or visit the web page at `http://www.php.net/manual/en/install.windows.php`.

Testing the Software

After you've successfully installed PHP, either as an Apache module or a standalone binary, you should test it to ensure that all required extensions have been successfully compiled in.

You can do this by creating a PHP script containing the following lines:

```
<?php
// name this file "verify.php"
phpinfo();
?>
```

Then, depending on how you chose to compile PHP, do one of the following:

- If you compiled PHP as an Apache module, copy this file to your web server's document root (in this example, `/usr/local/apache/htdocs/`) and then access it by pointing your web browser to `http://your_web_server/verify.php`.

- If you compiled PHP as a standalone binary, execute this script from the command line:

  ```
  $ /usr/local/bin/php verify.php
  ```

In either case, the output should be an HTML page that looks like Figure A.1.

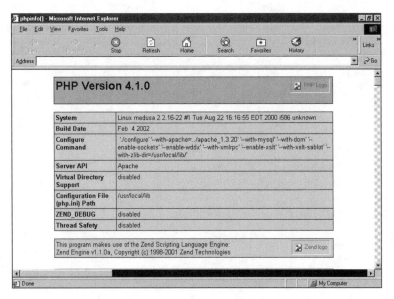

Figure A.1   The output of a `phpinfo()` call.

Examine this output to ensure that all the extensions you need are active.

"Without freedom, no art; art lives only on the restraints it imposes on itself, and dies of all others."

~ALBERT CAMUS

B

Open Source Licenses

THE OPEN SOURCE COMMUNITY IS A WONDERFUL thing to behold. Comprised of independent developers from all over the world, it is a rich, varied, and continuously evolving repository of software, ideas, and knowledge. Backed by all this enthusiasm and expertise, it's no wonder that many open source software projects are faster, are more robust, and have a richer feature set than their commercial counterparts.

The various open source applications and projects discussed within this book are all products of this community effort. All are available free of charge online, and all are licensed under different open-source licenses. This appendix contains the relevant license agreements.

GNU General Public License (GPL)

This license agreement applies to the following open source project described in this book: **eZXML**.
Version 2, June 1991
Copyright © 1989, 1991 Free Software Foundation, Inc. 59 Temple Place, Suite 330, Boston, MA 02111–1307 USA
Everyone is permitted to copy and distribute verbatim copies of this license document, but changing it is not allowed.

Preamble

The licenses for most software are designed to take away your freedom to share and change it. By contrast, the GNU General Public License is intended to guarantee your freedom to share and change free software—to make sure the software is free for all its users. This General Public License applies to most of the Free Software Foundation's software and to any other program whose authors commit to using it. (Some other Free Software Foundation software is covered by the GNU Library General Public License instead.) You can apply it to your programs, too.

When we speak of free software, we are referring to freedom, not price. Our General Public Licenses are designed to make sure that you have the freedom to distribute copies of free software (and charge for this service if you wish), that you receive source code or can get it if you want it, that you can change the software or use pieces of it in new free programs; and that you know you can do these things.

To protect your rights, we need to make restrictions that forbid anyone to deny you these rights or to ask you to surrender the rights. These restrictions translate to certain responsibilities for you if you distribute copies of the software, or if you modify it.

For example, if you distribute copies of such a program, whether gratis or for a fee, you must give the recipients all the rights that you have. You must make sure that they, too, receive or can get the source code. And you must show them these terms so they know their rights.

We protect your rights with two steps: (1) copyright the software, and (2) offer you this license which gives you legal permission to copy, distribute, and/or modify the software.

Also, for each author's protection and ours, we want to make certain that everyone understands that there is no warranty for this free software. If the software is modified by someone else and passed on, we want its recipients to know that what they have is not the original, so that any problems introduced by others will not reflect on the original authors' reputations.

Finally, any free program is threatened constantly by software patents. We wish to avoid the danger that redistributors of a free program will individually obtain patent licenses, in effect making the program proprietary. To prevent this, we have made it clear that any patent must be licensed for everyone's free use or not licensed at all. The precise terms and conditions for copying, distribution and modification follow.

GNU GENERAL PUBLIC LICENSE TERMS AND CONDITIONS FOR COPYING, DISTRIBUTION AND MODIFICATION

0. This License applies to any program or other work which contains a notice placed by the copyright holder saying it may be distributed under the terms of this General Public License. The "Program", below, refers to any such program or work, and a "work based on the Program" means either the Program or any

derivative work under copyright law: that is to say, a work containing the Program or a portion of it, either verbatim or with modifications and/or translated into another language. (Hereinafter, translation is included without limitation in the term "modification".) Each licensee is addressed as "you."

Activities other than copying, distribution, and modification are not covered by this License; they are outside its scope. The act of running the Program is not restricted, and the output from the Program is covered only if its contents constitute a work based on the Program (independent of having been made by running the Program). Whether that is true depends on what the Program does.

1. You may copy and distribute verbatim copies of the Program's source code as you receive it, in any medium, provided that you conspicuously and appropriately publish on each copy an appropriate copyright notice and disclaimer of warranty; keep intact all the notices that refer to this License and to the absence of any warranty; and give any other recipients of the Program a copy of this License along with the Program.

   You may charge a fee for the physical act of transferring a copy, and you may at your option offer warranty protection in exchange for a fee.

2. You may modify your copy or copies of the Program or any portion of it, thus forming a work based on the Program, and copy and distribute such modifications or work under the terms of Section 1 above, provided that you also meet all of these conditions:

   a) You must cause the modified files to carry prominent notices stating that you changed the files and the date of any change.

   b) You must cause any work that you distribute or publish, that in whole or in part contains or is derived from the Program or any part thereof, to be licensed as a whole at no charge to all third parties under the terms of this License.

   c) If the modified program normally reads commands interactively when run, you must cause it, when started running for such interactive use in the most ordinary way, to print or display an announcement including an appropriate copyright notice and a notice that there is no warranty (or else, saying that you provide a warranty) and that users may redistribute the program under these conditions, and telling the user how to view a copy of this License. (Exception: if the Program itself is interactive but does not normally print such an announcement, your work based on the Program is not required to print an announcement.)

These requirements apply to the modified work as a whole. If identifiable sections of that work are not derived from the Program, and can be reasonably considered independent and separate works in themselves, then this License, and its terms, do not apply to those sections when you distribute them as separate works. But when you distribute the same sections as part of a whole which is a work based on the Program, the distribution of the whole must be on the terms of this License, whose permissions for other licensees extend to the entire whole, and thus to each and every part regardless of who wrote it.

Thus, it is not the intent of this section to claim rights or contest your rights to work written entirely by you; rather, the intent is to exercise the right to control the distribution of derivative or collective works based on the Program.

In addition, mere aggregation of another work not based on the Program with the Program (or with a work based on the Program) on a volume of a storage or distribution medium does not bring the other work under the scope of this License.

3. You may copy and distribute the Program (or a work based on it, under Section 2) in object code or executable form under the terms of Sections 1 and 2 above provided that you also do one of the following:

   a) Accompany it with the complete corresponding machine-readable source code, which must be distributed under the terms of Sections 1 and 2 above on a medium customarily used for software interchange; or,

   b) Accompany it with a written offer, valid for at least three years, to give any third party, for a charge no more than your cost of physically performing source distribution, a complete machine-readable copy of the corresponding source code, to be distributed under the terms of Sections 1 and 2 above on a medium customarily used for software interchange; or,

   c) Accompany it with the information you received as to the offer to distribute corresponding source code. (This alternative is allowed only for noncommercial distribution and only if you received the program in object code or executable form with such an offer, in accord with Subsection b above.)

The source code for a work means the preferred form of the work for making modifications to it. For an executable work, complete source code means all the source code for all modules it contains, plus any associated interface definition files, plus the scripts used to control compilation and installation of the executable. However, as a special exception, the source code distributed need not include anything that is normally distributed (in either source or binary form) with the major components (compiler, kernel, and so on) of the operating system on which the executable runs, unless that component itself accompanies the executable.

If distribution of executable or object code is made by offering access to copy from a designated place, then offering equivalent access to copy the source code from the same place counts as distribution of the source code, even though third parties are not compelled to copy the source along with the object code.

4. You may not copy, modify, sublicense, or distribute the Program except as expressly provided under this License. Any attempt otherwise to copy, modify, sublicense or distribute the Program is void, and will automatically terminate your rights under this License. However, parties who have received copies, or rights, from you under this License will not have their licenses terminated so long as such parties remain in full compliance.

5. You are not required to accept this License, since you have not signed it. However, nothing else grants you permission to modify or distribute the Program or its derivative works. These actions are prohibited by law if you do not accept this License. Therefore, by modifying or distributing the Program (or any work based on the Program), you indicate your acceptance of this License to do so, and all its terms and conditions for copying, distributing or modifying the Program or works based on it.

6. Each time you redistribute the Program (or any work based on the Program), the recipient automatically receives a license from the original licensor to copy, distribute or modify the Program subject to these terms and conditions. You may not impose any further restrictions on the recipients' exercise of the rights granted herein. You are not responsible for enforcing compliance by third parties to this License.

7. If, as a consequence of a court judgment or allegation of patent infringement or for any other reason (not limited to patent issues), conditions are imposed on you (whether by court order, agreement or otherwise) that contradict the conditions of this License, they do not excuse you from the conditions of this License. If you cannot distribute so as to satisfy simultaneously your obligations under this License and any other pertinent obligations, then as a consequence you may not distribute the Program at all. For example, if a patent license would not permit royalty-free redistribution of the Program by all those who receive copies directly or indirectly through you, then the only way you could satisfy both it and this License would be to refrain entirely from distribution of the Program.

    If any portion of this section is held invalid or unenforceable under any particular circumstance, the balance of the section is intended to apply and the section as a whole is intended to apply in other circumstances.

    It is not the purpose of this section to induce you to infringe any patents or other property right claims or to contest validity of any such claims; this section has the sole purpose of protecting the integrity of the free software distribution system, which is implemented by public license practices. Many people have made generous contributions to the wide range of software distributed through that system in reliance on consistent application of that system; it is up to the author/donor to decide if he or she is willing to distribute software through any other system and a licensee cannot impose that choice.

This section is intended to make thoroughly clear what is believed to be a consequence of the rest of this License.

8. If the distribution and/or use of the Program is restricted in certain countries either by patents or by copyrighted interfaces, the original copyright holder who places the Program under this License may add an explicit geographical distribution limitation excluding those countries, so that distribution is permitted only in or among countries not thus excluded. In such case, this License incorporates the limitation as if written in the body of this License.

9. The Free Software Foundation may publish revised and/or new versions of the General Public License from time to time. Such new versions will be similar in spirit to the present version, but may differ in detail to address new problems or concerns.

Each version is given a distinguishing version number. If the Program specifies a version number of this License which applies to it and "any later version", you have the option of following the terms and conditions either of that version or of any later version published by the Free Software Foundation. If the Program does not specify a version number of this License, you may choose any version ever published by the Free Software Foundation.

10. If you wish to incorporate parts of the Program into other free programs whose distribution conditions are different, write to the author to ask for permission. For software which is copyrighted by the Free Software Foundation, write to the Free Software Foundation; we sometimes make exceptions for this. Our decision will be guided by the two goals of preserving the free status of all derivatives of our free software and of promoting the sharing and reuse of software generally.

NO WARRANTY

11. BECAUSE THE PROGRAM IS LICENSED FREE OF CHARGE, THERE IS NO WARRANTY FOR THE PROGRAM, TO THE EXTENT PERMITTED BY APPLICABLE LAW. EXCEPT WHEN OTHERWISE STATED IN WRITING THE COPYRIGHT HOLDERS AND/OR OTHER PARTIES PROVIDE THE PROGRAM "AS IS" WITHOUT WARRANTY OF ANY KIND, EITHER EXPRESSED OR IMPLIED, INCLUDING, BUT NOT LIMITED TO, THE IMPLIED WARRANTIES OF MERCHANTABILITY AND FITNESS FOR A PARTICULAR PURPOSE. THE ENTIRE RISK AS TO THE QUALITY AND PERFORMANCE OF THE PROGRAM IS WITH YOU. SHOULD THE PROGRAM PROVE DEFECTIVE, YOU ASSUME THE COST OF ALL NECESSARY SERVICING, REPAIR OR CORRECTION.

12. IN NO EVENT UNLESS REQUIRED BY APPLICABLE LAW OR AGREED TO IN WRITING WILL ANY COPYRIGHT HOLDER, OR ANY OTHER PARTY WHO MAY MODIFY AND/OR REDISTRIBUTE THE PROGRAM AS PERMITTED ABOVE, BE LIABLE TO YOU FOR DAMAGES, INCLUDING ANY GENERAL, SPECIAL, INCIDENTAL OR CONSEQUENTIAL DAMAGES ARISING OUT OF THE USE OR INABILITY TO USE THE PROGRAM (INCLUDING BUT NOT LIMITED TO LOSS OF DATA OR DATA BEING RENDERED INACCURATE OR LOSSES SUSTAINED BY YOU OR THIRD PARTIES OR A FAILURE OF THE PROGRAM TO OPERATE WITH ANY OTHER PROGRAMS), EVEN IF SUCH HOLDER OR OTHER PARTY HAS BEEN ADVISED OF THE POSSIBILITY OF SUCH DAMAGES.

END OF TERMS AND CONDITIONS

GNU Lesser General Public License (LGPL)

This license agreement applies to the following open source projects described in this book:
SOAPx4, **patTemplate**, *and* **patXMLRenderer**.

Version 2.1, February 1999

Copyright © 1991, 1999 Free Software Foundation, Inc.

59 Temple Place, Suite 330, Boston, MA 02111-1307 USA

Everyone is permitted to copy and distribute verbatim copies of this license document, but changing it is not allowed.

[This is the first released version of the Lesser GPL. It also counts as the successor of the GNU Library Public License, version 2, hence the version number 2.1.]

Preamble

The licenses for most software are designed to take away your freedom to share and change it. By contrast, the GNU General Public Licenses are intended to guarantee your freedom to share and change free software—to make sure the software is free for all its users.

This license, the Lesser General Public License, applies to some specially designated software packages—typically libraries—of the Free Software Foundation and other authors who decide to use it. You can use it too, but we suggest you first think carefully about whether this license or the ordinary General Public License is the better strategy to use in any particular case, based on the explanations below.

When we speak of free software, we are referring to freedom of use, not price. Our General Public Licenses are designed to make sure that you have the freedom to distribute copies of free software (and charge for this service if you wish); that you receive source code or can get it if you want it; that you can change the software and use pieces of it in new free programs; and that you are informed that you can do these things.

To protect your rights, we need to make restrictions that forbid distributors to deny you these rights or to ask you to surrender these rights. These restrictions translate to certain responsibilities for you if you distribute copies of the library or if you modify it.

For example, if you distribute copies of the library, whether gratis or for a fee, you must give the recipients all the rights that we gave you. You must make sure that they, too, receive or can get the source code. If you link other code with the library, you must provide complete object files to the recipients, so that they can relink them with the library after making changes to the library and recompiling it. And you must show them these terms so they know their rights.

We protect your rights with a two-step method: (1) we copyright the library, and (2) we offer you this license, which gives you legal permission to copy, distribute, and/or modify the library.

To protect each distributor, we want to make it very clear that there is no warranty for the free library. Also, if the library is modified by someone else and passed on, the recipients should know that what they have is not the original version, so that the original author's reputation will not be affected by problems that might be introduced by others.

Finally, software patents pose a constant threat to the existence of any free program. We wish to make sure that a company cannot effectively restrict the users of a free program by obtaining a restrictive license from a patent holder. Therefore, we insist that any patent license obtained for a version of the library must be consistent with the full freedom of use specified in this license.

Most GNU software, including some libraries, is covered by the ordinary GNU General Public License. This license, the GNU Lesser General Public License, applies to certain designated libraries, and is quite different from the ordinary General Public License. We use this license for certain libraries in order to permit linking those libraries into non-free programs.

When a program is linked with a library, whether statically or using a shared library, the combination of the two is legally speaking a combined work, a derivative of the original library. The ordinary General Public License therefore permits such linking only if the entire combination fits its criteria of freedom. The Lesser General Public License permits more lax criteria for linking other code with the library.

We call this license the "Lesser" General Public License because it does Less to protect the user's freedom than the ordinary General Public License. It also provides other free software developers Less of an advantage over competing non-free programs. These disadvantages are the reason we use the ordinary General Public License for many libraries. However, the Lesser license provides advantages in certain special circumstances.

For example, on rare occasions, there may be a special need to encourage the widest possible use of a certain library, so that it becomes a de-facto standard. To achieve this, non-free programs must be allowed to use the library. A more frequent case is that a free library does the same job as widely used non-free libraries. In this case, there is little to gain by limiting the free library to free software only, so we use the Lesser General Public License.

In other cases, permission to use a particular library in non-free programs enables a greater number of people to use a large body of free software. For example, permission to use the GNU C Library in non-free programs enables many more people to use the whole GNU operating system, as well as its variant, the GNU/Linux operating system.

Although the Lesser General Public License is Less protective of the users' freedom, it does ensure that the user of a program that is linked with the Library has the freedom and the wherewithal to run that program using a modified version of the Library.

The precise terms and conditions for copying, distribution and modification follow. Pay close attention to the difference between a "work based on the library" and a "work that uses the library." The former contains code derived from the library, whereas the latter must be combined with the library in order to run.

GNU LESSER GENERAL PUBLIC LICENSE TERMS AND CONDITIONS FOR COPYING, DISTRIBUTION AND MODIFICATION

0. This License Agreement applies to any software library or other program which contains a notice placed by the copyright holder or other authorized party saying it may be distributed under the terms of this Lesser General Public License (also called "this License"). Each licensee is addressed as "you."

   A "library" means a collection of software functions and/or data prepared so as to be conveniently linked with application programs (which use some of those functions and data) to form executables.

   The "Library", below, refers to any such software library or work which has been distributed under these terms. A "work based on the Library" means either the Library or any derivative work under copyright law: that is to say, a work containing the Library or a portion of it, either verbatim or with modifications, and/or translated straightforwardly into another language. (Hereinafter, translation is included without limitation in the term "modification".)

   "Source code" for a work means the preferred form of the work for making modifications to it. For a library, complete source code means all the source code for all modules it contains, plus any associated interface definition files, plus the scripts used to control compilation and installation of the library.

   Activities other than copying, distribution, and modification are not covered by this License; they are outside its scope. The act of running a program using the Library is not restricted, and output from such a program is covered only if its contents constitute a work based on the Library (independent of the use of the Library in a tool for writing it). Whether that is true depends on what the Library does and what the program that uses the Library does.

1. You may copy and distribute verbatim copies of the Library's complete source code as you receive it, in any medium, provided that you conspicuously and

appropriately publish on each copy an appropriate copyright notice and disclaimer of warranty; keep intact all the notices that refer to this License and to the absence of any warranty; and distribute a copy of this License along with the Library.

You may charge a fee for the physical act of transferring a copy, and you may at your option offer warranty protection in exchange for a fee.

2. You may modify your copy or copies of the Library or any portion of it, thus forming a work based on the Library, and copy and distribute such modifications or work under the terms of Section 1 above, provided that you also meet all of these conditions:

   a) The modified work must itself be a software library.

   b) You must cause the files modified to carry prominent notices stating that you changed the files and the date of any change.

   c) You must cause the whole of the work to be licensed at no charge to all third parties under the terms of this License.

   d) If a facility in the modified Library refers to a function or a table of data to be supplied by an application program that uses the facility, other than as an argument passed when the facility is invoked, then you must make a good faith effort to ensure that, in the event an application does not supply such function or table, the facility still operates, and performs whatever part of its purpose remains meaningful.

(For example, a function in a library to compute square roots has a purpose that is entirely well-defined independent of the application. Therefore, Subsection 2d requires that any application-supplied function or table used by this function must be optional: if the application does not supply it, the square root function must still compute square roots.)

These requirements apply to the modified work as a whole. If identifiable sections of that work are not derived from the Library, and can be reasonably considered independent and separate works in themselves, then this License, and its terms, do not apply to those sections when you distribute them as separate works. But when you distribute the same sections as part of a whole which is a work based on the Library, the distribution of the whole must be on the terms of this License, whose permissions for other licensees extend to the entire whole, and thus to each and every part regardless of who wrote it.

Thus, it is not the intent of this section to claim rights or contest your rights to work written entirely by you; rather, the intent is to exercise the right to control the distribution of derivative or collective works based on the Library.

In addition, mere aggregation of another work not based on the Library with the Library (or with a work based on the Library) on a volume of a storage or distribution medium does not bring the other work under the scope of this License.

3. You may opt to apply the terms of the ordinary GNU General Public License instead of this License to a given copy of the Library. To do this, you must alter all the notices that refer to this License, so that they refer to the ordinary GNU General Public License, version 2, instead of to this License. (If a newer version than version 2 of the ordinary GNU General Public License has appeared, then you can specify that version instead if you wish.) Do not make any other change in these notices.

    Once this change is made in a given copy, it is irreversible for that copy, so the ordinary GNU General Public License applies to all subsequent copies and derivative works made from that copy.

    This option is useful when you wish to copy part of the code of the Library into a program that is not a library.

4. You may copy and distribute the Library (or a portion or derivative of it, under Section 2) in object code or executable form under the terms of Sections 1 and 2 above provided that you accompany it with the complete corresponding machine-readable source code, which must be distributed under the terms of Sections 1 and 2 above on a medium customarily used for software interchange.

    If distribution of object code is made by offering access to copy from a designated place, then offering equivalent access to copy the source code from the same place satisfies the requirement to distribute the source code, even though third parties are not compelled to copy the source along with the object code.

5. A program that contains no derivative of any portion of the Library, but is designed to work with the Library by being compiled or linked with it, is called a "work that uses the Library." Such a work, in isolation, is not a derivative work of the Library, and therefore falls outside the scope of this License.

    However, linking a "work that uses the Library" with the Library creates an executable that is a derivative of the Library (because it contains portions of the Library), rather than a "work that uses the library." The executable is therefore covered by this License. Section 6 states terms for distribution of such executables.

    When a "work that uses the Library" uses material from a header file that is part of the Library, the object code for the work may be a derivative work of the Library even though the source code is not. Whether this is true is especially significant if the work can be linked without the Library, or if the work is itself a library. The threshold for this to be true is not precisely defined by law.

    If such an object file uses only numerical parameters, data structure layouts and accessors, and small macros and small inline functions (ten lines or less in length), then the use of the object file is unrestricted, regardless of whether it is legally a derivative work. (Executables containing this object code plus portions of the Library will still fall under Section 6.)

Otherwise, if the work is a derivative of the Library, you may distribute the object code for the work under the terms of Section 6. Any executables containing that work also fall under Section 6, whether or not they are linked directly with the Library itself.

6. As an exception to the Sections above, you may also combine or link a "work that uses the Library" with the Library to produce a work containing portions of the Library, and distribute that work under terms of your choice, provided that the terms permit modification of the work for the customer's own use and reverse engineering for debugging such modifications.

You must give prominent notice with each copy of the work that the Library is used in it and that the Library and its use are covered by this License. You must supply a copy of this License. If the work during execution displays copyright notices, you must include the copyright notice for the Library among them, as well as a reference directing the user to the copy of this License. Also, you must do one of these things:

a) Accompany the work with the complete corresponding machine-readable source code for the Library including whatever changes were used in the work (which must be distributed under Sections 1 and 2 above); and, if the work is an executable linked with the Library, with the complete machine-readable "work that uses the Library," as object code, and/or source code, so that the user can modify the Library and then relink to produce a modified executable containing the modified Library. (It is understood that the user who changes the contents of definitions files in the Library will not necessarily be able to recompile the application to use the modified definitions.)

b) Use a suitable shared library mechanism for linking with the Library. A suitable mechanism is one that (1) uses at run time a copy of the library already present on the user's computer system, rather than copying library functions into the executable, and (2) will operate properly with a modified version of the library, if the user installs one, as long as the modified version is interface-compatible with the version that the work was made with.

c) Accompany the work with a written offer, valid for at least three years, to give the same user the materials specified in Subsection 6a, above, for a charge no more than the cost of performing this distribution.

d) If distribution of the work is made by offering access to copy from a designated place, offer equivalent access to copy the above specified materials from the same place.

e) Verify that the user has already received a copy of these materials or that you have already sent this user a copy.

For an executable, the required form of the "work that uses the Library" must include any data and utility programs needed for reproducing the executable from it. However, as a special exception, the materials to be distributed need not include anything that is normally distributed (in either source or binary form) with the major components (compiler, kernel, and so on) of the operating system on which the executable runs, unless that component itself accompanies the executable.

It may happen that this requirement contradicts the license restrictions of other proprietary libraries that do not normally accompany the operating system. Such a contradiction means you cannot use both them and the Library together in an executable that you distribute.

7. You may place library facilities that are a work based on the Library side-by-side in a single library together with other library facilities not covered by this License, and distribute such a combined library, provided that the separate distribution of the work based on the Library and of the other library facilities is otherwise permitted, and provided that you do these two things:

   a) Accompany the combined library with a copy of the same work based on the Library, uncombined with any other library facilities. This must be distributed under the terms of the Sections above.

   b) Give prominent notice with the combined library of the fact that part of it is a work based on the Library, and explaining where to find the accompanying uncombined form of the same work.

8. You may not copy, modify, sublicense, link with, or distribute the Library except as expressly provided under this License. Any attempt otherwise to copy, modify, sublicense, link with, or distribute the Library is void, and will automatically terminate your rights under this License. However, parties who have received copies, or rights, from you under this License will not have their licenses terminated so long as such parties remain in full compliance.

9. You are not required to accept this License, since you have not signed it. However, nothing else grants you permission to modify or distribute the Library or its derivative works. These actions are prohibited by law if you do not accept this License. Therefore, by modifying or distributing the Library (or any work based on the Library), you indicate your acceptance of this License to do so, and all its terms and conditions for copying, distributing, or modifying the Library or works based on it.

10. Each time you redistribute the Library (or any work based on the Library), the recipient automatically receives a license from the original licensor to copy, distribute, link with, or modify the Library subject to these terms and conditions. You may not impose any further restrictions on the recipients' exercise of the rights granted herein. You are not responsible for enforcing compliance by third parties with this License.

11. If, as a consequence of a court judgment or allegation of patent infringement or for any other reason (not limited to patent issues), conditions are imposed on you (whether by court order, agreement or otherwise) that contradict the conditions of this License, they do not excuse you from the conditions of this License. If you cannot distribute so as to satisfy simultaneously your obligations under this License and any other pertinent obligations, then as a consequence you may not distribute the Library at all. For example, if a patent license would not permit royalty-free redistribution of the Library by all those who receive copies directly or indirectly through you, then the only way you could satisfy both it and this License would be to refrain entirely from distribution of the Library.

    If any portion of this section is held invalid or unenforceable under any particular circumstance, the balance of the section is intended to apply, and the section as a whole is intended to apply in other circumstances. It is not the purpose of this section to induce you to infringe any patents or other property right claims or to contest validity of any such claims; this section has the sole purpose of protecting the integrity of the free software distribution system which is implemented by public license practices. Many people have made generous contributions to the wide range of software distributed through that system in reliance on consistent application of that system; it is up to the author/donor to decide if he or she is willing to distribute software through any other system and a licensee cannot impose that choice. This section is intended to make thoroughly clear what is believed to be a consequence of the rest of this License.

12. If the distribution and/or use of the Library is restricted in certain countries either by patents or by copyrighted interfaces, the original copyright holder who places the Library under this License may add an explicit geographical distribution limitation excluding those countries, so that distribution is permitted only in or among countries not thus excluded. In such case, this License incorporates the limitation as if written in the body of this License.

13. The Free Software Foundation may publish revised and/or new versions of the Lesser General Public License from time to time. Such new versions will be similar in spirit to the present version, but may differ in detail to address new problems or concerns.

    Each version is given a distinguishing version number. If the Library specifies a version number of this License which applies to it and "any later version," you have the option of following the terms and conditions either of that version or of any later version published by the Free Software Foundation. If the Library does not specify a license version number, you may choose any version ever published by the Free Software Foundation.

14. If you wish to incorporate parts of the Library into other free programs whose distribution conditions are incompatible with these, write to the author to ask for permission. For software which is copyrighted by the Free Software

Foundation, write to the Free Software Foundation; we sometimes make exceptions for this. Our decision will be guided by the two goals of preserving the free status of all derivatives of our free software and of promoting the sharing and reuse of software generally.

NO WARRANTY

15. BECAUSE THE LIBRARY IS LICENSED FREE OF CHARGE, THERE IS NO WARRANTY FOR THE LIBRARY, TO THE EXTENT PERMITTED BY APPLICABLE LAW. EXCEPT WHEN OTHERWISE STATED IN WRITING THE COPYRIGHT HOLDERS AND/OR OTHER PARTIES PROVIDE THE LIBRARY "AS IS" WITHOUT WARRANTY OF ANY KIND, EITHER EXPRESSED OR IMPLIED, INCLUDING, BUT NOT LIMITED TO, THE IMPLIED WARRANTIES OF MERCHANTABILITY AND FITNESS FOR A PARTICULAR PURPOSE. THE ENTIRE RISK AS TO THE QUALITY AND PERFORMANCE OF THE LIBRARY IS WITH YOU. SHOULD THE LIBRARY PROVE DEFECTIVE, YOU ASSUME THE COST OF ALL NECESSARY SERVICING, REPAIR, OR CORRECTION.

16. IN NO EVENT UNLESS REQUIRED BY APPLICABLE LAW OR AGREED TO IN WRITING WILL ANY COPYRIGHT HOLDER, OR ANY OTHER PARTY WHO MAY MODIFY AND/OR REDISTRIBUTE THE LIBRARY AS PERMITTED ABOVE, BE LIABLE TO YOU FOR DAMAGES, INCLUDING ANY GENERAL, SPECIAL, INCIDENTAL, OR CONSEQUENTIAL DAMAGES ARISING OUT OF THE USE OR INABILITY TO USE THE LIBRARY (INCLUDING BUT NOT LIMITED TO LOSS OF DATA OR DATA BEING RENDERED INACCURATE OR LOSSES SUSTAINED BY YOU OR THIRD PARTIES OR A FAILURE OF THE LIBRARY TO OPERATE WITH ANY OTHER SOFTWARE), EVEN IF SUCH HOLDER OR OTHER PARTY HAS BEEN ADVISED OF THE POSSIBILITY OF SUCH DAMAGES.

    END OF TERMS AND CONDITIONS

Mozilla Public License – Version 1.1

This license agreement applies to the following open source project described in this book: **PHP.XPath**.

1. **Definitions.**

    1.0.1. **"Commercial Use"** means distribution or otherwise making the Covered Code available to a third party.

1.1.   **"Contributor"** means each entity that creates or contributes to the creation of Modifications.

1.2.   **"Contributor Version"** means the combination of the Original Code, prior Modifications used by a Contributor, and the Modifications made by that particular Contributor.

1.3.   **"Covered Code"** means the Original Code or Modifications or the combination of the Original Code and Modifications, in each case including portions thereof.

1.4.   **"Electronic Distribution Mechanism"** means a mechanism generally accepted in the software development community for the electronic transfer of data.

1.5.   **"Executable"** means Covered Code in any form other than Source Code.

1.6.   **"Initial Developer"** means the individual or entity identified as the Initial Developer in the Source Code notice required by **Exhibit A**.

1.7.   **"Larger Work"** means a work which combines Covered Code or portions thereof with code not governed by the terms of this License.

1.8.   **"License"** means this document.

1.8.1. **"Licensable"** means having the right to grant, to the maximum extent possible, whether at the time of the initial grant or subsequently acquired, any and all of the rights conveyed herein.

1.9.   **"Modifications"** means any addition to or deletion from the substance or structure of either the Original Code or any previous Modifications. When Covered Code is released as a series of files, a Modification is:

A.   Any addition to or deletion from the contents of a file containing Original Code or previous Modifications.

B.   Any new file that contains any part of the Original Code or previous Modifications.

1.10. **"Original Code"** means Source Code of computer software code which is described in the Source Code notice required by **Exhibit A** as Original Code, and which, at the time of its release under this License is not already Covered Code governed by this License.

1.10.1. **"Patent Claims"** means any patent claim(s), now owned or hereafter acquired, including without limitation, method, process, and apparatus claims, in any patent Licensable by grantor.

1.11. **"Source Code"** means the preferred form of the Covered Code for making modifications to it, including all modules it contains, plus any associated interface definition files, scripts used to control compilation and installation of an Executable, or source code differential comparisons against either the Original Code or another well known, available Covered Code of the Contributor's choice. The Source Code can be in a compressed or archival form, provided the appropriate decompression or de-archiving software is widely available for no charge.

1.12. **"You" (or "Your")** means an individual or a legal entity exercising rights under, and complying with all of the terms of, this License or a future version of this License issued under Section 6.1. For legal entities, "You" includes any entity which controls, is controlled by, or is under common control with You. For purposes of this definition, "control" means (a) the power, direct or indirect, to cause the direction or management of such entity, whether by contract or otherwise, or (b) ownership of more than fifty percent (50%) of the outstanding shares or beneficial ownership of such entity.

2. Source Code License.

2.1. **The Initial Developer Grant.** The Initial Developer hereby grants You a world-wide, royalty-free, non-exclusive license, subject to third party intellectual property claims:

(a) under intellectual property rights (other than patent or trademark) Licensable by Initial Developer to use, reproduce, modify, display, perform, sublicense and distribute the Original Code (or portions thereof) with or without Modifications, and/or as part of a Larger Work; and

(b) under Patents Claims infringed by the making, using or selling of Original Code, to make, have made, use, practice, sell, and offer for sale, and/or otherwise dispose of the Original Code (or portions thereof).

(c) the licenses granted in this Section 2.1(a) and (b) are effective on the date Initial Developer first distributes Original Code under the terms of this License.

(d) Notwithstanding Section 2.1(b) above, no patent license is granted: 1) for code that You delete from the Original Code; 2) separate from the Original Code; or 3) for infringements caused by: i) the modification of the Original Code or ii) the combination of the Original Code with other software or devices.

2.2. **Contributor Grant.** Subject to third party intellectual property claims, each Contributor hereby grants You a world-wide, royalty-free, non-exclusive license

(a) under intellectual property rights (other than patent or trademark) Licensable by Contributor, to use, reproduce, modify, display, perform, sublicense and distribute the Modifications created by such Contributor (or portions thereof) either on an unmodified basis, with other Modifications, as Covered Code and/or as part of a Larger Work; and

(b) under Patent Claims infringed by the making, using, or selling of Modifications made by that Contributor either alone and/or in combination with its Contributor Version (or portions of such combination), to make, use, sell, offer for sale, have made, and/or otherwise dispose of: 1) Modifications made by that Contributor (or portions thereof); and 2) the combination of Modifications made by that Contributor with its Contributor Version (or portions of such combination).

(c) the licenses granted in Sections 2.2(a) and 2.2(b) are effective on the date Contributor first makes Commercial Use of the Covered Code.

(d) Notwithstanding Section 2.2(b) above, no patent license is granted: 1) for any code that Contributor has deleted from the Contributor Version; 2) separate from the Contributor Version; 3) for infringements caused by: i) third party modifications of Contributor Version or ii) the combination of Modifications made by that Contributor with other software (except as part of the Contributor Version) or other devices; or 4) under Patent Claims infringed by Covered Code in the absence of Modifications made by that Contributor.

3. Distribution Obligations.

3.1. **Application of License.** The Modifications which You create or to which You contribute are governed by the terms of this License, including without limitation Section **2.2**. The Source Code version of Covered Code may be distributed only under the terms of this License or a future version of this License released under Section **6.1**, and You must include a copy of this License with every copy of the Source Code You distribute. You may not offer or impose any terms on any Source Code version that alters or restricts the applicable version of this License or the recipients' rights hereunder. However, You may include an additional document offering the additional rights described in Section **3.5**.

3.2. **Availability of Source Code.** Any Modification which You create or to which You contribute must be made available in Source Code form under the terms of this License either on the same media as an Executable version or via an accepted Electronic Distribution Mechanism to anyone to whom you made an Executable version available; and if made available via Electronic Distribution Mechanism, must remain available for at least twelve (12) months after the date it initially became available, or at least six (6) months after a subsequent version of that particular Modification has been made available to such recipients. You are responsible for ensuring that the Source Code version remains available even if the Electronic Distribution Mechanism is maintained by a third party.

3.3. **Description of Modifications.** You must cause all Covered Code to which You contribute to contain a file documenting the changes You made to create that Covered Code and the date of any change. You must include a prominent statement that the Modification is derived, directly or indirectly, from Original Code provided by the Initial Developer and including the name of the Initial Developer in (a) the Source Code, and (b) in any notice in an Executable version or related documentation in which You describe the origin or ownership of the Covered Code.

3.4. **Intellectual Property Matters**

(a) **Third Party Claims.** If Contributor has knowledge that a license under a third party's intellectual property rights is required to exercise the rights granted by such Contributor under Sections 2.1 or 2.2, Contributor must include a text file with the Source Code distribution titled "LEGAL" which describes the claim and the party making the claim in sufficient detail that a recipient will know whom to contact. If Contributor obtains such knowledge after the Modification is made available as described in Section 3.2, Contributor shall promptly modify the LEGAL file in all copies Contributor makes available thereafter and shall take other steps (such as notifying appropriate mailing lists or newsgroups) reasonably calculated to inform those who received the Covered Code that new knowledge has been obtained.

(b) **Contributor APIs.** If Contributor's Modifications include an application programming interface and Contributor has knowledge of patent licenses which are reasonably necessary to implement that API, Contributor must also include this information in the LEGAL file.

(c) **Representations.** Contributor represents that, except as disclosed pursuant to Section 3.4(a) above, Contributor believes that Contributor's Modifications are Contributor's original creation(s) and/or Contributor has sufficient rights to grant the rights conveyed by this License.

3.5. **Required Notices.** You must duplicate the notice in **Exhibit A** in each file of the Source Code. If it is not possible to put such notice in a particular Source Code file due to its structure, then You must include such notice in a location (such as a relevant directory) where a user would be likely to look for such a notice. If You created one or more Modification(s) You may add your name as a Contributor to the notice described in **Exhibit A**. You must also duplicate this License in any documentation for the Source Code where You describe recipients' rights or ownership rights relating to Covered Code. You may choose to offer, and to charge a fee for, warranty, support, indemnity or liability obligations to one or more recipients of Covered Code. However, You may do so only on Your own behalf, and not on behalf of the Initial Developer or any Contributor. You must make it absolutely clear than any such warranty, support, indemnity or liability obligation is offered by You alone, and You hereby agree to indemnify the Initial Developer and every Contributor for any liability incurred by the Initial Developer or such Contributor as a result of warranty, support, indemnity or liability terms You offer.

3.6. **Distribution of Executable Versions.** You may distribute Covered Code in Executable form only if the requirements of Section **3.1-3.5** have been met for that Covered Code, and if You include a notice stating that the Source Code version of the Covered Code is available under the terms of this License, including a description of how and where You have fulfilled the obligations of Section **3.2**. The notice must be conspicuously included in any notice in an Executable version, related documentation or collateral in which You describe recipients' rights relating to the Covered Code. You may distribute the Executable version of Covered Code or ownership rights under a license of Your choice, which may contain terms different from this License, provided that You are in compliance with the terms of this License and that the license for the Executable version does not attempt to limit or alter the recipient's rights in the Source Code version from the rights set forth in this License. If You distribute the Executable version under a different license You must make it absolutely clear that any terms which differ from this License are offered by You alone, not by the Initial Developer or any Contributor. You hereby agree to indemnify the Initial Developer and every Contributor for any liability incurred by the Initial Developer or such Contributor as a result of any such terms You offer.

3.7. **Larger Works.** You may create a Larger Work by combining Covered Code with other code not governed by the terms of this License and distribute the Larger Work as a single product. In such a case, You must make sure the requirements of this License are fulfilled for the Covered Code.

4. Inability to Comply Due to Statute or Regulation. If it is impossible for You to comply with any of the terms of this License with respect to some or all of the Covered Code due to statute, judicial order, or regulation then You must: (a) comply with the terms of this License to the maximum extent possible; and (b) describe the limitations and the code they affect. Such description must be included in the LEGAL file described in Section **3.4** and must be included with all distributions of the Source Code. Except to the extent prohibited by statute or regulation, such description must be sufficiently detailed for a recipient of ordinary skill to be able to understand it.

5. **Application of this License.** This License applies to code to which the Initial Developer has attached the notice in **Exhibit A** and to related Covered Code.

6. **Versions of the License.**

    6.1. **New Versions**. Netscape Communications Corporation ("Netscape") may publish revised and/or new versions of the License from time to time. Each version will be given a distinguishing version number.

    6.2. **Effect of New Versions**. Once Covered Code has been published under a particular version of the License, You may always continue to use it under the terms of that version. You may also choose to use such Covered Code under the terms of any subsequent version of the License published by Netscape. No one other than Netscape has the right to modify the terms applicable to Covered Code created under this License.

    6.3. **Derivative Works**. If You create or use a modified version of this License (which you may only do in order to apply it to code which is not already Covered Code governed by this License), You must (a) rename Your license so that the phrases "Mozilla", "MOZILLAPL", "MOZPL", "Netscape", "MPL", "NPL" or any confusingly similar phrase do not appear in your license (except to note that your license differs from this License) and (b) otherwise make it clear that Your version of the license contains terms which differ from the Mozilla Public License and Netscape Public License. (Filling in the name of the Initial Developer, Original Code or Contributor in the notice described in **Exhibit A** shall not of themselves be deemed to be modifications of this License.)

7. **DISCLAIMER OF WARRANTY.** COVERED CODE IS PROVIDED UNDER THIS LICENSE ON AN "AS IS" BASIS, WITHOUT WARRANTY OF ANY KIND, EITHER EXPRESSED OR IMPLIED, INCLUDING, WITHOUT LIMITATION, WARRANTIES THAT THE COVERED CODE IS FREE OF DEFECTS, MERCHANTABLE, FIT FOR A PARTICULAR PURPOSE OR NON-INFRINGING. THE ENTIRE RISK AS TO THE QUALITY AND PERFORMANCE OF THE COVERED CODE IS WITH YOU. SHOULD ANY COVERED CODE PROVE DEFECTIVE IN ANY RESPECT, YOU (NOT THE INITIAL DEVELOPER OR ANY OTHER CONTRIBUTOR) ASSUME THE COST OF ANY NECESSARY SERVICING, REPAIR OR CORRECTION. THIS DISCLAIMER OF WARRANTY CONSTITUTES AN ESSENTIAL PART OF THIS LICENSE. NO USE OF ANY COVERED CODE IS AUTHORIZED HEREUNDER EXCEPT UNDER THIS DISCLAIMER.

8. **TERMINATION.**

    8.1. This License and the rights granted hereunder will terminate automatically if You fail to comply with terms herein and fail to cure such breach within 30 days of becoming aware of the breach. All sublicenses to the Covered Code which are properly granted shall survive any termination of this License. Provisions which, by their nature, must remain in effect beyond the termination of this License shall survive.

8.2. If You initiate litigation by asserting a patent infringement claim (excluding declatory judgment actions) against Initial Developer or a Contributor (the Initial Developer or Contributor against whom You file such action is referred to as "Participant") alleging that:

(a) such Participant's Contributor Version directly or indirectly infringes any patent, then any and all rights granted by such Participant to You under Sections 2.1 and/or 2.2 of this License shall, upon 60 days notice from Participant terminate prospectively, unless if within 60 days after receipt of notice You either: (i) agree in writing to pay Participant a mutually agreeable reasonable royalty for Your past and future use of Modifications made by such Participant, or (ii) withdraw Your litigation claim with respect to the Contributor Version against such Participant. If within 60 days of notice, a reasonable royalty and payment arrangement are not mutually agreed upon in writing by the parties or the litigation claim is not withdrawn, the rights granted by Participant to You under Sections 2.1 and/or 2.2 automatically terminate at the expiration of the 60 day notice period specified above.

(b) any software, hardware, or device, other than such Participant's Contributor Version, directly or indirectly infringes any patent, then any rights granted to You by such Participant under Sections 2.1(b) and 2.2(b) are revoked effective as of the date You first made, used, sold, distributed, or had made, Modifications made by that Participant.

8.3. If You assert a patent infringement claim against Participant alleging that such Participant's Contributor Version directly or indirectly infringes any patent where such claim is resolved (such as by license or settlement) prior to the initiation of patent infringement litigation, then the reasonable value of the licenses granted by such Participant under Sections 2.1 or 2.2 shall be taken into account in determining the amount or value of any payment or license.

8.4. In the event of termination under Sections 8.1 or 8.2 above, all end user license agreements (excluding distributors and resellers) which have been validly granted by You or any distributor hereunder prior to termination shall survive termination.

9. **LIMITATION OF LIABILITY.** UNDER NO CIRCUMSTANCES AND UNDER NO LEGAL THEORY, WHETHER TORT (INCLUDING NEGLI-GENCE), CONTRACT, OR OTHERWISE, SHALL YOU, THE INITIAL DEVELOPER, ANY OTHER CONTRIBUTOR, OR ANY DISTRIBUTOR OF COVERED CODE, OR ANY SUPPLIER OF ANY OF SUCH PARTIES, BE LIABLE TO ANY PERSON FOR ANY INDIRECT, SPECIAL, INCI-DENTAL, OR CONSEQUENTIAL DAMAGES OF ANY CHARACTER INCLUDING, WITHOUT LIMITATION, DAMAGES FOR LOSS OF GOODWILL, WORK STOPPAGE, COMPUTER FAILURE OR MAL-FUNCTION, OR ANY AND ALL OTHER COMMERCIAL DAMAGES OR LOSSES, EVEN IF SUCH PARTY SHALL HAVE BEEN INFORMED OF THE POSSIBILITY OF SUCH DAMAGES. THIS LIMITATION OF LIABILITY SHALL NOT APPLY TO LIABILITY FOR DEATH OR PER-SONAL INJURY RESULTING FROM SUCH PARTY'S NEGLIGENCE TO THE EXTENT APPLICABLE LAW PROHIBITS SUCH LIMITATION. SOME JURISDICTIONS DO NOT ALLOW THE EXCLUSION OR LIMI-TATION OF INCIDENTAL OR CONSEQUENTIAL DAMAGES, SO THIS EXCLUSION AND LIMITATION MAY NOT APPLY TO YOU.

10. **U.S. GOVERNMENT END USERS.** The Covered Code is a "commercial item," as that term is defined in 48 C.F.R. 2.101 (Oct. 1995), consisting of "commercial computer software" and "commercial computer software docu-mentation," as such terms are used in 48 C.F.R. 12.212 (Sept. 1995). Consistent with 48 C.F.R. 12.212 and 48 C.F.R. 227.7202-1 through 227.7202-4 (June 1995), all U.S. Government End Users acquire Covered Code with only those rights set forth herein.

11. **MISCELLANEOUS.** This License represents the complete agreement con-cerning subject matter hereof. If any provision of this License is held to be unenforceable, such provision shall be reformed only to the extent necessary to make it enforceable. This License shall be governed by California law provisions (except to the extent applicable law, if any, provides otherwise), excluding its conflict-of-law provisions. With respect to disputes in which at least one party is a citizen of, or an entity chartered or registered to do business in the United States of America, any litigation relating to this License shall be subject to the jurisdiction of the Federal Courts of the Northern District of California, with venue lying in Santa Clara County, California, with the losing party responsible for costs, including without limitation, court costs and reasonable attorneys' fees and expenses. The application of the United Nations Convention on Contracts for the International Sale of Goods is expressly excluded. Any law or regulation which provides that the language of a contract shall be construed against the drafter shall not apply to this License.

12. **RESPONSIBILITY FOR CLAIMS.** As between Initial Developer and the Contributors, each party is responsible for claims and damages arising, directly or indirectly, out of its utilization of rights under this License and You agree to work with Initial Developer and Contributors to distribute such responsibility on an equitable basis. Nothing herein is intended or shall be deemed to constitute any admission of liability.

13. **MULTIPLE-LICENSED CODE.** Initial Developer may designate portions of the Covered Code as "Multiple-Licensed." "Multiple-Licensed" means that the Initial Developer permits you to utilize portions of the Covered Code under Your choice of the NPL or the alternative licenses, if any, specified by the Initial Developer in the file described in Exhibit A.

BSD License

This license agreement applies to the following open source projects described in this book:
XML-RPC for PHP, and **Metabase**.
Redistribution and use in source and binary forms, with or without modification, are permitted provided that the following conditions are met:

- Redistributions of source code must retain the above copyright notice, this list of conditions and the following disclaimer.

- Redistributions in binary form must reproduce the above copyright notice, this list of conditions and the following disclaimer in the documentation and/or other materials provided with the distribution.

For XML-RPC for PHP

- Neither the name of the "XML-RPC for PHP" nor the names of its contributors may be used to endorse or promote products derived from this software without specific prior written permission.

For Metabase

- Neither the name of Manuel Lemos nor the names of his contributors may be used to endorse or promote products derived from this software without specific prior written permission.

THIS SOFTWARE IS PROVIDED BY THE COPYRIGHT HOLDERS AND
CONTRIBUTORS "AS IS" AND ANY EXPRESS OR IMPLIED WARRANTIES,
INCLUDING, BUT NOT LIMITED TO, THE IMPLIED WARRANTIES OF
MERCHANTABILITY AND FITNESS FOR A PARTICULAR PURPOSE ARE
DISCLAIMED. IN NO EVENT SHALL THE COPYRIGHT OWNER OR CON-
TRIBUTORS BE LIABLE FOR ANY DIRECT, INDIRECT, INCIDENTAL, SPE-
CIAL, EXEMPLARY, OR CONSEQUENTIAL DAMAGES (INCLUDING, BUT
NOT LIMITED TO, PROCUREMENT OF SUBSTITUTE GOODS OR SER-
VICES; LOSS OF USE, DATA, OR PROFITS; OR BUSINESS INTERRUPTION)
HOWEVER CAUSED AND ON ANY THEORY OF LIABILITY, WHETHER IN
CONTRACT, STRICT LIABILITY, OR TORT (INCLUDING NEGLIGENCE
OR OTHERWISE) ARISING IN ANY WAY OUT OF THE USE OF THIS SOFT-
WARE, EVEN IF ADVISED OF THE POSSIBILITY OF SUCH DAMAGE.

*"What's in a name? That which we call a rose
By any other name would smell as sweet."*

~WILLIAM SHAKESPEARE, *ROMEO AND JULIET*

C

Glossary

American Standard Code for Information Interchange (ASCII) A format for text display that consists of a set of 128 characters.

associative array An array whose keys are strings rather than integers (sometimes referred to as a "hash" or "hash table").

BASE64 An encoding scheme for representing any type of data as ASCII text, so that it may be easily transmitted across the Internet.

callback function A function registered with the SAX parser as the handler for a specific type of event.

case folding In the context of an XML document, converting element names to uppercase to make them more consistent.

Cocoon A Java-based content publishing framework, with support for a variety of different data sources (including XML and databases).

Component Object Model (COM) A component-based software architecture model for integrated, reusable client and server objects.

deserialization The process of converting a serialized object back into its original representation. In the context of WDDX, the process of converting a WDDX packet into language-specific data structures.

Document Object Model (DOM) A tree-based approach to XML processing.

Document Type Definition (DTD) A document specifying conformance rules for an XML document to be considered valid.

entity reference   A text string that serves as the placeholder for an entity (for example, the string < serves as a placeholder for the less-than symbol <).

Extensible Stylesheet Language (XSL)   A language used to format and present XML data. The language consists of three components: XPath, XSLT, and XSL-FO.

external entity   An entity whose definition exists in a different file.

File Transfer Protocol (FTP)   A protocol for transferring files over the Internet.

GNU General Public License (GPL)   A software license that allows developers to easily share, modify, and reuse free software.

Internet Message Access Protocol (IMAP)   A protocol for reading email on a remote server (without first having to download it to your local machine).

Java Virtual Machine (JVM)   Software that interfaces between Java bytecode and a specific hardware platform.

Lesser General Public License (LGPL)   A variant of the GPL that allows derivative products to use alternate licenses (whereas works based on a GPL project will always remain under the terms of the GPL).

location path   An XPath address that consists of axes, node tests, and predicates.

Microsoft Component Object Model   *See* Component Object Model (COM)

named buffer   A storage area in memory that is accessible by name.

node   A branch or leaf in the XML document tree.

Portable Document Format (PDF)   A standard file format for electronic documents popularized by Adobe Systems, Inc.

Post Office Protocol (POP)   An Internet protocol for downloading email to your local machine.

processing instruction (PI)   Information or command embedded within an XML document.

RedHat Package Manager (RPM)   An open software packaging system designed to simplify software distribution and updates.

Relational Database Management System (RDBMS)   An application designed to administer a series of linked, or related, databases and tables.

Remote Procedure Call (RPC)   A client-server architecture for invoking remote procedures across a network.

Resource Description Framework (RDF)   An XML-based metadata language designed to describe content on the World Wide Web.

Scalable Vector Graphics (SVG)   An XML-based language for describing vector graphics.

serialization   The process of converting an object into a byte stream suitable for transmission or storage. In the context of WDDX, the process of converting a data structure into a WDDX packet.

Simple API for XML (SAX)   An event-based interface to XML processing.

Simple Mail Transfer Protocol (SMTP)   A protocol for sending email.

Simple Object Access Protocol (SOAP)   An emerging W3C standard for XML-based information exchange.

SMIL *See* Synchronized Multimedia Integration Language

source encoding Character encoding used by PHP when parsing an XML document.

Standardized General Markup Language (SGML) A standard for the creation of markup languages.

Structured Query Language (SQL) A standard, widely used programming language to access and manipulate database records.

stylesheet A set of rules or templates that define the formatting and appearance of a document.

SVG *See* Scalable Vector Graphics

Synchronized Multimedia Integration Language (SMIL) A markup language used for synchronized multimedia presentations.

target encoding Character encoding used by callback functions when parsing the XML data passed to them.

unparsed entity An entity that references data (usually binary data) that should *not* be processed by the parser.

Web Distributed Data Exchange (WDDX) An XML-based technology for data transfer over the Web.

Web Standards Description Language (WSDL) An XML-based language for describing network services.

Wireless Markup Language (WML) A presentation language for handheld devices (PDAs, cellular phones, and so on) that is similar to HTML.

XML–RPC A protocol for encoding RPC requests and decoding RPC responses using XML.

XML Schema A blueprint for a specific "class" of XML documents that is similar to (though far more powerful than) a Document Type Definition (DTD).

XPath A language for accessing different parts of an XML document, usually on the basis of specific user-defined criteria. XPath is a part of the W3C's XSL specification.

XSL *See* Extensible Stylesheet Language

XSL Formatting Objects (XSL-FO) A language that specifies formatting information for an XSLT result tree (most often used for printable documents). XSL-FO is a part of the W3C's XSL specification.

XSL Transformations (XSLT) A language that specifies the rules whereby an XML source tree is converted into a new result tree. XSLT is a part of the W3C's XSL specification.

Index

Symbols

A

B

C

listings

M

VOICES THAT MATTER

HOW TO CONTACT US

VISIT OUR WEB SITE

WWW.NEWRIDERS.COM

On our web site, you'll find information about our other books, authors, tables of contents, and book errata. You will also find information about book registration and how to purchase our books, both domestically and internationally.

EMAIL US

Contact us at: **nrfeedback@newriders.com**

- If you have comments or questions about this book
- To report errors that you have found in this book
- If you have a book proposal to submit or are interested in writing for New Riders
- If you are an expert in a computer topic or technology and are interested in being a technical editor who reviews manuscripts for technical accuracy

Contact us at: **nreducation@newriders.com**

- If you are an instructor from an educational institution who wants to preview New Riders books for classroom use. Email should include your name, title, school, department, address, phone number, office days/hours, text in use, and enrollment, along with your request for desk/examination copies and/or additional information.

Contact us at: **nrmedia@newriders.com**

- If you are a member of the media who is interested in reviewing copies of New Riders books. Send your name, mailing address, and email address, along with the name of the publication or web site you work for.

BULK PURCHASES/CORPORATE SALES

The publisher offers discounts on this book when ordered in quantity for bulk purchases and special sales. For sales within the U.S., please contact: Corporate and Government Sales (800) 382-3419 or **corpsales@pearsontechgroup.com**. Outside of the U.S., please contact: International Sales (317) 581-3793 or **international@pearsontechgroup.com**.

WRITE TO US

New Riders Publishing
201 W. 103rd St.
Indianapolis, IN 46290-1097

CALL/FAX US

Toll-free (800) 571-5840
If outside U.S. (317) 581-3500
Ask for New Riders
FAX: (317) 581-4663

New Riders

WWW.NEWRIDERS.COM

Solutions from experts you know and trust.

www.informit.com

New Riders has partnered with InformIT.com to bring technical information to your desktop. Drawing on New Riders authors and reviewers to provide additional information on topics you're interested in, InformIT.com has free, in-depth information you won't find anywhere else.

Expert Access.
Free Content.

- **Master the skills you need, when you need them**

- **Call on resources from some of the best minds in the industry**

- **Get answers when you need them, using InformIT's comprehensive library or live experts online**

- **Go above and beyond what you find in New Riders books, extending your knowledge**

As an **InformIT** partner, **New Riders** has shared the wisdom and knowledge of our authors with you online. Visit **InformIT.com** to see what you're missing.

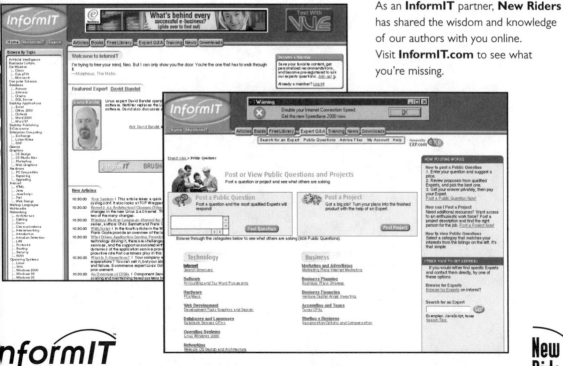

www.informit.com ▪ www.newriders.com

Colophon

Pictured on the cover of this book is a photograph of Stonehenge, one of the oldest and best-preserved megalithic structures in the world. Located on the Salisbury Plain in Wiltshire, England, this ancient British icon consists of a series of concentric rings constructed from gigantic sarsen stones and smaller bluestones. The sarsen stones that make up the outer circle of the henge weigh as much as 25 tons each and are said to have been transported at least twenty miles over steep hills. Estimates suggest that it would have taken approximately 600 men to move each stone and many millions of hours of labor to build the entire structure.

The original purpose of Stonehenge is unclear, although many theories swirl around this mysterious landmark. Some theorists suggest that it was constructed as a temple for worshipping ancient earth deities; others credit it with being an ancient burial ground for noblemen; and still others refer to it as a gigantic sun clock, a primitive calculator, or an astronomical observatory used to mark events on a prehistoric calendar. Whatever its original purpose, the ruined structure, with some of its upright stones rising to a height of over 18 feet, still remains an awe-inspiring—and thought-provoking—sight.

This book was written and edited in Microsoft Word, and laid out in QuarkXPress. The font used for the body text is Bembo and Mono. It was printed on 50# Husky Offset Smooth paper at VonHoffman Graphics Inc., in Owensville, Missouri. Prepress consisted of PostScript computer-to-plate technology (filmless process). The cover was printed at Moore Langen Printing in Terre Haute, Indiana, on 12 pt., coated on one side.